Carolyn F. Swift, PhD

Sexual Assault and Abuse: Sociocultural Context of Prevention

*Pre-publication
REVIEWS,
COMMENTARIES,
EVALUATIONS . . .*

"**T**his valuable collection, edited by one of the pioneers of sexual assault research, tackles the crucial subject of prevention from an ecological perspective. Not only are the ideas for prevention original, but they are also empowering."

Mary P. Koss, PhD
*Professor, The University
of Arizona, Health Sciences
Center, Tucson, Arizona*

"**N**ot just another compilation of research and clinical observations on sexual assault and abuse, this edited volume actually delivers a cornucopia for all who are concerned with the primary prevention of these damaging and degrading acts. The book incorporates but importantly transcends feminist analyses. Each chapter, in its own fashion, illuminates and elaborates the theme that prevention strategies need to incorporate the sociocultural environment within which sexual assault/abuse occurs. This ecological approach–particularly in application to preventing development of sexually abusive behavior in young males–is vintage Carolyn Swift, presented forcefully and incisively here in her own two co-authored chapters.

Epidemiologists and mental health policy makers will appreciate how the entire first section of the book (authored by Swift, Albee, Ryan-Finn, and Russell) delineates in sharp relief the long-muddled issues of prevention in this difficult and poignant arena. Service providers will be able to draw upon chapters by other eminent contributors (e.g., Becerra, Wyatt, Bond, and Conte) to reshape their prevention programs through incorporating deeper and more dynamic understandings of ethnic cultures, organizational cultures, and offender perspectives. Social scientists, even those only marginally interested in sexual assault/abuse, will learn much about how a research literature–e.g., that on the effects of pornography–is politically reworked in the crucible of national policy deliberations, through the concluding chapter by Einsiedel."

George J. McCall, PhD
Professor of Sociology and Public Policy Administration,
University of Missouri-St. Louis

Sexual Assault and Abuse: Sociocultural Context of Prevention

The *Prevention in Human Services* series:

Sexual Assault and Abuse: Sociocultural Context of Prevention

Carolyn F. Swift
Editor

The Haworth Press, Inc.
New York • London

Sexual Assault and Abuse: Sociocultural Context of Prevention, has also been published as *Prevention in Human Services* Volume 12, Number 2 1995.

The Haworth Press, Inc., 10 Alice Street, Binghamton, NY 13904-1580 USA

Library of Congress Cataloging-in-Publication Data

Sexual assault and abuse : sociocultural context of prevention / Carolyn F. Swift.
     p. cm.
    Includes bibliographical references and index.
    ISBN 1-56024-762-2 (alk. paper)
    1. Sex crimes–United States–Prevention. 2. Sex crimes–United States I. Swift, Carolyn F.
HV6592. S485 1995
364.1'53'0973–dc20
                                         95-33472
                                           CIP

INDEXING & ABSTRACTING

Contributions to this publication are selectively indexed or abstracted in print, electronic, online, or CD-ROM version(s) of the reference tools and information services listed below. This list is current as of the copyright date of this publication. See the end of this section for additional notes.

- *Abstracts of Research in Pastoral Care & Counseling*, Loyola College, 7135 Minstrel Way, Suite 101, Columbia, MD 21045

- *Child Development Abstracts & Bibliography*, University of Kansas, 2 Bailey Hall, Lawrence, KS 66045

- *Excerpta Medica/Secondary Publishing Division*, Elsevier Science Inc., Secondary Publishing Division, 655 Avenue of the Americas, New York, NY 10010

- *INTERNET ACCESS (& additional networks) Bulletin Board for Libraries ("BUBL"), coverage of information resources on INTERNET, JANET, and other networks.*
  - JANET X.29:UK.AC.BATH.BUBL or 00006012101300
  - TELNET: BUBL.BATH.AC.UK or 138.38.32.45 login 'bubl'
  - Gopher: BUBL.BATH.AC.UK (138.32.32.45). Port 7070
  - World Wide Web: http://www.bubl.bath.ac.uk./BUBL/home.html
  - NISSWAIS: telnetniss.ac.uk (for the NISS gateway), The Andersonian Library, Curran Building, 101 Saint James Road, Glasgow G4 ONS, Scotland

- *Inventory of Marriage and Family Literature (online and hard copy)*, National Council on Family Relations, 3989 Central Avenue NE, Suite 550, Minneapolis, MN 55421

- *Mental Health Abstracts (online through DIALOG)*, IFI/Plenum Data Company, 3202 Kirkwood Highway, Wilmington, DE 19808

- *NIAAA Alcohol and Alcohol Problems Science Database (ETOH)*, National Institute on Alcohol Abuse and Alcoholism, 1400 Eye Street NW, Suite 600, Washington, DC 20005

- *Referativnyi Zhurnal (Abstracts Journal of the Institute of Scientific Information of the Republic of Russia)*, The Institute of Scientific Information, Baltijskaja ul., 14, Moscow A-219, Republic of Russia

(continued)

- *RMDB DATABASE (Reliance Medical Information)*, Reliance Medical Information, Inc. (RMI), 100 Putman Green, Greenwich, CT 06830
- *Social Planning/Policy & Development Abstracts (SOPODA)*, Sociological Abstracts, Inc., P. O. Box 22206, San Diego, CA 92192-0206
- *Social Work Abstracts*, National Association of Social Workers, 750 First Street NW, 8th Floor, Washington, DC 20002
- *Sociological Abstracts (SA)*, Sociological Abstracts, Inc., P. O. Box 22206, San Diego, CA 92192-0206
- *SOMED (social medicine) Database*, Institute fur Dokumentation, Postfach 20 10 12, D-33548 Bielefeld, Germany
- *Violence and Abuse Abstracts: A Review of Current Literature on Interpersonal Violence (VAA)*, Sage Publications, Inc., 2455 Teller Road, Newbury Park, CA 91320

SPECIAL BIBLIOGRAPHIC NOTES

*related to special journal issues (separates)
and indexing/abstracting*

☐ indexing/abstracting services in this list will also cover material in any "separate" that is co-published simultaneously with Haworth's special thematic journal issue or DocuSerial. Indexing/abstracting usually covers material at the article/chapter level.

☐ monographic co-editions are intended for either non-subscribers or libraries which intend to purchase a second copy for their circulating collections.

☐ monographic co-editions are reported to all jobbers/wholesalers/approval plans. The source journal is listed as the "series" to assist the prevention of duplicate purchasing in the same manner utilized for books-in-series.

☐ to facilitate user/access services all indexing/abstracting services are encouraged to utilize the co-indexing entry note indicated at the bottom of the first page of each article/chapter/contribution.

☐ this is intended to assist a library user of any reference tool (whether print, electronic, online, or CD-ROM) to locate the monographic version if the library has purchased this version but not a subscription to the source journal.

☐ individual articles/chapters in any Haworth publication are also available through the Haworth Document Delivery Services (HDDS).

Sexual Assault and Abuse: Sociocultural Context of Prevention

CONTENTS

ALL HAWORTH BOOKS AND JOURNALS
ARE PRINTED ON CERTIFIED
ACID-FREE PAPER

ABOUT THE EDITOR

Carolyn F. Swift, PhD, is a Research Associate at the Schiefelbusch Institute for Lifespan Studies at the University of Kansas, Adjunct Professor at the Union Institute in Cincinnati, Ohio, and former Director of the Stone Center for Developmental Services and Studies at Wellesley College in Wellesley, Massachusetts. Her primary work has been in the prevention of child sexual abuse, rape, and woman battering, topics on which she has published widely. Dr. Swift received the Award for Distinguished Contribution to the Practice of Community Psychology by the Society for Community Research and Action of the American Psychological Association and the Award for Distinguished Contribution to the Field of Consultation, Education, and Prevention by the National Council of Community Mental Health Centers. She is a fellow of the American Psychological Association and of the American Association of Preventive Psychology.

Foreword

Through its many forms and victims, across centuries, continents and cultures, sexual assault embodies a universal theme: the violent enforcement of an unequal power relationship. It is not surprising that a basic theme of rape prevention strategies is the empowerment of those targeted as victims. These two themes–the abuse of power and empowerment–are consistently found in prevention literature on rape, and they appear as themes in this work as well.

Diverging from much of the literature on the prevention of sexual assault, the articles in this collection share the theme of expanding rape prevention strategies to incorporate the total environment–sociocultural as well as physical–within which rape occurs. This volume includes emerging approaches to rape prevention that encompass the ecology of rape. Whether these are victim- or rapist-focused approaches, they share a perspective that places behavior in the context of the multidimensional factors that shape it. A related theme is the recognition that prevention programs need to go beyond individual interventions to community-wide or system interventions. A comprehensive program to prevent sexual assault requires interventions at multiple levels–individuals, families, groups, organizations, and communities. Ultimately, preventive approaches need to change the sociocultural system that creates and maintains sexual assault and abuse.

In the Introduction Albee and Swift present a brief history of primary prevention in the field of public health. They outline basic prevention strategies, and identify some of the sociocultural factors that affect the incidence of sexual assault and abuse. In their discus-

[Haworth co-indexing entry note]: "Foreword." Swift, Carolyn F. Co-published simultaneously in *Prevention in Human Services* (The Haworth Press, Inc.) Vol. 12, No. 2, 1995, pp. xi-xvi; and: *Sexual Assault and Abuse: Sociocultural Context of Prevention* (ed: Carolyn F. Swift) The Haworth Press, Inc., 1995, pp. xi-xvi. Single or multiple copies of this article are available from The Haworth Document Delivery Service [1-800-342-9678, 9:00 a.m.-5:00 p.m. (EST)].

xi

sion of the misuse of power as the cause of much human misery, they identify the gender power imbalance in patriarchal societies as the "cause of the causes" of sexual victimization. Acknowledging the recency of scientific attention to the fields of sexual assault prevention, Albee and Swift project some starting points for designing programs to prevent sexual abuse.

The articles in this volume are grouped in two sections. Articles in the first section focus primarily on perpetrators, exploring some of the sociocultural causes and correlates of sexually assaultive behavior and their implications for prevention. Articles in the second section explore some of the sociocultural conditions connected with sexual victimization, and project interventions to reduce vulnerability. This volume is not intended as a comprehensive review of the sociocultural factors that contribute to a rape culture, but rather as a source that examines some of these factors, and projects preventive interventions to change them, with the ultimate goal of reducing the incidence of sexual assault and abuse.

Because primary prevention research focuses on populations rather than individuals, it promotes the systematic study of risk factors. Advancing from an individual to an epidemiological analysis of sexual assault and abuse permits new insights into both causes and possible prevention approaches. The population frame makes it easier to ask old questions in new ways. The question, "Why do men rape?" is translated to, "What are the developmental processes that interact with risk factors to produce raping behavior in boys and men?" This query eventually leads to the prevention question, "What sorts of interventions could change the outcome?"

Swift and Ryan-Finn explore some of the issues raised by these questions, and in seeking answers, review research associated with correlates of sexually abusive behavior. Their goal is to document perpetrator prevention as an essential component in the prevention of sexual abuse. Since this approach–preventing the development of sexually abusive behavior in boys and men–is only beginning to receive research attention, definitive answers to the questions posed above are premature. The authors discuss some of the major factors linked with the development of sexually abusive behavior, and expand on three: the sociocultural power inequities between women and men, the effects on children and young men of media exposure to sexual violence against women, and a history of childhood sexual abuse in boys and men. In the subsequent discussion of prevention approaches, educational, media, and legislative interventions are considered.

Diana Russell, in addressing the issue of why men rape, identifies pornography as one of the causes. Although this article was published originally in 1988, the significance it carries for rape prevention is major, and Russell has updated it for this publication. According to Russell, pornography fits four conditions that must be met for rape to occur: it predisposes men to rape, it undermines their internal, and their social inhibitions against raping, and it undermines potential victims' abilities to avoid rape. A substantial body of research supports this analysis. Russell's distinction between pornography and erotica is critical to her proof of the negative effects of pornography on the health and safety of women and children. Support of this country's first amendment rights has ruled out anti-pornography legislation in the United States to date. The value of Russell's work for prevention purposes is in clearly charting the destructive connection between pornography and the health and safety of women and children. When the destructive phenomenon itself cannot be eradicated, what prevention measures are available? This chapter sets out issues to which there are no easy answers.

While Russell focuses on the *content* of pornography, Einsiedel uses pornography to illustrate the *process* by which social science research has contributed to the formulation of public policy decisions. Public policy development–a level of intervention with significant impact on sociocultural norms and practices–presents opportunities for social scientists committed to prevention goals. Einsiedel describes the use of social science research and researchers in the 1970 and 1986 United States presidential commissions on pornography. An irony in comparing the two commissions, which were only 16 years apart, is that their conclusions about the effects of pornography were "diametrically opposed." The 1970 commission found that exposing youth and adults to explicit sexual materials *does not lead* to criminal sexual behavior. The 1986 commission found that exposure to sexually explicit material that is degrading or violent *does lead* to acts of violence against women. A critical difference in the two commissions is the revised definition of pornography (as distinct from erotica) used by the 1986 commission. Key differences between the two commissions include their definitions of pornography, their purposes, resources, staffs, and the political context of their work.

The second section of this volume deals with issues connected more directly with victims–such as the conditions or risk factors that increase vulnerability to sexual victimization. Most of the risks identified are related to membership in demographic groups. The primary demographic risk factor for sexual victimization, gender, is addressed throughout the volume. Other demographic risks addressed in this section include age, ethnicity, and status as an employee or student. Previous sexual victimization is also a significant risk factor in predicting future sexual victimization. The authors outline prevention approaches designed to reduce victimization risks.

Wyatt, Notgrass and Gordon present data on sexual revictimization in a population of African American women. Their research highlights ways in which developmental processes shape the risk factors that affect individuals and contribute to behavior. The study documents the negative consequences of sexual revictimization experienced by a sample of African American women before and after age 18. A review of the social and historical context of their sexual victimization establishes their vulnerability through both gender and minority ethnicity, and suggests a dual prevention strategy. The sexual enslavement of African American women documented in this country's history has effects which continue to influence the ways in which today's African American women are viewed sexually, as well as ways in which they may view themselves sexually. This legacy invites reflection on the meaning, in prevention terms, of "revictimization," since this term automatically carries the label of secondary prevention. If a racist society judges African American women to be marked negatively by the sexual victimization of their enslaved foremothers, then for many African American women sexual victimization begins at birth, and any subsequent sexual victimization is a *re*victimization. The concept of sexual revictimization challenges the relevance and usefulness of prevention theory's traditional distinction between primary and secondary prevention. The prevention of sexual victimization of

African American women requires reductions in both the incidence of sexual attacks, and in the stereotyped attitudes and beliefs about their sexual behavior. Recognizing the need for interventions across multiple levels, Wyatt, Notgrass and Gordon suggest prevention approaches directed to individuals, groups, organizations, communities, and society at large.

Becerra and Iglehart address the issue of intrafamilial child sexual abuse within Hispanic families in Los Angeles. In addressing this issue Becerra and Iglehart stress the necessity of implementing culture- and language-sensitive programs. The authors report the results of a Los Angeles study with Hispanic and white non-Hispanic families in which intrafamilial child sexual abuse was reported. The conditions here that contribute to risk include victims' young age and their membership in families that include boys and men who are perpetrators. Although the two samples differ in ways that reflect immigrant- and class-status, there are cultural differences between the two samples that must be recognized and addressed in working with Hispanic communities. Becerra and Iglehart propose a culturally and linguistically sensitive public information campaign as a primary prevention initiative. This program would educate Hispanic audiences about (1) incest, its incidence and prevalence, the negative consequences for victims and their families, the social and legal penalties for perpetrators, and the resources available within the community to prevent and treat the problem; (2) strengthening family relationships; and (3) developing coping mechanisms to deal with stress.

The term sexual harassment is relatively new, but the practices it describes are old. Bond deals with features of the worksite and academia that impact on sexual harassment. Moving beyond individual characteristics, she documents the embeddedness of sexual harassment in systemic relationship and environmental conditions. Although she identifies gender inequality as a primary factor in sexual harassment, she notes the multiple power bases from which harassment comes. In addition to gender power, power rooted in position, ethnicity, age and physical superiority compounds victimization. A major structural issue is the gender composition of the workplace. No simple formula applies here. Preliminary research shows that women in work settings where they are either invisible or a majority are less frequently harassed than women in settings where they are a *noticeable minority*. Findings such as these lead to an exploration of the function of sexual harassment in the work-place. Bond's approach to prevention in organizational settings is one of empowerment. Critical to her goal of developing empowering organizational climates are changes in values across all ecological levels–individuals, relationships, and work groups–with organizational support for the changes.

Although the scientific study of rape is of very recent origin, major progress has been made in the last decade. Prevention research has also reached a new level of sophistication, both in the general field and in the area of sexual assault/abuse prevention. These advances are reflected in the articles in this collection, which present emerging *approaches* to the prevention of rape and other sexual abuse. At this stage of the field's development there are no large-scale preventive interventions that have been subjected to rigorous experimental tests. What have evolved in this field are directions for future prevention research and action programs that converge on changing the social, political, economic, and religious environments that now support a rape culture.

I want to thank the contributors to this volume, whose work demonstrates the complexity of the prevention task. I also wish to acknowledge my appreciation to Rob Hess, editor of the *Prevention in Human Services* series, who has been an unflagging advocate for this volume.

Carolyn F. Swift
Institute for Life Span Studies
University of Kansas

Introduction

George W. Albee
University of Vermont

Carolyn F. Swift
University of Kansas

Both prevention and sexual abuse have developed along parallel tracks as fields of study. Although both deal with centuries-old practices, only within the last quarter century have they become subjects of research in the behavioral sciences. Initial assumptions in each case tended to be simplistic (i.e., single causal) and to reflect prevalent cultural beliefs. Both are emerging from these early stages to increasing sophistication in theory and methods (McCall, 1993). The issues raised in the prevention of sexual assault are complex, and will not be resolved quickly or easily. Below we outline a prevention paradigm and trace its implications for the prevention of sexual abuse.

The term prevention in behavioral science and the human service professions sometimes connotes a narrow and restricted definition and sometimes a broader range of concepts. We have borrowed the terms primary

---

Address correspondence to George W. Albee, 7157 Longboat Drive North, Longboat Key, FL 34228.

Parts of this essay have been adapted from the introduction to G. Albee, H. Leitenberg and S. Gordon (Eds.) (1986). *Fostering mature sexuality and preventing sexual problems*, Hanover, NH: The University Press of New England. Used with permission of copyright owner, The Vermont Conference on the Primary Prevention of Psychopathology.

[Haworth co-indexing entry note]: "Introduction." Albee, George W., and Carolyn F. Swift. Co-published simultaneously in *Prevention in Human Services* (The Haworth Press, Inc.) Vol. 12, No. 2, 1995, pp. 1-11; and: *Sexual Assault and Abuse: Sociocultural Context of Prevention* (ed: Carolyn F. Swift) The Haworth Press, Inc., 1995, pp. 1-11. Single or multiple copies of this article are available from The Haworth Document Delivery Service [1-800-342-9678, 9:00 a.m.-5:00 p.m. (EST)].

1

prevention, secondary prevention, and tertiary prevention from the field of public health. We suggest that *primary prevention* involves working with *groups* of non-affected persons, or with social conditions, to prevent the development of subsequent disturbance, that *secondary prevention* means early crisis intervention with those individuals who are suffering stress in order to prevent the development of full-fledged disorders, and *tertiary prevention* means intervention after serious individual damage has already occurred in order to relieve, insofar as possible, the handicapping consequences of the full-bloom disorder. One unfortunate consequence of this broad application of the term "prevention" is that it has resulted in endless confusion about what research or programs should be called prevention inasmuch as practically every kind of behavioral science or human service effort could appropriately be classified under one or another of the broad rubrics described.

In recent years a more narrow usage of the term prevention has gained acceptance in the field of behavioral disorders. Under this more restricted usage, the terms prevention and primary prevention have come to be used interchangeably and there is general agreement that the characteristics of primary prevention include work with groups of non-affected persons including those at high risk for the condition or conditions to be prevented. The effort is to reduce the subsequent *incidence* (new cases) of disorder or damage, the whole process being subject to appropriate follow-up and evaluation.

Clearly our efforts must begin to focus on *primary prevention* if ever we are to reduce the *incidence* of sexual abuse. Efforts at primary prevention intended to reduce the incidence of undesirable behavior are not usually directed at specific at-risk individuals but at all members of specified groups. Our purpose, in primary prevention, is to reduce the rate of the undesirable condition or behavior in the entire group.

The following formula (Albee, 1984) has been useful as a way of categorizing prevention efforts:

$$\text{Reducing Incidence} = \frac{\text{organic factors} + \text{stress} + \text{exploitation}}{\text{social competence} + \text{self-esteem} + \text{support networks}}$$

The equation suggests three ways to reduce the incidence of disturbed behavior or mental illness: (1) reduce the levels of stress and exploitation, (2) increase the levels of social competence, self-esteem and social networking, or (3) some combination of these. The main tools for primary prevention are education, social engineering, and social/political change. Primary prevention efforts are based on the assumption that reducing stress and exploitation and giving people better resources for coping are effective ways to prevent social difficulties. So is helping them to develop good self-esteem and find support groups.

A major argument for a primary prevention approach is based on an analogy: the success that has been achieved in reducing or wiping out other plagues that have afflicted humankind over the centuries. It is accepted public health doctrine that (a) widespread plagues afflicting large numbers of people are *never* brought under control or eliminated through intensive treatment of individuals and (b) successful efforts at eradicating widespread disorders *cannot* be achieved by attempts at increasing the number of persons trained in individual intervention. Over the past 200 years widespread successes have been achieved in improving the health and life expectancy of persons especially in the industrial nations. Life expectancy has been increased, unnecessary and premature death has been reduced, and major infectious diseases have been eliminated or brought largely under control. While the propaganda mills of the health care industry tout the triumphs of high-technology medicine applied to individuals–heart transplants, coronary by-pass surgery, CAT-scanners, kidney dialysis–the fact is that it has been the quiet sanitary revolution, improvements in sewage disposal, water purification, nutrition, and the control of the spread of contagious diseases, that truly have resulted in dramatic improvements in the health of populations. Anyone familiar with the history of health care recognizes that it is *primary prevention*, not treatment, that deserves the credit for the major improvement in the health of populations.

The strategies for effective primary prevention in the field of health are simple and straightforward. Generally they involve (1) finding the noxious agent and rendering it powerless in some way, (2) strengthening the host by building up resistance to fight off the noxious agent when it reaches the person, and (3) preventing transmission of the noxious agent to the host.

The heroes and heroines in the field of public health are persons who have applied one or more of these basic techniques in ways that have reduced or eliminated epidemics. In what was perhaps the most famous act in the history of public health, John Snow in 1854 observed that a cholera epidemic in London seemed centered around a particular section of the city. Suspecting that the water supply was involved, he chained and then later removed the handle from the Broad Street pump, thereby requiring Londoners in that neighborhood to go some distance away to draw their water from another well. As a consequence, he stopped a cholera epidemic before, it should be noted, the specific noxious agent causing cholera had been identified. This and subsequent demonstrations of water-borne noxious agents has led to the purification of the water supply with incalculable benefits in the prevention of disease.

The *second* public health strategy, strengthening the host, is illustrated by the concepts of immunity and immunization. An observation was made in England that one group of persons was singularly free of the widespread plague of smallpox. The young women who milked cows were somehow immune to the dreaded scourge. Further investigation revealed that they contracted cowpox, a relatively mild related disease, and that somehow this made them resistant. This observation led eventually to immunization through vaccination. It now seems certain that smallpox has been eliminated from the face of the earth. The last person to have smallpox was a man in Ethiopia whose picture appeared in newspapers around the world a few years ago. When he recovered, and his various contacts failed to develop symptoms of this disease, the World Health Organization declared smallpox eradicated, and barring the escape of smallpox germs from bacteriological laboratories, or their deliberate spread, the human race is probably permanently free.

The *third* strategy, prevention of transmission, can be illustrated by the work of a young Hungarian physician named Semmelweiss. He long suspected that the puerperal fevers often associated with the process of childbirth might result from the contamination of the mother by the unwashed hands of the physicians who delivered babies. This insight preceded any sophisticated awareness of the presence of disease germs in the unseen world of microbiology. Physicians were wont to go directly from the dissecting room to the obstetrical delivery room with unwashed hands contaminated by all sorts of virulent organisms. Semmelweiss urged the simple step of careful hand-washing prior to delivery. Because his suggestion was regarded as impertinent, a challenge to the authority of senior physicians, he was dismissed from his post. But his observations and recommendations eventually carried the day so that the antisepsis of hospitals is now firmly entrenched. Currently, efforts at preventing the transmission of AIDS have focused on education on the use of condoms, or clean needles, to prevent transmission of the noxious agent to the bloodstream.

LOOKING FOR THE CAUSE OF THE CAUSES

Joffe (1982) has suggested an extremely important concept that we must consider in efforts at primary prevention. He has asked us to learn to seek the *cause of the causes.* Very often in examining a particular condition that we want to prevent we halt our efforts when we have found one or more specific proximate causes. Thus if we are interested in preventing sexual harassment we may discover that men are most commonly the harassers and women the victims, that men often have positions of power over the women they harass, and that the women targeted are most often under 35 years of age (Gutek, 1985). We conclude that we have identified some conditions that may suggest important "causes." This may lead us to institute preventive programs involving sexual harassment training at the worksite, organizational policies prohibiting sexual harassment, and the development of procedures for dealing with harassment. But we fail to take the critical step of trying to identify the cause of the causes. If we do not ask what are the conditions that are responsible for the inferior status of women in our society, for the special vulnerability of young women to sexual harassment, and for the violent acts perpetrated by men against women, then we are not dealing with the important cause of causes.

In a similar way, we may identify specific epidemiological factors associated with other forms of sexual abuse. But we may neglect searching for the cause of causes. One such higher order cause clearly is the gender power imbalance in our society with its emphasis on the importance of male domination of females, the emphasis in the mass media on male violence and female passivity, and the pervasive subtle sexism that is everywhere as present as the air we breathe and the water we drink. What is the cause of the causes? To many, the power imbalance between genders is as fixed a part of their world as air and water, based on differences in the physical capacities of men and women. Instead of celebrating these differences and using them to promote the strengths of each gender to benefit society, they are used in patriarchal cultures to justify the subjugation and maltreatment of women and children, with devastating and violent effects, particularly in sexual and other interpersonal behavior. The gender power imbalance will not be easily changed. What causes this imbalance and what can we do about it?

Our society is characterized by hierarchal relations of all kinds, but especially between men and "their women and children." Madonna Kolbenschlag (1979) has argued that all oppression ultimately is a reflection of the uneven power relations that exist between women and men. From the days of the Greeks, when slaves and women were considered by men to be irrational species, to modern religious androlatry, social violence preserves and sustains hierarchal relations emphasizing male superiority and power. When an agency of the federal government recently classified jobs according to social desirability, nuclear physics was at the top and child care was at the bottom. Recent changes in the economic system further advance the process of the "feminization of poverty" and the masculinization of war and medicine. The federal government now proposes that it retain responsibility for a greatly reduced level of support for welfare, which negatively affects most heavily women and children.

It seems reasonable to conclude from the available data (see Leitenberg, 1984) that those societies that emphasize a rigid patriarchal, male-dominated hierarchal social structure will have the highest rates of rape and child molestation while those societies that are most equalitarian will have the lowest rates. Prescott (1979) argues from cross-cultural studies that societies that are most strong in their opposition to women's rights also are the strongest in their opposition to abortion, and are, at the same time, more likely to treat their enemies with a high level of cruelty, and they tend to practice slavery. He says: ". . . it is perhaps not surprising to discover that cultures that enslave women to the bondage of compulsory pregnancy also practice other forms of human slavery" (1979, p. 317). He reports that every culture that punishes abortion is patrilineal while nearly three quarters of those cultures that do *not* punish abortion are matrilineal.

Sexual abuse is a specific form of exploitation in patriarchal societies by the more powerful male of the less powerful woman and child. It is an extreme form of the culturally-sanctioned exploitation and oppression of women and children characteristic of our patriarchy. Too frequently the society, supporting patriarchal myth systems, blames the victims. The victims, not the perpetrators, are stigmatized. The victims suffer a variety of damaging consequences to their personhood and their self-esteem. A recent study (Saunders, Villeponteaux, Lipovsky, Kilpatrick & Veronen, 1992) found clear evidence that early sexual assault was related to later adult psychopathology in women.[1]

Less overt, more symbolic, rape occurs with great frequency in our patriarchy. Our society provides a subtle but nurturant climate for the exploitation of the weak by the powerful along multiple demographic dimensions–gender, ethnicity, age, sexual orientation. Unequal pay for equal work, sexual harassment in the work place, the kitchen, and the bedroom and the consistent depiction of sexist and racist imagery in the media all contribute to reinforcing the exploitation of women by men. Women of color in this country, particularly African-American women, suffer the double discrimination of female gender and minority ethnicity. This discrimination is reflected in the history of sexual exploitation of African American women in the United States, and in their reluctance to disclose their sexual victimization for fear they will not be believed (Wyatt, 1992; Wyatt, Notgrass & Gordon, this volume).

Media role models for women emphasize passivity and submission. Those for men emphasize aggression and dominance. These images, and the constant media modeling of men as warriors and as powerful manipulators of machines and people, provide social pressure on men to act out dominance over others; in the sexual arena such actions have resulted in the chronic victimization of women and children. Russell (this volume) notes that exposure to the media pairing of violence and sex reduces men's inhibitions to rape. She documents studies showing that a majority (up to 65%) of college men have indicated they would rape if they could be assured of not being caught.

Only a small proportion of men who are potential rapists actually carry out the overt act with a stranger-victim. A larger number act out in their own circle of family and friends, thereby helping to produce new generations of emotionally disturbed persons. The most visible population of those affected are the women and children who suffer the sexual abuse. But the population of boys who witness (or become aware of) their fathers'/brothers'/uncles' violence against their mothers, sisters and friends are also scarred; they're at risk for developing the exploitive behavior to which they've been exposed (although the burden of risk for cycling violence into future generations, and the factors contributing to it, are only now beginning to be identified–see MacEwen, 1994; Vander Mey, 1988). Through their modeling of women-focused violence rapists contribute to the production of new generations of rape-prone males. The cycle of sexual abuse is perpetuated by the patriarchal sanction of violence against women, as reflected both in the low rates of arrest, conviction and incarceration for males who commit these acts, and in the glorification of this behavior in the media. Rapists function as societal storm troopers to maintain the patriarchal power men wield over women in our society (Brownmiller, 1975). A priority strategy for preventionists is to analyze and intervene in the process of development that results in sexually abusive behavior in males.

Sexual abuse is the by-product of a misogynous society where male supremacy is the rule. When over half the population is relegated to inferior status at birth, when gender is perceived as primarily a form of power relationship, where women and children are seen as powerless and as possessions of the patriarchal male, we find high rates of sexual abuse. Sexual abuse is clearly affected by the pornography that stresses the power inequality between the sexes, and by the idealization in our mass media of the powerful man and the powerless, passive, little-girl woman.

In the prevention of sexual abuse, the high risk groups are women and children, who are nearly always the intended victims. Prevention efforts have historically been directed to women–who are taught to restrict their behavior to reduce their chances of rape (avoid unlit streets, wear more conservative clothes, travel in groups, etc.), and to children–who are directed to identify good from bad bodily touches, and to say no to perpetrator approaches. The ecology of rape dictates that prevention strategy be focused on boys and men, who are the perpetrators.

But what kind of strategy? If we take the position that both rape and child molestation are extreme examples of the widespread exploitation of populations perceived to be less powerful and thus potential victims by males who are themselves often caricatures of widely adopted male sex roles, then our prevention strategy, over the long haul, will have to involve efforts to effect a redistribution of power between women and men to change the cultural definition of appropriate male behavior. In an equalitarian society, where children grow up with healthier sexual knowledge and experience and where the society emphasizes sex education that focuses on the acceptability of sexual pleasure in equalitarian relationships, we would expect a reduction in incidence of these damaging behaviors. But such an agenda will immediately run into opposition from those who enjoy and benefit from the present unequal distribution of power, from religious fundamentalists and patriarchs in general, and from all institutions that have deeply ingrained patterns of male domination. In addition, if the society's power brokers benefit from the exploitation of women as underpaid and exploited labor, then efforts at equalization of rights threaten the very economic foundations of the society. We find that prevention means political action and social change (Joffe & Albee, 1981) and we must remind ourselves that power is not given up easily.

In some ways, the prevention of sexual abuse may be accomplished, in significant measure, by building competencies and coping skills in the potential victims, by forming support groups that provide potential victims with the strength and skill to avoid danger or to resist attack. The women's movement and the civil rights movement have achieved some successes because they have helped individuals, who might otherwise have felt isolated and alone against their exploiters, to form support networks that encourage social change, social action, and competence feelings. The Anita Hill-Clarence Thomas hearing raised the consciousness of the nation by showing a credible victim, Ms. Hill, being harassed by an all white male Senate committee. Subsequently the number of harassment accusations has risen considerably.

The federal crime bill, passed in August, 1994, provides fiscal support ($1.6 billion) to fight violence against women. Prevention efforts are addressed through the bill's rape education and community prevention programs, and through the sanctions the bill creates to deter sex offenses through more rigorous enforcement and longer sentences. It represents a legislative advance in preventing sexual assault, through its specific prevention provisions, and through the federal resources it provides to support women's efforts to live violence-free lives.

Legislation, and women's efforts to protect themselves and their children, are necessary but not sufficient means to eliminate sexual abuse. Men must also change, and become partners with women in eradicating sexual abuse from male behavioral repertoires. While few scientific data bear directly on the development of prevention efforts in this field, it is clear that a major cause of sexual abuse is a patriarchal machismo system that devalues women and children and regards them as male possessions. Prevention efforts must stress the development of an equalitarian society that educates its children about human sexuality–particularly the rewards of consensual sexual relationships.

After a thorough review of the literature on the sexual victimization of children, Leitenberg (1984) asks the fundamental question for preventionists:

> . . . sexual abuse of children is only one component of a much larger issue. How can people live so that unequal physical, financial, emotional and social power was never used at someone else's expense? If that ideal were realized, then children would never be abused in any way by adults, sexually or otherwise. (1984, p. 71)

We will hear the same kinds of resistance to programs of primary prevention of sexual abuse as have been mounted in the broad field of preventing psychopathology. We can expect to hear that (1) not enough money is available for prevention–we need to spend our limited resources on the treatment of victims; (2) we cannot prevent sexual abuse if we do not know its cause, and so we should conduct research that looks especially for genetic and biochemical factors causing sexual abuse; (3) what is being proposed involves system change and this is not the province of behavioral scientists or mental health professionals–we should leave political and social change to those better qualified; and (4) there is no evidence that efforts at preventing sexual abuse really work and so we cannot undertake a major effort until better evidence is available.

The messages to be delivered to those who want change focus on (1) eliminating the social, economic, and political power differentials between women and men, (2) acting on the need for better sex education of children, (3) developing methods to inoculate children from the media pairing of sex and violence against women and children, (4) recognizing the importance of sex as a natural and pleasurable human activity, and (5) helping people to integrate sex responsibly into their lives.

Underlying all this is a revolutionary message: The underlying sexist and exploitive cause of the causes must be challenged and eliminated. Mary Daly (1978) identifies the cause of the causes:

> The fact is that we live in a profoundly anti-female society, a misogynist "civilization" in which men collectively victimize women, attacking us as personifications of their own paranoid fears, as The Enemy. Within this society it is men who rape, who sap women's energy, who deny women economic and political power. (1978, p. 29)

If we are to prevent sexual abuse we must prevent sexism by finding effective ways to redistribute and equalize gender power.

NOTE

1. A number of recent studies of men and women who were sexually abused in childhood (Briere et al., 1988; Hunter, 1991; Urquiza & Crowley, cited in Finkelhor, 1990) report finding few or no differences between the two groups on a variety of assessment instruments, although some found differences between abused and nonabused samples. Young, Bergandi and Titus (1994) found few gender differences between latency age girls and boys in a comparison of the effects of sexual abuse, although they confirmed that the abused children reported more problems with peer interactions and depression than a control group of nonabused children. Because of the relative invisibility of young male sexual abuse victims in the literature–until quite recently–it is not possible to assess their subsequent psychopathology in any definitive way, but emerging studies appear to show comparable reactions to those of young female victims.

REFERENCES

Albee, G. (1984). A model for classifying prevention programs. In J. Joffe, G. Albee, & L. Kelly (Eds.), *Readings in primary prevention of psychopathology: Basic concepts.* Hanover, NH: University Press of New England.

Briere, J., Evans, D., Runtz, M., & Wall, T. (1988). Symptomatology in men who were molested as children: A comparison study. *American Journal of Orthopsychiatry, 58*, 457-461.

Brownmiller, S. (1975). *Against our will: Men, women and rape.* New York: Simon and Schuster.

Daly, M. (1978). *Gyn/Ecology: The metaethics of radical feminism.* Boston: Beacon Press.

Finkelhor, D. (1990). Early and long-term effects of child sexual abuse: An update. *Professional Psychology, 21*, 325-330.

Gutek, B. (1985). *Sex and the workplace*. San Francisco: Jossey-Bass.

Hunter, J. (1991). A comparison of psychosocial maladjustment of adult males and females sexually molested as children. *Journal of Interpersonal Violence, 6*, 205-217.

Joffe, J. (1982). Approaches to prevention of adverse developmental consequences of genetic and prenatal factors. In L. Bond & J. Joffe (Eds.), *Facilitating infant and early childhood development*. Hanover, NH: University Press of New England.

Joffe, J. & Albee, G. (Eds.) (1981). *Prevention through political action and social change*. Hanover, NH: University Press of New England.

Kolbenschlag, M. (1979). *Kiss Sleeping Beauty goodbye*. New York: Doubleday.

Leitenberg, H. (1984). Sexual victimization of children: Pedophilia and incest. In J. Geer, J. Heiman & H. Leitenberg (Eds.), *Human sexual behavior*. Englewood Cliffs, NJ: Prentice-Hall.

MacEwen, K. (1994). Refining the intergenerational transmission hypothesis. *Journal of Interpersonal Violence, 9*, 350-365.

McCall, G. (1993). Risk factors and sexual assault prevention. *Journal of Interpersonal Violence, 8*, 277-295.

Prescott, J. (1979). Appendices 3 and 4. In S. Gordon, P. Scales & K. Everly (Eds.), *The sexual adolescent: Communicating with teenagers about sex* (2nd ed.). North Scituate, MA: Duxbury.

Saunders, B., Villeponteaux, L., Lipovsky, J., Kilpatrick, D., & Veronen, L. (1992). Child sexual assault as a risk factor for mental disorders among women. *Journal of Interpersonal Violence, 7*, 189-204.

Vander Mey, B. (1988). The sexual victimization of male children: A review of previous research. *Child Abuse & Neglect, 12*, 61-72.

Wyatt, G. (1992). The sociocultural context of African American and White American Women's Rape. *Journal of Social Issues, 48*, 77-91.

Young, R., Bergandi, T. & Titus, T. Comparison of the effects of sexual abuse on male and female latency-aged children. *Journal of Interpersonal Violence, 9*, 291-306.

Perpetrator Prevention: Stopping the Development of Sexually Abusive Behavior

Carolyn F. Swift

University of Kansas

Kimberly Ryan-Finn

University of Washington

SUMMARY. This paper documents perpetrator prevention as an essential component in the prevention of sexual assault and abuse. Traditional approaches to the prevention of sexual abuse have focused primarily on changing the behavior of potential victims. Preventive interventions that have the potential for changing the behavior of potential perpetrators are explored. Although there is little empirical work to review in the prevention of perpetrator development in boys and men, some of the correlates of sexually abusing behavior are identified and related research highlighted. Three of the risk factors linked with sexually abusive behavior are explored: gender inequity, the negative effects on children and young men of media exposure to violence–particularly sexual violence against women, and the increased risk of sexually abusive behavior by males with a history of childhood sexual abuse. Preventive interventions to reduce these risks are considered. The incorporation of perpetrator prevention into an ecological approach to the prevention of sexual

---

Address correspondence to Carolyn Swift, 1102 Hilltop Drive, Lawrence, KS 66044.

[Haworth co-indexing entry note]: "Perpetrator Prevention: Stopping the Development of Sexually Abusive Behavior." Swift, Carolyn F., and Kimberly Ryan-Finn. Co-published simultaneously in *Prevention in Human Services* (The Haworth Press, Inc.) Vol. 12, No. 2, 1995, pp. 13-44; and: *Sexual Assault and Abuse: Sociocultural Context of Prevention* (ed: Carolyn F. Swift) The Haworth Press, Inc., 1995, pp. 13-44. Single or multiple copies of this article are available from The Haworth Document Delivery Service [1-800-342-9678, 9:00 a.m.-5:00 p.m. (EST)].

13

abuse is discussed. *[Article copies available from The Haworth Document Delivery Service: 1-800-342-9678.]*

INTRODUCTION

Sexual abuse is not a modern phenomenon. It crosses historical eras, geographic boundaries, and the demographics of race, class and education. One demographic factor that sexual abuse rarely crosses is that of the gender of the abuser. Over 90% of sexual abusers are male (Koss, 1990). For this reason references to sexual abusers in this paper are to males. Victims are predominantly female, although recent research is yielding increasing proportions of victimized boys and men. Although sexual victimization is centuries old, it is only in the last few decades that the scientific and professional communities have begun to acknowledge and address the problem on a population-wide scale. Understandably, initial attention has gone to the identification and treatment of victims. More recently the research community has begun to examine possibilities for preventing sexual abuse. Since multiple factors affect the incidence of sexual abuse, no one prevention approach will eliminate it. Preventive interventions in multiple domains–social, cultural, economic, political, and religious–will be required to achieve a significant reduction in sexual abuse.

Our primary objective in this paper is to document perpetrator prevention as an essential component in the primary prevention of sexual abuse. Traditional approaches to the prevention of sexual abuse have generally ignored the role of the perpetrator or assumed his behavior to be unchangeable; until recently the small body of work that focused on perpetrators used convicted sex offenders as participants–a small percentage of those who commit sexual assault or abuse. A secondary objective of this paper is to place sexual abuse prevention in the context of an ecological approach (Bond, this volume), an approach that integrates the perpetrator and the victim in the context of their social, economic, and cultural environment. Over the last few decades prevention efforts have focused primarily on changing the behavior of potential victims. There have been some efforts to change environmental variables affecting sexual abuse, ranging from increased use of street lights to rape reform laws. The least pursued approach is that of changing the behavior of perpetrators–sexually abusing men and boys.

We begin by reviewing the problem of sexual abuse. We then address models of primary prevention, and outline approaches to the primary prevention of sexual abuse. The body of the article is devoted to exploring prevention approaches that have the potential for changing the behavior of potential perpetrators. Although there is little empirical work to review in the prevention of perpetrator development in boys and men, we identify some of the correlates of sexually abusing behavior and highlight related research. We conclude with suggestions for incorporating perpetrator prevention into an ecological approach to the prevention of sexual abuse.

BACKGROUND

Sexual Abuse

The term sexual abuse here includes sexual assault, sexual harassment and any other form of contact or interaction in which an individual is used without their consent for the sexual stimulation of the perpetrator or another person. The United States common law and the FBI Criminal Code define sexual assault, the legal term for rape, as the forcible carnal knowledge of a female against her will. In her careful review of rape prevalence studies, Koss (1993) arrives at a 14% prevalence rate for women–as a middle ground between diverging research estimates ranging from 8% to over 20%. According to Kilpatrick (1993) more than half a million (680,000) women were raped during a one year period. Sexual coercion by a friend or acquaintance–e.g., date rape–is common. Over half of the sexual assaults of adult and college age women are committed by romantic partners, and half (49%) of child sexual assaults are committed by persons known to the victim (Koss, 1990).

Although the scientific study of rape is of very recent origin, major progress has been made in the last decade. Current theory and practice reflect the etiological significance of multiple variables and multilevel interventions. Epidemiological research has replaced studies of incarcerated rapists and clinical case studies of victims as the legitimate method of estimating incidence and prevalence. Definitions and methodologies are being reexamined (Koss, 1992; Muehlenhard, Powch, Phelps & Giusti, 1992; White & Farmer, 1992), and sociocultural factors impacting on rape are being explored and assessed (George, Winfield & Blazer, 1992; Sorenson & Siegel, 1992; Wyatt, 1992).

Primary Prevention Approaches

Public Health Model. The classic primary prevention paradigm,[1] based on the public health model of the prevention of physical disease (Anthony, 1990; Gordon, 1952), requires altering one of three elements: a noxious stressor, a host population on which the stressor impacts, and the environment in which the stressor and host co-exist. According to this model, disease or disorder is a result of stressors such as bacteria, viruses, or chemical agents acting on host populations. Three prevention strategies, corresponding to each of the three elements, are to eliminate or reduce the power of the noxious stressor, strengthen the host population to resist the stressor or alter the environment so as to prevent the transmission of the disease from stressor to host.[2]

Currently in the United States the most widely used strategy to prevent sexual abuse focuses on strengthening the host population of women and children to resist or avoid the stressor–the male abuser. Research over the last 20 years has demonstrated that women who assertively defend themselves when attacked or mobilize their resources to escape stand a greater chance of not being raped than women who do not (Bart & O'Brien, 1985; Ullman & Knight, 1993). Many women have avoided victimization through increased defensive skills. But not all women and children access these measures easily. Those at the extreme ends of the life cycle and some with physical or mental disabilities are defenseless against sexual abuse. Although self-defense programs for women and children are vital components in the prevention of sexual abuse, they are not sufficient measures, in themselves, to eliminate it.

The transmission prevention strategy focuses on altering the shared environment of the stressor and the host. In the context of sexual abuse this strategy has most often meant changing the physical environment– e.g., increasing the use of street lights and police patrols. Changes in the physical environment may increase the safety of some neighborhoods, but this may occur at the expense of surrounding neighborhoods, which then become vulnerable to crime displacement. Another common transmission prevention strategy, also directed at controlling the physical environment, involves physically separating women from situations with historically high risk for sexual abuse. These efforts focus on restricting and controlling women's activities. Certain times, places and situations–being outside alone at night, or in certain areas of cities, or alone in bars–carry increased risk for sexual assaults. Attempts to prevent rape by restricting women's freedom hold little probability for developing effective interventions in today's society. Although transmission prevention efforts have traditionally focused on the physical environment, some efforts at changing the sociocultural environment of sexual abuse have been incorporated into legislation. Expanding the application of the transmission prevention model to other areas of the sociocultural environment–changing traditional gender values, with their inherent inequities, to egalitarian values, for example–is an essential component in an ecological approach to sexual abuse prevention.

Stressor-focused interventions, which in the context of sexual abuse mean perpetrator prevention, are the least used of the three public health strategies in preventing sexual abuse. Sexual abusers cannot be targeted for eradication in the same way that bacteria or viruses can. Nevertheless there is a wide continuum between eliminating abusers from the population and permitting them to continue their behavior with little risk of negative consequences. Researchers and public policy scholars are increasingly supporting prevention programs focused on the perpetrators, as exemplified in the following:

> Among the most promising interventions to reduce girls' and young women's risk of victimization are ones that are directed toward boys and men as potential victimizers. Traditional prevention programs directed at girls and women center on victimization prevention that, although important, implies that girls and women are responsible for their victimization. It is important to focus preventive interventions on the perpetrators or likely perpetrators as well as on the victims or potential victims. (American Psychological Association Commission on Violence and Youth, 1993, p. 49)

> Although tremendous resources have been enlisted to respond to the incidence and impact of both child sexual abuse and adult sexual assaults, intervention strategies have failed to prevent the occurrence, and prevention strategies have been aimed at potential victims. While self-protection and defense, reporting, prosecution, and treatment programs are certainly called for in response to the problem, the ultimate solution is to prevent the development of new offenders so that future generations are no longer at risk. While recent intervention responses have been descriptive and reactive, the only pro-active approach to sexual abuse prevention is perpetration prevention. (Ryan, 1991b, pp. 393-394)

Fischhoff, Furby and Morgan (1987), in their report of a survey of rape strategies, project a typology of rape prevention that includes altering societal beliefs and attitudes as well as the structural characteristics of society that maintain rape. Conte, Rosen and Saperstein (1986) note that the conditions which produce child sexual abuse are deeply embedded in our culture. "While many prevention professionals recognize that fundamental change in power relationships in families and in society from a sexist to equalitarian distribution will be necessary to prevent sexual victimization, ultimately as a professional group, not enough has been done to link political and cultural life and sexual victimization" (1986, p. 153). Sparks and Bar On (1985) point out that we "must find ways of intervening to alter the conditions in our communities that continue to produce offenders" (1985, p. 2).

Although the need for prevention programs focusing on potential offenders is clear, there are almost no preventive interventions designed along these lines. Prevention of the development of sexually abusing behavior requires major changes across social, economic, political and religious institutions. An initial step to an ecological approach to the prevention of sexual abuse requires interventions targeted to boys and men and to the relevant environmental stressors that impact on them to shape their sexual behavior.

Gordon's Classification System for Disease Prevention. The classic public health model's categories of stressor-host-environment do not address the relative risks, costs, or benefits of intervention. Gordon's (1983) classification system takes these considerations into account for interventions directed to the primary prevention of physical disease.[3] His three types of preventive interventions are based on the risks and costs associated with intervening with an entire population (*universal* preventive interventions), population subgroups with higher than average risk for developing the disease (*selective* preventive interventions), and individuals with risk factors or abnormalities that place them at high risk for developing the disease (*indicated* preventive interventions). We find it useful to adapt Gordon's classification system to the prevention of sexual abuse.

Universal interventions–those applied to an entire population or group– are acceptable for all members in terms of the balance of benefits versus risks and costs. Examples include public information campaigns (cancer, AIDS), automobile seatbelts, and immunizations. Universal interventions have several advantages. First, targeting everyone means that it is not necessary to identify or obtain access to subgroups of the population. The universal interventions of public education and municipal water treatment, for example, generally include all members of a community. Access to such services is built into the infrastructure of local communities through legislation, policies and procedures. Prohibiting sexual abuse through legislation provides universal sanctions to deter the abuse. Implementing a classroom intervention throughout a school district is an effective means of ensuring that students in that district are exposed to the same instruction and provided with the same resources.

A second advantage of universal interventions is that they avoid stigmatizing people who may be at risk, through demography or history, for developing the dysfunction targeted for prevention. This is an important point in child sexual abuse, since most men whose life circumstances or histories place them at higher risk for developing into sexual abusers–e.g., child victims of sexual abuse, stepfathers–do not develop abusive behavior. The trade-offs of universal interventions are their acceptability in terms of risks and costs–issues best decided on a case by case basis. Universal interventions, through education, legislation and the electronic and print media, offer the potential for changing gender stereotypes, achieving egalitarian gender values, providing sex education, and ultimately reducing the incidence of sexual abuse.

Gordon's *selective* preventive interventions are applicable to population subgroups whose members are at higher risk than the general population for developing the dysfunction.[4] In the context of preventing the development of sexually abusive behavior, boys and men with a history of child sexual abuse may be appropriate targets for selective preventive interventions. Gordon's *indicated* preventive interventions could be applied to individuals who–through screening for example–exhibit abnormalities that place them at particularly high risk for becoming sex abusers. In our discussion of the prevention of the development of sexually abusive behavior we have drawn from both the public health prevention model, and Gordon's classification system.

The Evolution of Approaches to Rape Prevention

The last quarter century has seen accelerated changes in gender relationships. Approaches to sexual assault prevention during this time have mirrored the generational shifts in gender roles and sexual values. These shifts are most dramatically shown in the evolution of two implicit assumptions that dominated rape research through the mid-1970s, dictating both the level of research and the target of intervention. The first assumption was that individuals were the nexus for change, rather than communities or systems. The destructive influences of society's differential gender-values were not integrated into rape prevention theory or research prior to the mid-1970s, and this contributed to the focus of prevention efforts on individuals, rather than on communities or on the system itself. The second assumption identified the victim as the pivot of prevention efforts, rather than the perpetrator or the rape supportive environment. Reducing the incidence of sexual assault meant changing the behavior of potential victims. Rape was thought to be the pathological behavior of a disturbed male; victims were seen as women and children who had contributed in some way–from carelessness or poor judgment to provocative dress–to their victimization.

The decade of the 1990s has seen these assumptions radically altered. As the rates of violent crime and sexual abuse have increased and the phenomena of date rape, marital rape and sexual harassment have become increasingly public, it is clear that these acts are more accurately conceptualized as social pathologies than as individual acts of depravity (Gordon & Riger, 1989). There is increasing recognition that the primary prevention of sexual abuse requires changing the behavior of the perpetrator (APA Commission on Violence and Youth, 1993; McCall, 1993; Ryan, 1991b). To do this, the variables which control the development of sexually abusing behavior in boys and men must be identified and changed. Preventive approaches must go beyond changing individuals to changing the system that creates and maintains sexual abuse.

CORRELATES OF THE DEVELOPMENT
OF SEXUALLY ABUSIVE BEHAVIOR IN BOYS AND MEN

The development of sexually abusive behavior stems from factors at both the system- and the individual-level. At the system level, factors range from women's status in society to sex education for children. At the core of sexual abuse is the inferior status ascribed to women and girls in patriarchal societies. This ascribed status results in gender inequities across multiple domains. These inequities are embedded within society through differential sex role socialization, creating a gender power imbalance that is a major support for a rape culture (Hansen & O'Leary, 1985). "An important contributing factor to girls' vulnerability is the historical pattern of social dominance of males over females in the United States. Significant risk is produced by the intersection of this inequality of status with the physical and emotional vulnerability of youth and with the socialization of girls to be compliant" (APA Commission on Violence and Youth, 1993, p. 49).

Another major factor that contributes to the development of sexual abuse is the tendency—most visibly prevalent in males—to resolve conflict by physical means. This practice supports systemic violence in our society, including sexual violence. Of all the industrialized countries, the United States has the highest rate of interpersonal violence (APA Commission on Violence and Youth, 1993). A related systemic factor is the unremitting media pairing of sex with violence against women, which negatively influences not only adolescent and adult males (Russell, this volume), but provides child viewers with early exposure to this destructive connection. The cumulative effects on boys and girls of repeated exposures to television, film, fiction, rock music, and computer games exploiting this connection are unknown. However, research with male students indicates a correlation between viewing electronic media depictions of sexual violence against women and insensitivity toward female victims of violence (Russell, this volume).

Society's failure to provide accurate information and education to children about sexuality is another systemic factor underlying sexual abuse (Albee, Gordon & Leitenberg, 1983). Until a few decades ago, public schools in this country made minimal attempts to educate children about human sexuality. Those that did rarely went beyond brief explanations of pubertal development and human reproduction. The evolution of adolescent sexual behavior over the last few decades has forced a re-examination of this policy. With the increase of sexual activity at earlier ages have come commensurate increases in teenage pregnancy, abortion and sexually transmitted diseases–including AIDS. A separate but related development has been the increasing visibility of child sexual abuse and date rape. Public response to these problems has begun to coalesce around prevention efforts, which have included a focus on sex education in the schools. Broadening the sex education curricula in public schools to include the importance of consensual sexual relationships and the emotional, physical, social and legal consequences of sexual behavior as well as the mechanics of intercourse and reproduction, would be positive steps toward reducing sexual violence in our society (Cohn, 1986).

A broad spectrum of individual factors has been linked to the development of sexually abusive behavior. These include a history of childhood sexual abuse (Araji & Finkelhor, 1986; Finkelhor, 1990; Risin & Koss, 1987), stepfather status (Finkelhor & Baron, 1986; Gordon, 1989; Russell, 1986), exposure to the pairing of violence or degradation with sexual activities–either through personal experience or through exposure to pornography (APA Commission on Violence and Youth, 1993; Hoberman, 1990; Huston et al., 1992; Russell, 1993), alcohol/drug use (Koss & Gaines, 1993; Muehlenhard & Linton, 1987), social isolation (Finkelhor & Baron, 1986), dysfunctional families, lack of social skills–especially in managing anger and aggression–and restricted capacity to empathize (Ryan & Lane, 1991).

It is beyond the scope of this article to address all of these factors. Below we look at interventions that attempt to reduce or eliminate three of the factors linked with sexually abusive behavior: gender inequity, the negative effects on children of media exposure to violence–particularly sexual violence against women, and the increased risk of sexually abusive behavior by boys and men with a history of childhood sexual abuse.

INTERVENTIONS TO PREVENT THE DEVELOPMENT OF SEXUALLY ABUSIVE BEHAVIOR

We turn to consideration of interventions to prevent the development of sexually abusive behavior in boys and men. Acknowledging the narrow range of intervention studies available, we have taken examples from the fields of education, legislation and the media. Some of these interventions are designed to reduce the incidence of sexual abuse directly. More often they are directed to changing one or more of the correlates of sexually abusing behavior or its development, reflecting the current beginning state of knowledge in the field. In most instances empirical evidence is available to assess outcome.

We first review the relationship between sexual abuse and gender inequity. We then present examples of educational interventions that offer promise for reducing gender stereotypes in school-age children. Emerging results of a study with adolescent sex offenders are reviewed in the context of educational interventions adaptable to primary prevention goals. Next we turn to legislative interventions that build a world with more egalitarian gender values, and improve women's status in pursuing justice against sexual abusers. We review some innovative interventions to reduce the impact on children and young men of media content depicting sexual violence against women. Finally we consider preventive interventions targeted to males with a history of childhood sexual abuse.

Promoting Gender Equity

A factor that encompasses many others in the analysis of sexual abuse is that of male power and dominance (Brownmiller, 1975; Russell, 1984). Sexual abuse is one result of the devastating effects of the unequal division of power between females and males in a society that condones the use of violence in settling conflicts. The process of sex role socialization incorporates the patriarchal values of male dominance and female submission. From earliest childhood girls and boys learn that to be female is to be inferior. Men are socialized to be predatory, to find aggression, or even assault, a source of sexual arousal (Russell, 1984). Women are socialized in very different ways–to take care of relationships first, and themselves second (Miller, 1987). Traditionally males have taken aggressive roles in seeking and consummating sexual relationships. From courtship rituals to wartime rape they have exercised force and authority to control women and children sexually (Brownmiller, 1975). Russell has noted that rape is not so much a deviant act as an overconforming one: "It is an extreme acting-out of qualities regarded as masculine . . . aggression, force, power, strength, toughness, dominance, competitiveness. To win, to be superior, to conquer, and to control demonstrate masculinity to those who subscribe to common cultural notions of masculinity; this constitutes the *masculinity mystique"* (1984, pp. 117-118). Since patriarchal values are built on a hierarchy of power, with a few men at the top and many at the bottom, there are many men who are relatively powerless within the system. Sex offenders are often described as believing they do not meet the ideals of masculinity in our society (Finkelhor, 1983; Russell, 1984). Sex may be the arena where traditional notions of masculinity are most intensely played out, particularly by men who feel powerless in the rest of their lives, and whose masculinity is threatened by this sense of powerlessness. It is clear that efforts to prevent sexual abuse must address both inter- and intra-gender power issues.

Gender inequity is only one form of inequity in our society. Other forms underlie racism, age discrimination, homophobia, and discrimination against those who are differently abled. Reducing any one of these is a formidable undertaking, one that becomes even more complicated when inequities are compounded.[5] Acknowledging this reality, gender inequity is a critical issue in the prevention of sexual assault.

Educational Interventions. Presenting children with unbiased gender information provides optimum conditions for the development of healthy attitudes and beliefs about themselves and others, and contributes to the elimination of discriminatory customs and values associated with gender that threaten the safety and welfare of women and children in our society. Such information aids in correcting both discriminatory gender beliefs and attitudes, and the gender role socialization that reinforces these beliefs and attitudes. Since over half of adult sex offenders begin their sex crimes during adolescence or before (Ryan, 1991a), it is important to intervene in early childhood.

Research has demonstrated the negative effects of traditional sex roles (Broverman, Vogel, Broverman, Clarkson & Rosenkrantz, 1972; Hare-Mustin & Marecek 1990; Lott, 1990; O'Leary, Unger & Wallston, 1985):

> "Feminine" traits have been shown to be associated with low self-esteem, high anxiety, low social acceptance, and traditional career choices, which are themselves lower in earning power, status, and prestige (citation omitted). Negative consequences of gender typing for males have concerned difficulties in school adjustment and dys-functions with respect to self-expression and interpersonal relation-ships (citation omitted). Thus, for most people, the belief that indi-viduals should be socialized to acquire "gender-appropriate" traits and behaviors has been replaced by the belief that psychologically

> healthy individuals are those who demonstrate flexibility in attitudes and behaviors, easily crossing traditional gender lines. (Liben & Bigler, 1987, p. 90)

Children develop schemata–"learned expectations that guide perception, memory, and inference" (Calvert & Huston, 1987, p. 79)–about gender at an early age (Liben & Signorella, 1987). A key issue is their ability to perceive activities as appropriate for either sex according to skills and interests. The capacity to conceptualize occupations and activities in gender-free ways demonstrates children's flexibility with regard to their gender schemata. Such flexibility is critical in reducing the sex-role stereotyping that underlies sexual abuse.

Significant differences in children's flexibility in processing information inconsistent with traditional gender stereotypes appear to be related to the children's level of gender-stereotyping (Signorella, 1987). High-stereotype children–those with high levels of traditional gender stereotypes–have significantly more difficulty remembering depictions of women and men in nontraditional gender roles than low-stereotype children. Although research in identifying children with high- and low-gender stereotyping is still in preliminary stages, it appears that factors such as the occupational and marital status of mothers, and the presence of siblings, as well as exposure to media, affect gender stereotyping. Children whose mothers work outside the home or are single parents tend to be less gender stereotyped (Huston, 1983; Katz, 1987), as are those with an other-sex sibling or girls with no siblings (Katz, 1987). Heavy television viewing appears to raise the level of gender stereotyping in children (Calvert & Huston, 1987), reflecting the reality of television content.

A variety of factors influence the probability of changing children's gender schemata. Non-school influences include the child's sex; developmental level; parental gender attitudes, beliefs and behaviors; and family constellation–single parent, mother working outside the home, presence of siblings (Katz, 1987). School influences range from teacher variables such as sex, ethnicity, expectations of gender behavior, level of personal contacts with students, and classroom teaching style, to other variables such as curricula, academic counseling and access to athletic programs (Meece, 1987). What is required in the schools is a comprehensive approach addressing both the obvious issues–such as curricula, and equal support and access for both girls and boys to mathematics and physics courses as well as athletic programs–and less obvious issues such as staffing patterns. It is unrealistic to expect brief interventions exposing children to nontraditional sex roles to bring about major or lasting shifts in embedded gender schemata when these schemata continue to be supported formally and informally within the school system, the home, and the broader society. It is therefore encouraging to note that significant changes in children's sex role preferences and gender stereotypes have been demonstrated by a variety of brief interventions.

Marcia Guttentag and her colleagues (Guttentag, 1977; Guttentag et al., 1976) conducted an experiment in preventing sexism. They integrated a six-week developmental curriculum into coeducational classes of kinder-gartners, fifth and ninth grade children. The intervention focused on changing sex-stereotypes in three areas: occupational, familial, and socioemotional roles. Their results were complex, but on the whole, positive. Although girls showed more consistent changes than boys in their views of occupational roles, teachers at each grade level who believed in the philosophy of the curriculum and who implemented it regularly were successful in changing student attitudes. "In a ninth grade classroom where the teacher used the nonsexist curriculum regularly and enthusiastically, in fact, there were significant attitudinal changes, and not only in girls; boys, too, changed to nonstereotyped views in all three areas" (Guttentag, 1977, p. 251). Guttentag concludes:

> It is clear that the schools can be used in a primary preventive role. Even a brief nonsexist intervention, implemented throughout a school, can have marked effects on sexist stereotypes of children and adolescents . . . The mental health costs of sexism are high. The schools are a socializing instrument that can serve immediately in the primary prevention of sexism. (p. 252)

The problems created by highly stereotyped beliefs and attitudes go beyond a feminist agenda for equality. In addition to perpetuating negative gender stereotypes, such attitudes interfere with children's information processing. Children tend to forget or distort information that is incompatible with their stereotypes. For example, Bigler and Liben (1990, 1992) introduced elementary school children to rules for sorting occupations based on skills and interests rather than gender. By exposing children to this procedure prior to presenting them with counterstereotypic occupational examples, these investigators succeeded in reducing children's gender-typing of occupations. Bigler (in press) extended the finding that children's classification skills can reduce gender stereotyping in occupations: in a test of Bem's (1983) suggestion that society's use of gender as a functional category increases gender stereotyping, Bigler pretested elementary school children on gender stereotyping and classification skill, and assigned them to three types of classrooms:

(1) functional use of male and female groups, (2) functional use of "red" and "green" groups, or (3) no explicit groups. After four weeks, children completed posttest measures of gender and inter-group attitudes. As predicted, the functional use of gender categories led to increases in gender stereotyping, particularly among those children with less advanced classification skills. The functional use of color categories did not result in highly stereotypic perceptions of groups. (in press, p. 2)

These results give pause to parents and teachers about the typical class-room practice of forming lines, assigning tasks or dividing groups of children by sex. The practice reinforces gender stereotyping, and thereby perpetuates the unequal treatment of boys and girls. It also disrupts children's capacities to process information.

Schools can be a major source of confirmation, as well as alteration, of the gender schemata children bring from home, from their neighborhood, and from the media to which they are exposed. Meece's (1987) comment on the role of schools in shaping children's gender schemata alerts preventionists to the problems of school environments on this issue:

Schools have been slow in adapting to recent changes in the social roles of men and women. As a result, schools may be exposing children to masculine and feminine images that are even more rigid and more polarized than those currently held in the wider society. Furthermore, the school setting does not seem to provide children with many opportunities to perform behaviors not associated with their gender. Therefore, schools seem to play an important role in reinforcing rigid gender distinctions, while neglecting children's need for developing greater flexibility in gender role conceptions. (1987, p. 67)

In addition to school-based strategies there are educational strategies developed outside the classroom that could be adapted for classroom use. Emerging research with adolescent sex offenders provides some clues about learned sexual behavior for primary prevention education efforts. In a pilot study, Weinrott and Riggan (1991) were successful in reducing adolescent sex offenders' arousal to children in a laboratory situation, and in increasing participants' understanding of the severity of their crimes, particularly in their impact on others. Although this study worked with sex offenders as participants, and thus was not a primary prevention effort,[6] the intervention could be adapted to primary prevention goals–i.e., preventing the development of sexually abusive behavior in boys and adolescent males.

Strategies in the Weinrott and Riggan pilot study included (1) preparing adolescents for appropriate (consensual) sexual relationships, (2) changing distorted thinking about human sexuality, and (3) decreasing deviant sexual fantasies. The first strategy functions to eliminate force from sexual relationships, and is consonant with the preventive objective of equalizing gender power. The two "corrective" strategies also lend themselves to prevention translation. Educating children about sexuality–particularly about the negative consequences, interpersonally and legally, of using force in sexual relationships, and the benefits of consensual sexual relationships–holds promise for reducing distorted thinking about sexual behavior. The third strategy, decreasing deviant sexual fantasies, could be addressed by preventive interventions with children to block the development of such fantasies. One approach would be to alter children's attitudes about the veracity and integrity of media content, particularly televised violence (Huesmann, Eron, Klein, Brice & Fischer, 1983; Linz, Arluk & Donnerstein, 1990), to reduce its impact. Linz, Wilson and Donnerstein (1992) have conceptualized a media literacy program to inoculate high school students against the effects of sexually violent material.

Weinrott and Riggan's pilot study presented sex offenders with a set of negative consequences that have been relatively invisible in our society, some because they have been essentially unenforced. Through repeated showings of videotapes (using actors) offenders were exposed to the law enforcement consequences of arrest, conviction, and incarceration. They were also exposed to videotaped enactments of victims' trauma, and the anxiety and grief of families and friends. Over a period of time repeated exposures reduced the adolescent abuser's arousal to inappropriate sexual partners, and increased his awareness of the unsuitability of his behavior. Success with related strategies has been described by Johnson (1989) and Hunter and Goodwin (1992). This work suggests the preventive value of sex education with children and adolescents, and the importance of articulating both the benefits of consensual sexual behavior, and the negative consequences of sexually abusive behavior.

In sum, interventions that educate children about human sexuality may serve to block deviate sexual behavior. Educational interventions also have the potential for reducing the sexist, racist, and heterosexist beliefs, attitudes and behaviors that support sexual assault. Routinely presenting school children with unbiased gender information should contribute to reductions in gender stereotyping and thus promote gender equity. Reductions in stereotypic attitudes and behaviors, in turn, would provide a solid foundation for building a sexually safe society.

Legislative Interventions

The legal system both reflects and shapes societal beliefs, and is a powerful tool in implementing social change. In the last 15 years new legislation has broadened the definition of sexual offenses (e.g., to include marital rape and sexual harassment), made sexual abuse a more serious offense (e.g., through more uniform and more severe sentencing), and attempted to make prosecution less intimidating for victims (e.g., through rape-shield laws). Current research raises controversy about the efficacy of reform of rape laws and their enforcement (Goldberg-Ambrose, 1992). Although these laws have met with mixed success, the new laws have led to increased visibility for sexual abuse crimes. Anita Hill was an exemplar for many other women in her protest of sexual harassment. The history of civil rights legislation is instructive here–it may take generations for legal remedies to be effective. Even so, the reform of laws dealing with rape and other sexual abuse is an important formal step in announcing society's revised limits on sexual abuse. As Loh (1981) noted in a review of rape reform laws, legislation can, and often does, serve as a "catalyst for attitude change . . . The criminal law serves not only a general deterrent function. It also has a 'moral or sociopedagogic' purpose to reflect and shape moral values and beliefs of society" (1981, p. 50).

The federal Crime Bill (Summary of Revised Crime Conference Report, 1994) passed in August, 1994, constitutes a watershed fiscally and symbolically for its declaration of support for women to live violence-free lives. The $1.6 billion it provides to fight violence against women is directed to law enforcement through multiple channels: training of police, prosecutors and judges; increased security in public places; civil rights remedies for victims of felonies motivated by gender bias; reciprocity between states for enforcing court "stay-away orders;" and extension of rape shield laws to civil cases and to all criminal cases to bar irrelevant questions about a victim's sexual history. The bill increases or creates new penalties for sex offenses and assaults against children, and requires sex offenders and child molesters to pay restitution to their victims. Prevention is addressed directly through the bill's rape education and community prevention programs, and indirectly through the sanctions it creates to deter sex offenses through more rigorous enforcement and longer sentences.

Although pornography involving adults is legal in this country, the Canadian Supreme Court has taken a pioneering approach to controlling pornography. The Canadian Court ruled unanimously in 1992 that obscenity is defined by the *harm it causes to women:* " 'Materials portraying women as a class of objects for sexual exploitation and abuse have a negative impact on the individual's sense of self-worth and acceptance,' read the court's landmark opinion, the first time a court has established the precedent that a threat to the equality and safety of women 'is a substantial concern which justifies restricting the otherwise full exercise of the freedom of expression' " (Hill & Silver, 1992, p. 285).

In addition to legislation targeted directly to the prevention of sexual assault, legal efforts to reduce gender inequity in economic and political domains also contribute to the prevention goal. The federal parental leave policy is an example of how legal intervention can impact on societal values (Caplan-Cotenoff, 1991). In addition to the greater stability of care provided in childbirth and family emergencies, this policy helps women attain equal access to jobs and protects them from pregnancy discrimination, allows men to play a larger role in child care, and gives both men and women greater freedom to pursue careers without giving up their family lives.

One expected outcome of this legislation is a reduction in the prevalence of sex-role stereotypes. Prevailing attitudes often discriminate against men who seek to play a larger role in their child's upbringing, and tend to force women to choose between career and family. A study by Parker and Parker (cited in Gilgun & Gordon, 1985) revealed that increases in the daily care of children by males correlated with a decrease in sexually abusive behavior towards those children. According to available data,[7] countries with nationwide parental leave policies had fewer rapes than the United States (Caplan-Cotenoff, 1991; Russell, 1984).

Reducing the Negative Impact of Sexually Violent or Degrading Media Content

The electronic media are extremely powerful forces in shaping and influencing social behavior. Over the last two decades a body of research has established a scientific consensus that exposure to television violence leads a significant portion of child viewers to learn both violent and victim behaviors (Huston et al., 1992; Pearl, Bouthilet & Lazar, 1982; Surgeon General's Scientific Advisory Committee on Television and Social Behavior, 1972; APA Commission on Violence & Youth, 1993). Confronted with these data, some researchers have piloted programs to reduce the impact of televised violence on children.

The exposure of the public to constant sexualized images of women in demeaning and degrading circumstances–through advertisements, television shows, movies, and magazines–has a negative impact on cultural attitudes toward and treatment of women. It is unclear what effects such media images have on children at varying ages, and on their developing sexuality. The literature on this subject is sparse (Martinson, 1991). Nevertheless, there now exists a large body of research, much of which is reviewed by Russell in this volume (see also Russell, 1993), documenting the misogynistic effects of pornography on the fantasies and behaviors of adult males. It is not unlikely that a similar process occurs when children are bombarded with "soft" pornographic media content, such as MTV, girl- and woman-slashing movies, television soap operas and action-adventure programs. Of particular concern is the finding of a relationship between exposure to televised violence in childhood and the subsequent development of violent behavior in adolescence and adulthood (Huesmann, 1986; Huesmann, Eron, Lefkowitz & Walder, 1984).

Because of the freedom of expression that is a cornerstone of our democracy it is difficult if not impossible to censor or control the dissemination of pornography in our society, although there have been efforts to do so (Dworkin & MacKinnon, 1993; Hill & Silver, 1993; MacKinnon, 1985). Complicating the situation is the shifting definition of pornography across recent decades. Nudity and the depiction of consensual, non-degrading sexual interactions between adults were labelled as pornography as recently as 10-20 years ago. Although these traditional labels are still in use, sexually explicit but nonviolent and nondegrading material is increasingly being treated not as pornography, but as erotica, and considered an acceptable feature of entertainment and/or aesthetic appreciation in movies, television, literature and the visual arts. In this shifting ecology of acceptable sexual behavior it is important to keep in mind that it is the definition of pornography as material endorsing degrading or abusive sexual behavior that is associated with the sexual abuse of women and children (Einsiedel, this volume; Russell, this volume).

The laws of classical and instrumental conditioning support the conclusion that repeated portrayals of abuser-victim sexual interactions, paired with portrayals of victims deriving pleasure from these activities, can lead viewers to believe that abusive sex is enjoyable for all parties concerned, and can lead to attempts to emulate the observed behavior.

> Films that depict women as erotically surrendering to a rapist and willingly being raped have been shown to increase men's beliefs that women desire rape and deserve sexual abuse. Male youth who view sexualized violence or depictions of rape on television or in film are more likely to display callousness toward female victims of violence, especially rape. Laboratory studies also have shown an increase in men's aggression against women after exposure to vio-

lent sexual displays. (APA Commission on Violence and Youth, 1993, p. 34)

Confronted with the cumulative evidence, some researchers have developed programs to reduce the impact of televised/filmed violence on children. Two very different approaches to controlling children's exposure or reactions to violent television or film content are limiting their exposure, and teaching them techniques to critique the violence they have seen. Putting lock boxes on television sets to control the reception of certain channels or programs is designed to help parents control their children's viewing habits. As welcome as this product may be to many parents, there are many other parents who will not access this device. Many children will continue to be left in homes with little guidance for their television viewing experiences.

Huesmann, Eron, Klein, Brice and Fischer (1983) took the second approach. They altered child viewers' attitudes and behaviors toward television violence through an experiment based on dissonance theory as developed in counter-attitudinal advocacy research. Children in the experimental group first learned about the unreality of televised violence and about alternative solutions. They then wrote persuasive essays about the differences between television and real life, and videotaped their essays for other children who had allegedly been "fooled" by television into imitating the violence. When the videotapes were played for all the children, the experimental children saw themselves publicly taking antiviolence positions. The result for children in the experimental group was a significant decline in aggressive behavior and a significant increase in attitudes about the harmfulness of televised violence. Linz, Arluk and Donnerstein (1990) adapted this intervention to college males exposed to a variety of sexually violent media images. Their results were consistent with the earlier study. Experimenters were successful in reducing acceptance of slasher films and rape myths, and in sensitizing experimental participants to the plight of a videotaped rape victim.

Linz, Wilson and Donnerstein (1992), in their review of sexual violence in the mass media, identify and evaluate three types of interventions to prevent the acceptance by our youth of sexual violence as normative behavior: legal restrictions, informational labeling of media products as to their violence and/or sexual content, and educational interventions. They reject the first two on a variety of grounds and conclude by proposing a research program to test a formal educational curriculum for adolescents to be administered through high schools. They conceptualize their media literacy program as a way of inoculating adolescents against the effects of sexually violent material.

The most realistic approach to reducing the harm caused by pornography today involves increased scientific attention to the effects of pornography on human behavior, and continuous education of the public about the results of this research. Mobilizing communities to prevent specific social and health problems is an effective strategy for change. Precedent documents the evolution of community response from initial passivity to active disapproval when the public is adequately informed of behavior that threatens the common welfare. Drunken driving, elder discrimination, and heart disease are all problems for which behavioral solutions at the community level have proven to be effective. Community response to these problems has been brought about by a range of dedicated groups and individuals, from grassroots organizations to university-based action research programs. These groups include Mothers Against Drunk Driving (MADD), the Grey Panthers and the American Association of Retired Persons (AARP), and the Stanford Health Disease project (Farquhar et al., 1985; Flora, Maccoby & Farquhar, 1989).

Such community mobilization has produced laws and policies that cumulatively erode the beliefs, attitudes and eventually the behaviors that threaten the common welfare. An example in the context of sexual behavior is the access children and adolescents initially had to telephone numbers with a 900 area code featuring explicit descriptions of sex acts. Community protest, primarily from parents, led to a policy which bars access by individual households to telephone numbers with a 900 area code in the United States on the request of the customer.

There is no simple solution to the problems raised by the pairing of sex and violence in pornography or in the softer "porn" available in television advertising and programs, videotapes and movies, and the print media. The mass media itself can be used to promote the adoption of prosocial behavior (Johnston & Ettema, 1982; Sprafkin, Swift & Hess, 1983), prevent the negative effects of sexually violent programming, and thus be a part of the solution. Embarking on a massive public education campaign is only one of a series of interventions needed to bring about the changes in public attitudes, beliefs, and behaviors that will ultimately lead to a sexually safe society.

Intervening with Boys and Men with a History of Childhood Sexual Abuse

In addition to interventions to prevent the development of sexually abusive behavior on a population-wide level, preventive interventions should be implemented for boys and men who are at higher than average risk for developing the behavior. A history of sexual abuse in childhood appears to be a risk factor for developing sexually abusive behavior later in life. There is increasing evidence that men who have been sexually abused as children commit sexual abuse at a higher rate than men without such histories. Finkelhor (1980) reported that rates of childhood abuse for sex offenders are two to five times higher (19-48%) than in non-offending populations (10%). An estimate of the prevalence of childhood sexual victimization of males is provided in a study by Risin and Koss (1987), who found that 7.3% of a representative national sample of adult male students in higher education reported an abusive childhood sexual experience. According to these authors, "The men who reported the highest level of adult sexual aggression reported more childhood sexual experiences and an earlier age of first sexual intercourse" (1987, p. 322).

Urquiza and Crowley (cited in Finkelhor, 1990) found that one-fourth of their sample of male college students who reported being sexually victimized as children also reported having sexual fantasies about children, compared with less than a tenth (9%) of the sample of nonvictimized men. In addition, twice as many of the victimized men expressed a desire to engage in sexual activities with a child, compared with the nonvictimized men (13% versus 6%). Pedophilic participants in an interview study of nonincarcerated paraphiliacs (Abel et al., 1987) reported molesting boys at a much higher rate than girls. The authors note that "Since only limited resources are available to provide assessment and treatment for child molesters, it would be advantageous to target those individuals who molest boys specifically since effective treatment of this group would dramatically reduce the total number of current and future child molestations" (1987, p. 22).

Sexual abuse has multiple causes. In any one instance a complex set of conditions, including systemic as well as individual factors–history, stress, resources, and opportunity–may combine to produce sexual abuse. Acknowledging this complexity, it seems appropriate at our current stage of knowledge to recognize the sexual victimization of boys as a significant risk factor in the development of adult male sexual aggression, and to develop prevention programs based on this knowledge. Both universal and selective interventions (Gordon, 1983) are appropriate for this subgroup of boys and men.

One of the problems with prevention efforts is the difficulty in identifying boys who have been molested. It is well known that victimized girls often do not report their abuse, partly because of the stigma. The problem of non-reporting is compounded with boys. Added to the stigma is the male role they inherit–to control rather than be controlled, to be the initiating actor in sexual activity rather than the receiver, to protect their bodies from aggression. The fact that most sexual abusers are identified as male means that most boy victims are abused by males. This same-sex abuse is another factor that silences boy victims, who fear that their forced participation in sex may be interpreted as consensual, and will result in their being labelled as gay–an outcome that risks censure in a society that continues to discriminate against homosexual men and women.

Another problem in efforts to work with male victims of sexual abuse is the difficulty in timing interventions to precede their reenactment of abuse or other sexually aggressive behavior. Cavanaugh-Johnson (1987) found that child victims as young as five exhibit sexually abusive behaviors. Sandy Lane (1991) conducted a perpetration prevention program with boys aged seven to nine. Although all the participants had been sexually abused and were exhibiting sexualized behaviors, none were believed to have developed sexually abusive behaviors:

> In the beginning of this prevention program it was discovered that the original assumption had been naive. Each of the youth referred for help to avoid the potential of developing sexually abusive behaviors was in fact already perpetrating. The hope that the sexualized behaviors that resulted from early victimization or exposure to sexual stimuli were reactive expressions or even normative childhood sexual exploration was not validated . . . One wonders how young intervention must start to prevent the problem of sexual abuse. (1991. pp. 299-300)

Lane raises a problem familiar to prevention theorists and practitioners. At what point does the manifestation of risk become the early expression of the disorder?

Boys who fit the ambiguous category between abuse victim and incipient abuser may best be served by what Gordon (1983) calls *indicated* preventive interventions. A number of investigators have explored interventions with boys who have been sexually molested; in many of these studies the participants were themselves molesters (Hunter & Goodwin, 1992; Hunter & Santos. 1990; Ryan & Lane, 1991; Weinrott & Riggan, 1991). Two commonly used techniques are sensitization and satiation. The first sensitizes sexually abused boys, particularly abusers, to the impact of their behavior on themselves and others. Structured play therapy permits therapists to interrupt children's scenarios when they threaten to lead to sexual abuse, and to teach children to redirect their feelings constructively (Johnson, 1989). With adolescent abusers this has been done by repeated exposure to the negative consequences of sexual abuse, including impact on family and friends, through videotaped vignettes (Weinrott & Riggan, 1991).

The second common technique is to extinguish inappropriate sexual behavior through satiation therapy. Hunter and Goodwin (1992) implement this technique by asking adolescent abusers to repeat their deviant erotic fantasies into a tape recorder multiple times a week until the fantasies become boring and no longer arousing. Other techniques used with sexually abused children include group therapy in which therapists track and shape children's capacities to problem-solve, implement social skills, and cognitively control their behavior (Johnson, 1989). Such interventions require professionals with training and experience in working with sexually abused children.

Issues of professional training are relevant here: graduate curricula, field placement and internships available to student mental health professionals should routinely include education about child sexual abuse, its prevention and treatment. Medical and mental health professionals should be trained to identify males in the high risk categories and provide them with information about their risks and ways to avoid abusive behaviors. The education of high risk males and those within their life space would alert them to the precautions necessary to provide safe environments for themselves and those around them. Such education could also trigger more intensive interventions. In those subpopulations of boys and men whose histories or experiences flag them as in need of more intensive attention–i.e., those with multiple risk factors or boys whose sexual victimization was particularly traumatic, violent or lengthy–programs of individual intervention may be warranted.

Research into the identification of sexually abused children at earlier stages is necessary if primary prevention is to succeed. In this effort, preventive sex abuse education programs in schools have proved helpful in case-finding. Teachers in daycare and elementary schools should be trained in receiving children's accounts of sexual abuse and forwarding the information to the appropriate authorities in their communities.

Projected interventions with the risk population of boys and men and their significant others include informational print and video materials adapted to the appropriate risk factor and developmental level. These materials would provide guidance in avoiding abusive behaviors, as well as assistance in accessing resources to help in this process. Such video and print materials, made prominently available in community libraries, medical and mental health clinics and offices, could serve parents, teachers–and others who work with children–as education and referral resources. Resources to work with the population of sexually abused males are few at this time. Continuing research is needed to assist in their identification and treatment, and to reduce the risk they carry to repeat their own abuse with a new generation of victims.

CONCLUSION

The liberation of women through education, and through their economic and political advancement over the last few decades, has been critical in putting sexual abuse on the public agenda and keeping it there. The significance of this empowerment lies in the changes in women's roles. More women are embracing roles of agency and rejecting the culturally sanctioned roles of passivity and victimhood. Women's shifting gender roles have led to changes in the attitudes and behavior of both women and men. More women and more men are bringing up their daughters and sons to value women and their achievements, particularly in domains from which women have been traditionally excluded.

Although a society totally free of sexual exploitation may be utopian, the goal of significantly reducing the incidence of sexual abuse of women and children is within reach. Achieving this goal means changing the sexist values of our culture to egalitarian gender values, building the use of alternatives to violence in resolving conflict, and socializing children to practice these values. It also means providing children with information about sexual behavior–its emotional, physical, social and legal consequences–and with the skills to reduce the negative impact of exposure to media violence.

In the past the transmission prevention strategy as applied to sexual abuse has often penalized women by limiting their freedom of movement to particular times and places. Incorporating an ecological perspective of sexual abuse means changing the sociocultural, as well as the physical environment. Eliminating the inferior status ascribed to women would be a major step in eliminating gender inequities. Pursued further, this line of thinking ends up advocating more interventions of the "prevent-the-transmission-of-patriarchal-culture" type, rather than interventions of the "eliminate-the-stressor-or-reduce-its-impact" type. Over the long run, doing the former will accomplish the latter, in primary prevention terms.

An ecological approach to the prevention of sexual abuse requires addressing all three elements of the abusive situation. We have focused on changing the development of sexually abusing behavior in boys and men, since that approach has been relatively ignored in the prevention research community, as well as in the wider world. However reciprocal changes between men and women, and changes within the sociocultural environment, must also occur if the goals of primary prevention in the field of sexual abuse are to be met. This means developing interventions to:

1. change the sociocultural *environment* to achieve gender equity–eliminate the inferior gender status of girls and women and the consequent gender power imbalance (transmission-prevention focused strategy),
2. prevent the development of sexually abusive behavior in *males* (stressor-focused strategy), and
3. promote *women's* empowerment in achieving gender equity in both public and private domains; educate women and children to assert their rights to control their own bodies and protect themselves from sexual assault (host-focused strategies).

In the mid-1980s the National Committee for the Prevention of Child Abuse (NCPCA) held a conference on "Preventing Child Sexual Abuse: A Focus on the Potential Perpetrator." In the conference summary, Anne Cohn (1986) wrote:

The major focus of prevention efforts should be on *potential perpetrators* and on the *cultural and societal values* (emphasis added) which allow this problem to persist. The task is to reach out to the potential abusers and help them to understand the impact of their behavior, to control their behavior and to develop alternative and more appropriate behaviors. To date no concerted efforts to determine how to do so have been made. (1986, p. 559)

It has been a decade since the NCPCA conference. Although researchers have begun the lengthy process of identifying and documenting the variables that produce the development of sexually abusive behavior, the published studies provide more of an introduction to the subject than an explanation. Further research will identify additional variables and more effective interventions in the prevention of perpetrator development. As in any new field of inquiry, more questions are raised by initial research than are answered.

Preventionists in the field of sexual abuse have moved closer to consensus on the necessity of changing sociocultural gender values and expanding the prevention focus to include potential perpetrators. A consolidation of these gains–through the refinement of theory, research and practice to include the stressor population of potential abusers, the host population of potential victims, and the sociocultural and physical environment they share–would provide the foundation to test interventions incorporating an ecological perspective for the prevention of sexual abuse. Ultimately such an approach is needed to build a sexually safe environment for future generations.

NOTES

1. The public health concepts of "secondary" and "tertiary" prevention are seen as treatment, not prevention approaches, and therefore are not addressed here.

2. McCall (1993) has written a thoughtful analysis contrasting prevention approaches. We have chosen to work within the public health prevention model, since its focus has expanded to include disordered interpersonal behavior such as violence (Anthony, 1990), as well as physical and mental illness and disease.

3. Gordon's classification system is meant to apply only to *primary* prevention–i.e., it is incompatible with the public health model's secondary and tertiary prevention classification system. Gordon's classification system has been adapted by the Institute of Medicine (1994) to apply to mental disorder as well as physical disease.

4. Although gender creates a category of high risk for males in general in terms of the development of sexually abusive behavior (i.e., males have a higher risk of developing into sexual abusers than females), we have addressed the general population of boys and men primarily through universal interventions–e.g,, education, legislation, and the media.

5. See Wyatt, Notgrass, and Gordon (this volume) for a discussion of multiple issues involved in the intersection of racism and sexism in the United States. See also Bond (this volume) for additional discussion of the complexities of multiple power inequities in sexual harassment.

6. In their pilot study, using "vicarious sensitization," they exposed six adolescent sex offenders to audiotapes of crimes which evoked arousal to a child, followed immediately by aversive videotapes depicting adolescent sex offenders confronting a variety of negative consequences of their offenses–social, emotional, physical and legal. The results, based on phallometric data and self-report, showed a significant decrease in arousal to children for the participants compared to their pre-intervention behavior, as well as to a control group. An additional, unanticipated, result was participants' shifts in attitude about their own sexual behavior. All reported that the experiment helped them to better understand others' feelings about their behavior, which they saw, post-treatment, as more serious. This result is not thought to be manipulation by the subjects for early release or parole, since their primary therapists and parole officers were uninformed about their performance in the program. Preliminary results from the followup study using 69 subjects tend to confirm these findings (Weinrott, 1994).

7. The federal parental leave legislation has not been in effect long enough in this country to collect comparative data.

BIBLIOGRAPHY

Abel, G., Becker, J., Mittelman, M., Cunningham-Rathner, R., Rouleau, J. & Murphy, W. (1987). Self-reported sex crimes of nonincarcerated paraphiliacs. *Journal of Interpersonal Violence, 2*, 3-25.

Albee, G., Gordon, S. & Leitenberg, H. (Eds.). (1983). *Promoting sexual responsibility and preventing sexual problems.* Hanover, NH: University Press of New England.

American Psychological Association Commission on Violence & Youth. (1993). *Violence and youth: Psychology's response. I: Summary report.* Washington, DC: American Psychological Association.

Anthony, J. (1990). Prevention research in the context of epidemiology, with a discussion of public health models. In Peter Muehrer (Ed.), *Conceptual research models for preventing mental disorders* (pp. 1-32). DHHS Pub. No. (ADM) 90-1713. Washington, DC: The National Institute of Mental Health.

Araji, S. & Finkelhor, D. (1986). Abusers: A review of the research. In D. Finkelhor, S. Araji, L. Baron, A. Browne, S. Peters & G. Wyatt, *A sourcebook on child sexual abuse* (pp. 89-118). Beverly Hills, CA: Sage.

Bart, P. & O'Brien, P. (1985). *Stopping rape: Successful survival strategies.* (The Athene Series). Elmsford, NY: Pergamon.

Bem, S. (1983). Gender schema theory and its implications for child development: Raising gender-aschematic children in a gender-schematic society. *Signs, 8,* 598-616.

Bigler, R. (in press). The role of classification skill in moderating environmental influences on children's gender stereotyping: A study of the functional use of gender in the classroom. *Child Development.*

Bigler, R & Liben, L. (1990). The role of attitudes and interventions in gender-schematic processing. *Child Development, 61,* 1440-1452.

Bigler, R. & Liben, L. (1992). Cognitive mechanisms in children's gender stereotyping: Theoretical and educational implications of a cognitive-based intervention. *Child Development, 63,* 1351-1363.

Broverman, I., Vogel, S., Broverman, D., Clarkson, F., & Rosenkrantz, P. (1972). Sex-role stereotypes: A current appraisal. *The Journal of Social Issues, 28,* 59-78.

Brownmiller, S. (1975). *Against our will: Men, women and rape.* New York: Simon and Schuster.

Calvert, S. & Huston, A. (1987). Television and children's gender schemata. In L Liben & M. Signorella (Eds.), *Children's gender schemata* (pp. 75-88). San Francisco: Jossey-Bass.

Caplan-Cotenoff, S. (1991). Parental leave: The need for a national policy to foster sexual equality. *American Journal of Law & Medicine, 8*(1), 71-104.

Cavanaugh-Johnson, T. (1987). Child perpetrators: Children who molest children. *Child Abuse & Neglect, 12,* 219-230.

Cohn, A. (1986). Preventing adults from becoming sexual molesters. *Child Abuse & Neglect, 10,* 559-562.

Conte, J., Rosen, C. & Saperstein, L. (1986). An analysis of programs to prevent the sexual victimization of children. *Journal of Primary Prevention, 6,* 141-155.

Dworkin, A., & MacKinnon, C. (1993). Questions and answers. In D.E.H. Russell (Ed.), *Making violence sexy: Feminist views on pornography* (pp. 78-96). New York, NY: Teachers College Press.

Farquhar, J., Fortmann, S., Maccoby, N., Haskell, W., Williams, P., Flora, J., Taylor, C., Brown, B., Solomon, D., & Hulley, S. (1985). The Stanford Five City project: Design and methods. *American Journal of Epidemiology, 112,* 3223-3339.

Finkelhor, D. (1980). Risk factors in the sexual victimization of children. *Child Abuse & Neglect, 4,* 265-273.

Finkelhor, D. (1983). Common features of family abuse. In D. Finkelhor, R. Gelles, G. Hotaling & M. Straus (Eds.), *The dark side of families* (pp. 17-28). Beverly Hills, CA: Sage.

Finkelhor, D. (1990). Early and long-term effects of child sexual abuse: An update. *Professional Psychology, 21,* 325-330.

Finkelhor, D. & Baron, L. (1986). High-risk children. In D. Finkelhor, S. Araji, L. Baron, A. Browne, S. Peters & G. Wyatt, *A sourcebook on child sexual abuse* (pp. 60-88). Newbury Park, CA: Sage.

Fischhoff, B., Furby, L. & Morgan, M. (1987). Rape prevention: A typology of strategies. *Journal of Interpersonal Violence, 2,* 292-308.

Flora, J., Maccoby, N. & Farquhar, J. (1989). Cardiovascular disease prevention: The Stanford studies. In R. Rice & C. Atkin (Eds.), *Public communication campaigns.* Beverly Hills, CA: Sage.

George, L., Winfield, I., & Blazer, D. (1992). Sociocultural factors in sexual assault: Comparison of two representative samples of women. *Journal of Social Issues, 48,* 1, 105-125.

Gilgun, J. & Gordon, S. (1985). Sex education and the prevention of child sexual abuse. *Journal of Sex Education and Therapy, 11,* 46-52.

Goldberg-Ambrose. (1992). Unfinished business in rape law reform. *Journal of Social Issues, 48,* 173-185.

Gordon, J. (1952). The twentieth century—yesterday today and tomorrow. In Top, F. (Ed.), *The history of American epidemiology.* St. Louis, MO: C.V. Mosby.

Gordon, M. (1989). The family environment of sexual abuse: A comparison of natal and stepfather abuse. *Child Abuse & Neglect, 13,* 121-130.

Gordon, M. & Riger, S. (1989). *The female fear.* New York, NY: The Free Press.

Gordon, R. (1983). An operational classification of disease prevention. *Public Health Reports, 98,* 107-109.

Guttentag, M. (1977). The prevention of sexism. In G. Albee & J. Joffe (Eds.), *Primary prevention of psychopathology. Vol. 1: The issues* (pp. 238-253). Hanover, NH: University Press of New England.

Guttentag, M., Bray, H., Amsler, J., Donovan, V., Legge, G., Legge, W., Littenberg, R. & Stotsky, S. (1976). *Undoing sex stereotypes: A How-to-do-it guide with tested non-sexist curricula and teaching methods.* New York: McGraw-Hill.

Hansen, R. & O'Leary, V. (1985). Sex-determined attributions. In V. O'Leary, R. Unger & B. Wallston (Eds.), *Women, gender, and social psychology* (pp. 67-99). Hillsdale, NJ: Lawrence Erlbaum Associates.

Hare-Mustin, R. & Marecek, J. (1990). Gender and the meaning of difference: Postmodernism and psychology. In R. Hare-Mustin & J. Marecek (Eds.), *Making a difference: Psychology and the construction of gender* (pp. 22-64). New Haven: Yale University Press.

Hill, S. & Silver, N. (1993). Civil rights antipornography legislation: Addressing harm to women. In E. Buchwald, P. Fletcher & M. Roth (Eds.), *Transforming a rape culture* (pp. 282-299). Minneapolis, MN: Milkweed Editions.

Hoberman, H. (1990). Study group report on the impact of television violence on adolescents. *Journal of Adolescent Health Care, 11*, 45-49.

Huesmann, L. (1986). Psychological processes promoting the relation between exposure to media violence and aggressive behavior by the viewer. *Journal of Social Issues, 42*(3), 125-140.

Huesmann, L., Eron, L., Lefkowitz, M. & Walder, L. (1984). The stability of aggression over time and generations. *Developmental Psychology, 20*, 1120-1134.

Huesmann, L., Eron., L., Klein, R., Brice, P. & Fischer, P. (1983). Mitigating the imitation of aggressive behaviors by changing children's attitudes about media violence. *Journal of Personality and Social Psychology, 44*, 899-910.

Hunter, J. & Goodwin, D. (1992). The clinical utility of satiation therapy with juvenile sexual offenders: Variations and efficacy. *Annals of Sex Research, 5*(2), 71-80.

Hunter, J. & Santos, D. (1990). The use of specialized cognitive-behavioral therapies in the treatment of adolescent sexual offenders. *International Journal of Offender Therapy and Comparative Criminology, 34*, 239-247.

Huston, A. (1983). Sex typing. In P. Mussen (Ed.). *Handbook of child psychology. Vol. 4: Socialization, personality and social behavior* (4th Ed.). New York: Wiley.

Huston, A., Donnerstein, E., Fairchild, H., Feshbach, N., Katz, P., Murray, J., Rubinstein, E., Wilcox, B. & Zuckerman, D. (1992). *Big world, small screen: The role of television in American society*. Lincoln, NE: University of Nebraska Press.

Institute of Medicine. (1994). *Reducing risks for mental disorders: Frontiers for preventive intervention research*. Washington, DC: National Academy Press.

Johnson, T. (1989). Children who molest: A treatment program. *Journal of Interpersonal Violence, 4*, 185-203.

Johnston, J. & Ettema, J. (1982). *Positive images*. Newbury Park, CA: Sage.

Katz, P. (1987). Variations in family constellation: Effects on gender schemata. In L. Liben & M. Signorella (Eds.), *Children's Gender Schemata* (pp. 39-56). San Francisco: Jossey-Bass.

Kilpatrick, D. (1993). Introduction, special section: Rape. *Journal of Interpersonal Violence, 8*, 193-197.

Koss, M. (1990). The women's mental health research agenda. *American Psychologist, 45,* 374-380.

Koss, M. (1992). The underdetection of rape: Methodological choices influence incidence estimates. *Journal of Social Issues, 48,* 1, 61-75.

Koss, M. (1993). Detecting the scope of rape: A review of prevalence research methods. *Journal of Interpersonal Violence, 8,* 198-222.

Koss, M. & Gaines, J. (1993). The prediction of sexual aggression by alcohol use, athletic participation, and fraternity affiliation. *Journal of Interpersonal Violence, 8,* 94-108.

Lane, S. (1991). Special offender populations. In G. Ryan & S. Lane (Eds.), *Juvenile sexual offending: Causes, consequences, and correction* (pp. 299-332). Lexington, MA: Lexington Books.

Liben, L. & Bigler, R. (1987). Reformulating children's gender schemata. In L. Liben & M. Signorella (Eds.), *Children's gender schemata* (pp. 89-105). San Francisco: Jossey-Bass Inc.

Liben, L. & Signorella, M. (Eds.). (1987). *Children's gender schemata: New directions for child development.* San Francisco: Jossey-Bass.

Linz, D., Arluk, I. & Donnerstein, E. (1990). Mitigating the negative effects of sexually violent mass media through pre-exposure briefings. *Communication Research, 17,* 641-674.

Linz, D., Wilson, B. & Donnerstein, E. (1992). Sexual violence in the mass media: Legal solutions, warnings, and mitigation through education. *Journal of Social Issues, 48,* 145-171.

Loh, W. (1981). What has reform of rape legislation wrought? Truth in criminal labelling. *Journal of Social Issues, 37*(4), 28-52.

Lott, B. (1990). Dual natures of learned behavior. In R. Hare-Mustin & J. Marecek (Eds.), *Making a difference: Psychology and the construction of gender* (pp. 65-101). New Haven: Yale University Press.

MacKinnon, C. (1986). Pornography: Not a moral issue. *Women's Studies International Forum, 9,* 63-78.

Martinson, F. (1991). Normal sexual development in infancy and childhood. In G. Ryan & S. Lane (Eds.), *Juvenile sexual offending: Causes, consequences, and correction* (pp. 57-82). Lexington, MA: Lexington Books.

McCall, G. (1993). Risk factors and sexual assault prevention. *Journal of Interpersonal Violence, 8,* 277-295.

Meece, J. (1987). The influence of school experiences on the development of gender schemata. In L. Liben & M. Signorella (Eds.), *Children's Gender Schemata.* San Francisco: Jossey-Bass.

Miller, J. (1987). *Toward a new psychology of women* (2nd Ed.). Boston, MA: Beacon Press.

Muehlenhard, C. & Linton, M. (1987). Rape and sexual aggression in dating situations: Incidence and risk factors. *Journal of Counseling Psychology, 34,* 186-196.

Muehlenhard, C., Powch, I., Phelps, J., & Giusti, L. (1992). Definitions of rape: Scientific and political implications. *Journal of Social Issues, 48*, 1, 23-44.

O'Leary, V., Unger, R., & Wallston, B. (Eds.). (1985). *Women, gender, and social psychology.* Hillsdale, NJ: Lawrence Erlbaum Associates.

Pearl, D., Bouthilet, L. & Lazar, J. (1982). *Television and behavior: Ten years of scientific progress and implications for the Eighties. Vol. I.* U.S. Department of Health and Human Services, DHHS Publication No. (ADM) 82-1196. Washington, DC: National Institute of Mental Health.

Risin, L. & Koss, M. (1987). The sexual abuse of boys: Prevalence and descriptive characteristics of childhood victimizations. *Journal of Interpersonal Violence, 2,* 309-323.

Russell, D. E.H. (1984). *Sexual exploitation: Rape, child sexual abuse, and workplace harassment.* Beverly Hills, CA: Sage.

Russell, D.E.H. (1986). *The secret trauma: Incest in the lives of girls and women.* New York: Basic Books.

Russell, D.E.H. (Ed.). (1993). *Making violence sexy.* New York NY: Teachers College Press.

Ryan, G. (1991a). Juvenile sexual offenders: Defining the population. In G. Ryan & S. Lane (Eds.), *Juvenile sexual offending: Causes, consequences, and correction* (pp. 3-8). Lexington, MA; Lexington Books.

Ryan, G. (1991b). Perpetration prevention: Primary and secondary. In G. Ryan & S. Lane (Eds.), *Juvenile sexual offending: Causes, consequences, and correction* (pp. 393-408). Lexington, MA: Lexington Books.

Ryan, G. & Lane, S. (Eds.) (1991). *Juvenile sexual offending: Causes, consequences, and correction.* Lexington, MA: Lexington Books.

Sorenson, S., & Siegel, J. (1992). Gender, ethnicity and sexual assault: Findings from a Los Angeles study. *Journal of Social Issues, 48*(1), 93-104.

Sparks, C. & Bar On, B. (1985). *A social change approach to the prevention of sexual violence against women. Work in Progress,* Series No. 83-08). Wellesley, MA: Wellesley College, Stone Center for Developmental Services and Studies.

Sprafkin, J., Swift, C., & Hess, R. (Eds.) (1983). *Rx Television: Enhancing the Preventive Impact of TV.* New York, NY: The Haworth Press, Inc.

Summary of the Revised Crime Conference Report. (August, 1994). Capitol Building, Washington, DC: Office of Senator Nancy Kassebaum.

Surgeon General's Scientific Advisory Committee on Television and Social Behavior. (1972). *Television and growing up: The impact of televised violence.* Report to the Surgeon General, United States Public Health Service. Washington, DC: U.S. Government Printing Office.

Ullman, S. & Knight, R. (1993). The efficacy of women's resistance strategies in rape situations. *Psychology of Women Quarterly, 17*, 23-38.

Weinrott, M. (September 1,1994). Personal communication.

Weinrott, M. & Riggan, M. (1991, August). Vicarious sensitization: A new method to reduce deviant arousal in adolescent sex offenders. Paper presented at the Annual Convention of the American Psychological Association, San Francisco, CA.

White, J., & Farmer, R. (1992). Research methods: How they shape views of sexual violence. *Journal of Social Issues, 48*(1), 45-59.

Wyatt, G. (1992). The sociocultural context of African American and White American women's rape. *Journal of Social Issues, 48*(1), 77-91.

Pornography and Rape:
A Causal Model

Diana E. H. Russell

Mills College

SUMMARY. In order for rape to occur, a man must not only be predisposed to rape, but his internal and social inhibitions against acting out rape desires must be undermined. My theory is that pornography (1) predisposes some males to want to rape a woman or intensifies the predisposition in other males already so disposed; (2) undermines some males' *internal* inhibitions against acting out their rape desires; (3) undermines some males' *social* inhibitions against the acting out; and (4) undermines some potential victims' abilities to avoid or resist rape. Some of the research substantiating this theory is presented and discussed, and suggestions are made for further research.[1] *[Article copies available from The Haworth Document Delivery Service: 1-800-342-9678.]*

I don't need studies and statistics to tell me that there is a relationship between pornography and real violence against women. My body remembers.[2]

–Woman's testimony, 1983

Address correspondence to Diana Russell, Department of Sociology, Mills College, Oakland, CA 94613.

The author would like to thank the following people for their helpful suggestions in reading the previously published article on which this revised article is based: Catharine MacKinnon, Dorchen Leidholdt, Marny Hall, and Helen Longino. She would also like to thank Kris Wood for her editorial assistance.

[Haworth co-indexing entry note]: "Pornography and Rape: A Causal Model." Russell, Diana E. H. Co-published simultaneously in *Prevention in Human Services* (The Haworth Press, Inc.) Vol. 12, No. 2, 1995, pp. 45-91; and: *Sexual Assault and Abuse: Sociocultural Context of Prevention* (ed: Carolyn F. Swift) The Haworth Press, Inc., 1995, pp. 45-91. Single or multiple copies of this article are available from The Haworth Document Delivery Service [1-800-342-9678, 9:00 a.m.-5:00 p.m. (EST)].

45

> The relationship between particularly sexually violent images in the media and subsequent aggression . . . is much stronger statistically than the relationship between smoking and lung cancer.

–Edward Donnerstein, 1983

In this chapter I present my theoretical model of the causative role of pornography and describe some of the research that I believe substantiates this theory. First, I wish to point out that when addressing the question of whether or not pornography causes violence and sexual assault, many people fail to acknowledge that in many instances the actual *making* of pornography involves or even requires violence and sexual assault. Testimony by women and men involved in such activity provides numerous examples of this (*Public Hearings*, 1983; *Attorney General's Commission on Pornography*, 1986).

In one case, a man who said he had participated in over a hundred pornographic movies testified at the Commission hearings in Los Angeles as follows: "I, myself, have been on a couple of sets where the young ladies have been forced to do even anal sex scenes with a guy which (sic) is rather large and I have seen them crying in pain" (1986, p. 773). Another witness testified at the Los Angeles hearings as follows:

> Women and young girls were tortured and suffered permanent physical injuries to answer publisher demands for photographs depicting sadomasochistic abuse. When the torturer/photographer inquired of the publisher as to the types of depictions that would sell, the torturer/photographer was instructed to get similar existing publications and use the depiction therein for instruction. The torturer/photographer followed the publisher's instructions, tortured women and girls accordingly, and then sold the photographs to the publisher. The photographs were included in magazines sold nationally in pornographic outlets. (1986, pp. 787-88)

Peter Bogdanovich writes of *Playboy* "Playmate of the Year" Dorothy Stratten's response to her participation in a pornographic movie: "A key sequence in *Galaxina* called for Dorothy to be spread-eagled against a cold water tower. The producers insisted she remain bound there for several hours, day and night. In one shot of the completed film, the tears she cries are real" (1984, p. 59). Although this movie was not made for the so-called adult movie houses, I consider it pornography because of its sexist and degrading combination of sexuality and bondage.

A letter was sent to the United States Attorney General's Commission on Pornography reporting that: "A mother and father in South Oklahoma City forced their four daughters, ages ten to seventeen, to engage in family sex while pornographic pictures were being filmed" (1986, p. 780).

Nor should it be assumed that violence occurs only in the making of violent pornography. For example, although many people would classify the movie *Deep Throat* as nonviolent pornography because it does not portray rape or other violence, we now know from Linda Marchiano's two books (Lovelace, 1980; 1986), as well as from her public testimony (for example, *Public Hearings*, 1983), that this film is in fact a documentary of her rape from beginning to end. Many people, including some of the best researchers on pornography in this country, ignore the violence pornographers use in the manufacture of these misogynist materials (for example, see Malamuth & Donnerstein, 1984). Catharine MacKinnon points out the frequently forgotten fact (quoted in the epigraph above) that "before pornography became the pornographer's speech it was somebody's life" (1987, p. 179). Testimony presented at the hearings held on the anti-pornography civil rights ordinance in Minneapolis, Minnesota, in 1983 provides powerful evidence for the truth of this statement (*Public Hearings*, 1983).

MALES' PROPENSITY TO RAPE[3]

Why do I want to rape women? Because I am basically, as a male, a predator and all women look to men like prey. I fantasize about the expression on a woman's face when I "capture" her and she realizes she cannot escape. It's like I won, I own her.

–Male respondent, Shere Hite, 1981, p. 718

It is important to know the proclivities and the state of mind of those who read and view pornography. Research indicates that in today's society 25 to 30% of male college students in the United States and Canada admit that there is some likelihood they would rape a woman if they could get away with it.[4]

In the first of these studies conducted at the University of California at Los Angeles, the word *rape* was not used; instead, an account of rape was read to the male subjects, of whom 53% said there was some likelihood that they would behave in the same fashion as the man described in the story, if they could be sure of getting away with it (Malamuth, Haber, & Feshbach, 1980). Without this assurance, only 17% said they might emulate the rapist's behavior. It is helpful to know exactly what behavior these students said they might enact.

> Bill soon caught up with Susan and offered to escort her to her car. Susan politely refused him. Bill was enraged by the rejection. "Who the hell does this bitch think she is, turning me down," Bill thought to himself as he reached into his pocket and took out a Swiss army knife. With his left hand he placed the knife at her throat. "If you try to get away, I'll cut you," said Bill. Susan nodded her head, her eyes wild with terror.

The story then depicted the rape. There was a description of sexual acts with the victim continuously portrayed as clearly opposing the assault (Malamuth et al., 1980, p. 124).

In another study, 356 male students were asked: "If you could be assured that no one would know and that you could in no way be punished for engaging in the following acts, how likely, if at all, would you be to commit such acts?" (Briere & Malamuth, 1983). Among the sexual acts listed were the two of interest to these researchers: "forcing a female to do something she really didn't want to do" and "rape" (Briere & Malamuth, 1983). *Sixty percent of the sample indicated that under the right circumstances, there was some likelihood that they would rape, use force, or do both.*

In a study of high school males, 50% of those interviewed believed it acceptable "for a guy to hold a girl down and force her to have sexual intercourse in instances such as when 'she gets him sexually excited' or 'she says she's going to have sex with him and then changes her mind'" (Goodchilds & Zellman, 1984).

Some people dismiss the findings from these studies as "merely attitudinal." But this conclusion is incorrect. Malamuth has found that male subjects' self-reported likelihood of raping is correlated with physiological measures of sexual arousal by rape depictions. Clearly, erections cannot be considered attitudes. More specifically, the male students who say they might rape a woman if they could get away with it are significantly more likely than other male students to be sexually aroused by portrayals of rape. Indeed, these men were more sexually aroused by depictions of rape than by mutually consenting depictions. And when asked if they would find committing a rape sexually arousing, they said "yes" (Donnerstein, 1983, p. 7). They were also more likely than the other male subjects to admit to having used actual physical force to obtain sex with a woman. These latter data were self-reported, but because they refer to actual behavior they too cannot be dismissed as merely attitudinal.

Looking at sexual arousal data alone (as measured by penile tumescence), not its correlation with self-reported likelihood to rape, Malamuth reports that:

- About 10% of the population of male students are sexually aroused by "very extreme violence" with "a great deal of blood and gore" that "has very little of the sexual element" (1985, p. 95).
- About 20 to 30% show substantial sexual arousal by depictions of rape in which the woman never shows signs of arousal, only abhorrence (1985, p. 95).
- About 50 to 60% show some degree of sexual arousal by a rape depiction in which the victim is portrayed as becoming sexually aroused at the end (personal communication, August 18, 1986).

Given these findings, it is hardly surprising that after reviewing a whole series of related experiments, Neil Malamuth concluded that "the overall pattern of the data is . . . consistent with contentions that many men have a proclivity to rape" (1981b, p. 139).

Shere Hite (1981, p. 1123) provides data on men's self-reported desire to rape women from the general population outside the university laboratory. Distinguishing between those men who answered the question anonymously and those who revealed their identities, Hite reports the following answers by the anonymous group to her question, "Have you ever wanted to rape a woman?": 46% answered "yes" or "sometimes," 47% answered "no," and 7% said they had fantasies of rape, but presumably had not acted them out–yet.

For reasons unknown, the non-anonymous group of men reported slightly more interest in rape: 52% answered "yes" or "sometimes," 36% answered "no," and 11% reported having rape fantasies. Although Hite's survey was not based on a random sample, and therefore, like the experimental work cited above, cannot be generalized to the population at large, her finding that roughly half of the more than 7,000 men she surveyed admitted to having wanted to rape a woman one or more times suggests that men's propensity to rape is probably very widespread indeed.

Interestingly, Hite's percentages come quite close to my finding that 44% of a probability sample of 930 adult women residing in San Francisco reported having been the victim of one or more rapes or attempted rapes over the course of their lives (Russell, 1984).

The studies reviewed here suggest that at this time in the history of our culture, a substantial percentage of the male population has some desire or proclivity to rape females and/or to sexually abuse children. Indeed, some men in this culture consider themselves deviant for *not* wanting to rape a woman. For example, the answer of one of Hite's male respondents was: "I have never raped a woman, or wanted to. In this I guess *I am somewhat odd*. Many of my friends talk about rape a lot and fantasize about it. The whole idea leaves me cold" (1981, p. 719; my italics). Another replied: "I must admit a certain part of me would receive some sort of thrill at ripping the clothes from a woman and ravishing her. But I would probably collapse into tears of pity and weep with my victim, *unlike the traditional man*" (1981, p. 719; my italics).

Feminists are among the optimists who believe that males' proclivity to rape is largely a consequence of social and cultural forces, not biological ones. And, of course, having a *desire* to behave in a certain way is not the same as actually *behaving* in that way, particularly in the case of anti-social behavior. Nevertheless, it is helpful to have this kind of baseline information on the desires and predispositions of males, who are, after all, the chief consumers of pornography.

A DEFINITION OF PORNOGRAPHY

Feminists of the anti-pornography-equals-censorship school deliberately obfuscate any distinction between erotica and pornography, using the term erotica for all sexually explicit materials. In contrast, anti-pornography feminists consider it vitally important to distinguish between pornography and erotica. Many people have talked or written about the difficulty of defining these phenomena, declaring that, "One person's erotica is another person's pornography." This statement is often used to ridicule an anti-pornography stance. The implication is that if there is no consensus on a definition of pornography, its effects cannot be examined.

Yet there is no consensus on the definitions of many phenomena. Rape is an example. Legal definitions vary considerably in different states. The police often have their own definitions, which may differ from legal definitions. For example, if a woman is raped by someone she knows, the police often "unfound"[5] the case because they are skeptical about most acquaintance and date rapes. This skepticism does not come from the law—except in cases of marital rape.

If rape is defined as forced intercourse or attempts at forced intercourse, this leaves the problem of figuring out what exactly constitutes force. How does one measure it? What is the definition of intercourse? Does it include oral and anal intercourse, intercourse with a foreign object, digital intercourse, or is it limited to vaginal intercourse? How much penetration is necessary to qualify as intercourse? How does one determine if an attempt at rape versus some lesser sexual assault has occurred? How does one deal with the fact that the rapist and the victim often do not believe that a rape occurred, even when the definition of rape was met? For example, many rapists do not consider that forcing intercourse on an unwilling woman qualifies as rape because they think the woman's "no" means "yes." Many victims think they have not been raped when the perpetrator is their husband or lover, even while the law in some states considers such acts rape. Fortunately, few people argue that because rape is so difficult to define and there is no consensus on the best definition of it, it should therefore not be considered a heinous act, as well as illegal.

Similarly, millions of court cases have revolved around arguments as to whether a killing constitutes murder or manslaughter.[6] Just because it takes a court case to decide this question, no one argues that killing should therefore not be subject to legal sanctions.

In contrast, the often-quoted statement of one judge that although he could not necessarily define pornography, he could recognize it when he saw it, is frequently cited to support the view that pornography is entirely in the eyes of the beholder. Many people have argued that because there is no consensus on how to define pornography and/or because it can be difficult to determine whether or not the pornographic label is appropriate in particular cases, pornography should therefore not be subject to legal restraints, or even opprobrium.

Interestingly, lack of consensus did not prove to be an obstacle in making pictorial child pornography illegal. This makes it clear that the difficulty of defining pornography is yet one more strategy the pro-pornographers and their apologists employ in their efforts to derail those who oppose the harms of pornography, and to make their work appear futile.

Feminist philosopher Helen Longino formulated the following defini-tion of pornography–which is the most satisfactory one I have come across: "it is sexually explicit material that represents or describes degrad-ing or abusive sexual behavior so as to endorse and/or recommend the behavior as described" (1980, p. 44).

Erotica, on the other hand, refers to *material intended to be sexually arousing, but which is not degrading, abusive, sexist, or racist.* For exam-ple, the following types of material would not qualify as erotica: sexually arousing images in which women are consistently shown naked while men are clothed; women's genitals constantly being visible but not men's; men always playing the initiating, dominant role; images of women confined to young, white bodies that fit men's narrow concept of beauty, that is, very thin, large breasted, blonde women in passive poses. Such images are examples of *sexualized racism.*

The term *degrading sexual behavior* used in Longino's definition of pornography refers to sexual behavior that is humiliating, depraved, insulting, disrespectful, slave-like, for example, urinating or defecating on a woman, ejaculating in her face, treating her as sexually dirty or inferior, depicting her as slavishly taking orders from men[7] and eager to engage in whatever sex acts a man wants, calling her insulting names while engaging in sex, such as bitch, cunt, nigger, whore. This concept (degrading sexual behavior) also includes *sexual objectification*, the portrayal of human beings–usually women–as mere sex objects, such as "tits, cunt, and ass," not as multi-faceted human beings.

Abusive sexual behavior means to hurt by mistreatment. It includes sexual behavior that is painful, damaging, exploitative, brutal, cruel–for example, rape, child sexual abuse, violent, sado-masochistic, bondage, battery.

As Longino points out, "What is wrong with pornography, then, is its degrading and dehumanizing portrayal of women (and *not* its sexual content)" (1980, p. 45). Typically, in pornographic books, magazines, and films:

> women are represented as passive and as slavishly dependent upon men. The role of female characters is limited to the provision of sexual services to men. To the extent that women's sexual pleasure is represented at all, it is subordinated to that of men and is never an end in itself as is the sexual pleasure of men. What pleases women is the use of their bodies to satisfy male desires. While the sexual objectification of women is common to all pornography, women are the recipients of even worse treatment in violent pornography, in which women characters are killed, tortured, gang-raped, mutilated, bound, and otherwise abused, as a means of providing sexual stimulation or pleasure to the male characters. (Longino, 1980, p. 42)

A particularly important feature of Longino's definition is its clear differentiation between representations of abusive sexual behavior that are intended to educate and those that are intended to endorse or recommend the abusive or degrading sexual behavior portrayed. Without this critical defining criterion, pornography would include mainstream and educational movies such as *The Accused*, *The Rape of Love*, and *Not a Love Story*, which present realistic representations of degrading sexual behavior in order to portray their reprehensible nature. In short, "Not all sexually explicit material is pornography, nor is all material which contains representations of sexual abuse and degradation pornography" (Longino, 1980, p. 42).

The term *gorenography* was coined to apply to slasher movies in which violence is used to sexually titillate an audience by combining the violence with sexually provocative (but not sexually explicit) depictions of women (Caputi, 1987, p. 216). Since many mainstream movies also use violence as sexual titillation, gorenography is not confined to slasher movies–"a genre of film which is not sexually explicit but which features extreme violence against women, most commonly involving teenage girls being raped and stabbed to death, usually both" (Ebert & Siskel, 1980). *Gorenography is defined here as nonsexually explicit material that combines violence and sexual behavior in such a way as to eroticize the violence, and which is presented in such a manner as to condone the behavior portrayed or described.*

Both gorenography and pornography can be envisioned as lying on a continuum of sexually abusive/degrading representations. Snuff movies are at one end and sexually abusive and degrading portrayals of women that are nonviolent and non-sexually explicit are at the other end (for example, sexually objectifying ads, movies, magazines, and videos). Nonviolent pornography lies somewhere in the middle, while gorenography and violent pornography lie close to the snuff movie end. Terms do not exist for some of the phenomena on this continuum, for example, abusive and degrading portrayals of women which are neither sexually explicit nor violent.

Many feminists have stretched the conventional notion of pornography to include all types of images on this continuum. For example, members of the now defunct San Francisco-based Women Against Violence in Pornography and Media organization used to refer to sexist record covers, jokes, and billboards as pornographic (Lederer, 1980). However, I think communication becomes very confusing if feminist definitions of widely used concepts differ substantially from common usage.

This discussion of definitions has introduced the following variables[8]: (1) sexually explicit material; (2) sexually violent material; (3) degrading and abusive portrayals of women; (4) sexist material; (5) degradation, abuse, sexism or violence condoned. Nonviolent pornography is defined by terms 1, 3, 4, and 5. Violent pornography is defined by all these terms. Gorenography is defined by terms 2, 4, and 5. Erotica may be sexually explicit, but is otherwise defined by the absence of terms 2, 3, 4, and 5.

Interestingly, Canadian psychologists Charlene Senn and Lorraine Radtke found the distinction between pornography and erotica to be significant and meaningful to the women subjects in their experiment. After slides had been categorized as violent pornography, nonviolent pornography (sexist and dehumanizing), or erotica (nonsexist and nonviolent), these researchers found that the violent and nonviolent images had a negative effect on the mood states of their women subjects, whereas the erotic images had a positive effect (1986, pp. 15-16; also see Senn, 1993). Furthermore, the violent images had a greater negative impact than the nonviolent pornographic images [these differences were significant at $p <$ .05 (1986, p. 16)]. This shows that our conceptual distinction between pornography and erotica is both meaningful and operational.

THE CONTENT OF PORNOGRAPHY

I've seen some soft-porn movies, which seem to have the common theme that a great many women would really like to be raped, and after being thus 'awakened to sex' will become lascivious nympho-maniacs. That . . . provides a sort of rationale for rape: "they want it, and anyway, it's really doing them a favor"

–Male respondent, Hite, 1981, p. 787

Don Smith did a content analysis of 428 "adults only" paperbacks published between 1968 and 1974. His sample was limited to books that were readily accessible to the general public in the United States, excluding paperbacks that are usually available only in so-called adult book-stores (1976). He reported the following findings:

- One-fifth of all the sex episodes involved completed rape.
- The number of rapes increased with each year's output of newly published books.
- Of the sex episodes, 6% involved incestuous rape. The focus in the rape scenes was almost always on the victim's fear and terror, which became transformed by the rape into sexual passion. Over 97% of the rapes portrayed in these books resulted in orgasm for the victims. In three-quarters of these rapes, multiple orgasm occurred.
- Less than 3% of the rapists experienced any negative consequences, and many were rewarded.

A few years later, Neil Malamuth and Barry Spinner undertook a content analysis to determine the amount of sexual violence in cartoons and pictorials in *Penthouse* and *Playboy* magazines from June 1973 to December 1977 (1980). They found that:

- By 1977, about 5% of the pictorials and 10% of the cartoons were rated as sexually violent.

- Sexual violence in pictorials (but not in cartoons) increased significantly over the five-year period, "both in absolute numbers and as a percentage of the total number of pictorials."
- *Penthouse* contained over twice the percentage of sexually violent cartoons as *Playboy* (13 versus 6%).

In another study of 1,760 covers of heterosexual magazines published between 1971 and 1980, Park Dietz and B. Evans reported that bondage and confinement themes were evident in 17% of them (1982).

Finally, in a more recent content analysis of videos in Vancouver, Canada, T. S. Palys found that 19% of all the scenes coded in a sample of 150 sexually-oriented home videos involved aggression, and 13% involved sexual aggression (1986, pp. 26-27). [A "scene" was defined as "a thematically uninterrupted sequence of activity in a given physical context" (1986, p. 25). Only scenes involving sex, aggression, or sexual aggression were coded.]

Of all the sexually aggressive scenes in the "adult" videos, 46% involved bondage or confinement; 23%, slapping, hitting, spanking, or pulling hair; 22%, rape; 18%, sexual harassment; 4%, sadomasochism; and 3%, sexual mutilation. In comparison, 38% of all the sexually aggressive scenes in the triple-X videos involved bondage or confinement; 33%, slapping, hitting, spanking, or pulling hair; 31%, rape; 17%, sexual harassment; 14%, sadomasochism; and 3%, sexual mutilation (1986, p. 31).

While Palys's analysis focuses largely on the unexpected finding that "adult" videos "have a significantly greater absolute number of depictions of sexual aggression per movie than (have) triple-X videos," the more relevant point here is that violence against women in both types of pornographic videos is quite common, and that rape is one of the more prevalent forms of sexual violence depicted. Moreover, I would expect a comparable content analysis of videos in the United States to reveal more rape and other sexual violence than was found in this Canadian study, since the Canadian government has played a more active role than the United States government in trying to control pornography.

In addition, Palys reported that about 60% of the aggressors in the videos he studied were portrayed in a positive fashion as good people with positive attributes. And in 73% of the codable cases, they suffered no negative consequences for their aggressive behavior (1986, p. 32). Interestingly, Palys did not find an increase in the amount of sexual violence portrayed in these videos over time. However, as Palys points out, it was not clear whether this was because some proprietors had become sensitized to issues of sexual violence as a result of protests by Canadian women, or whether they hoped to avoid protests by selecting less violent fare in recent years (1986, p. 34).

In a comparison of the contents of sexual and nonsexual media violence, Malamuth (1986) points out the following important differences between them:

- The victim is usually female in pornography and male in nonsexual portrayals of violence on television (p. 5).
- "Victims of nonsexual aggression are usually shown as outraged by their experience and intent on avoiding victimization. They, and at times the perpetrators of the aggression, suffer from the violence" (p. 6). In contrast, "when sexual violence is portrayed, there is frequently the suggestion that, despite initial resistance, the victim secretly desired the abusive treatment and eventually derived pleasure from it" (p. 6).
- Unlike nonsexual violence, pornography is designed to arouse men sexually. Such arousal "might result in subliminal conditioning and cognitive changes in the consumer by associating physical pleasure with violence. Therefore, even sexual aggression depicted negatively may have harmful effects because of the sexual arousal induced by the explicitness of the depiction" (pp. 6-7).

In summary, experiments reveal that from 25 to 60% of male student subjects admit to some likelihood of raping or forcing sex acts on a woman if they can get away with it. Other studies show that pornography has become increasingly violent over the years–at least in the non-video media–and that it presents an extremely distorted view of rape and sexuality.

A THEORY ABOUT THE CAUSATIVE ROLE OF PORNOGRAPHY

Sociologist David Finkelhor has developed a very useful multicausal theory to explain the occurrence of child sexual abuse (1984). According to Finkelhor's model, in order for child sexual abuse to occur, four conditions have to be met. First, someone has to *want* to abuse a child sexually. Second, this person's internal inhibitions against acting out this desire have to be undermined. Third, this person's social inhibitions against acting out this desire (e.g., fear of being caught and punished) have to be undermined. Fourth, the would-be perpetrator has to undermine or overcome his or her chosen victim's capacity to avoid or resist the sexual abuse.

According to my theory, these conditions also have to be met in order for rape, battery, and other forms of sexual assault on adult women to occur (Russell, 1984). Although my theory can be applied to other forms of sexual abuse and violence against women besides rape, this formulation of it will focus on rape because most of the research relevant to my theory has been on this form of sexual assault.

In *Sexual Exploitation* (1984) I suggest many factors that may predispose a large number of men in the United States to want to rape or assault women sexually. Some examples discussed in this book are (1) biological factors, (2) childhood experiences of sexual abuse, (3) male sex-role socialization, (4) exposure to mass media that encourage rape (e.g., woman-slashing films), and (5) exposure to pornography. Here I will discuss only the role of pornography.

Although women have been known to rape both men and women, and have even more often been known to sexually abuse children, males are by far the predominant perpetrators of sexual assault as well as the biggest consumers of pornography (see, for example, Finkelhor, 1984; Russell, 1984). Hence, my theory will focus on male perpetrators.

A diagrammatic presentation of this theory appears in Figure 1. As previously noted, in order for rape to occur, a man not only must be predisposed to rape, but his internal and social inhibitions against acting out his rape desires must be undermined. My theory, in a nutshell, is that pornography (1) predisposes some men to want to rape women or intensifies the predisposition in other men already so predisposed; (2) it undermines some men's internal inhibitions against acting out their desire to rape; and (3) it undermines some men's social inhibitions against acting out their desire to rape.

THE MEANING OF "CAUSE"

Given the intense debate about whether or not pornography plays a causal role in rape, it is surprising that so few of those engaged in it ever state what they mean by "cause." A definition of the concept *simple causation* follows:

An event (or events) that precedes and results in the occurrence of another event. Whenever the first event (the cause) occurs, the second event (the effect) necessarily or inevitably follows. Moreover, in simple causation the second event does not occur unless the first event has occurred. Thus the cause is both the SUFFICIENT

CONDITION and the NECESSARY CONDITION for the occurrence of the effect. (Theodorson & Theodorson, 1979)

By this definition, pornography clearly does not cause rape, since it seems safe to assume that some unknown percentage of pornography consumers do not rape women, and that many rapes are unrelated to pornography.

The concept of *multiple causation* is more relevant to this question than simple causation.

With the conception of MULTIPLE CAUSATION, various possible causes may be seen for a given event, any one of which may be a sufficient but not necessary condition for the occurrence of the effect, or a necessary but not sufficient condition. In the case of multiple causation, then, the given effect may occur in the absence of all but one of the possible sufficient but not necessary causes; and, conversely, the given effect would not follow the occurrence of some but not all of the various necessary but not sufficient causes. (Theodorson & Theodorson, 1979)

In this article I will show that pornography is one of the possible sufficient (but not necessary) causes of (a) the desire to rape, and/or (b) the act of rape.

To illustrate (b), it may be helpful to present a hypothetical example. Let us say that Mr. A had been aware of a desire to rape women for some time but had never done so because he considered rape to be cruel and immoral. Let us suppose Mr. A then goes to see a typical pornographic movie in which women are depicted as becoming sexually aroused by rape, and that Mr. A becomes sexually excited by the rape scenes. Then let us suppose that the next time Mr. A is on a date, he feels a desire to rape the woman. He remembers the movie portrayal of women enjoying being raped. He reasons that if women secretly enjoy rape, it cannot be cruel or immoral as he had previously thought. So he rapes his date. Is this a case of pornography causing rape?

The answer is yes. Pornography, in this illustration, would be a sufficient, but not necessary, cause of Mr. A's act of rape. The belief that women like to be raped would have successfully undermined Mr. A's inhibitions against acting out his desire.

Since I have already presented the research on men's proclivity to rape, I will next discuss some of the evidence that pornography can be a sufficient (though not necessary) condition for men to desire rape (see the list on the far right side of Figure 1). I will mention when the research findings

FIGURE 1. Theoretical Model of Pornography as a Cause of Rape

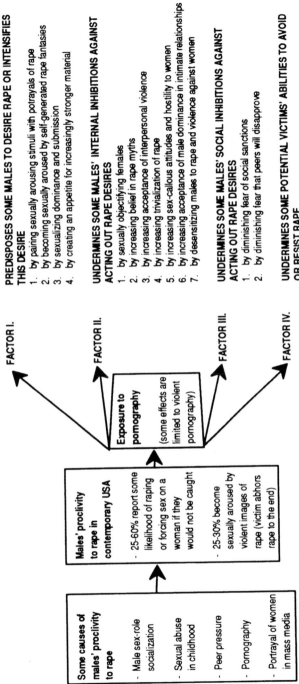

FACTOR I. → **PREDISPOSES SOME MALES TO DESIRE RAPE OR INTENSIFIES THIS DESIRE**
1. by pairing sexually arousing stimuli with portrayals of rape
2. by becoming sexually aroused by self-generated rape fantasies
3. by sexualizing dominance and submission
4. by creating an appetite for increasingly stronger material

FACTOR II. → **UNDERMINES SOME MALES' INTERNAL INHIBITIONS AGAINST ACTING OUT RAPE DESIRES**
1. by sexually objectifying females
2. by increasing belief in rape myths
3. by increasing acceptance of interpersonal violence
4. by increasing trivialization of rape
5. by increasing sex-callous attitudes and hostility to women
6. by increasing acceptance of male dominance in intimate relationships
7. by desensitizing males to rape and violence against women

FACTOR III. → **UNDERMINES SOME MALES' SOCIAL INHIBITIONS AGAINST ACTING OUT RAPE DESIRES**
1. by diminishing fear of social sanctions
2. by diminishing fear that peers will disapprove

FACTOR IV. → **UNDERMINES SOME POTENTIAL VICTIMS' ABILITIES TO AVOID OR RESIST RAPE**
1. by encouraging females to get into high rape-risk situations
2. by creating a pornography industry that requires female participation

Exposure to pornography (some effects are limited to violent pornography)

Males' proclivity to rape in contemporary USA
- 25-60% report some likelihood of raping or forcing sex on a woman if they would not be caught
- 25-30% become sexually aroused by violent images of rape (victim abhors rape to the end)

Some causes of males' proclivity to rape
- Male sex-role socialization
- Sexual abuse in childhood
- Peer pressure
- Pornography
- Portrayal of women in mass media

I describe apply to violent pornography and when to pornography that appears to the viewer to be nonviolent.

Earlier, I noted that research indicates that 60% of the male students tested say there is some likelihood that they would rape or force sex acts on a woman if they knew they could get away with it. High as this figure is, the percentage of men who *desire* to rape women would likely be significantly higher. There must be some men who would like to rape a woman, but who would have moral compunctions about so doing. However, a desire to rape can be assumed to be present in men who disclose some likelihood of raping women, but in addition to this desire they must have succeeded in evading some of their presumed internal or social inhibitions against rape in order to express some likelihood that they would do it.

I. The Role of Pornography in Predisposing Some Males to Want to Rape

> I went to a porno bookstore, put a quarter in a slot, and saw this porn movie. It was just a guy coming up from behind a girl and attacking her and raping her. That's when I started having rape fantasies. When I seen that movie, it was like somebody lit a fuse from my childhood on up. . . . I just went for it, went out and raped.

> –Rapist interviewed by Beneke, 1982, pp. 73-74

Factor I in my theoretical model contends that pornography can induce a desire to rape women in males who had no such desire previously, and that it can increase or intensify the desire to rape in males who already felt this desire. This section will provide the evidence for the three different ways in which pornography can induce this predisposition that are listed alongside Factor I in Figure 1.

(1) Pairing Sexually Arousing/Gratifying Stimuli with Rape

A simple application of the laws of social learning (e.g., classical conditioning, instrumental conditioning and social modeling), about which there is now considerable consensus among psychologists, suggests that viewers of pornography can develop arousal responses to depictions of rape, murder, child sexual abuse, or other assaultive behavior. Researcher S. Rachman of the Institute of Psychiatry, Maudsley Hospital, London, has demonstrated that male subjects can learn to become sexually aroused by seeing a picture of a woman's boot after repeatedly seeing women's boots in association with sexually arousing slides of nude females (Russell, 1984, p. 131). The laws of learning that operated in the acquisition of the boot fetish can also teach men who were not previously aroused by depictions of rape to become so. All it may take is the repeated association of rape with arousing portrayals of female nudity (or clothed females in provocative poses).

Even for men who are not sexually excited during movie portrayals of rape, masturbation subsequent to the movie reinforces the association. This constitutes what R. J. McGuire, J. M. Carlisle, and B. G. Young refer to as "masturbatory conditioning" (Cline, 1974, p. 210). The pleasurable experience of orgasm–an expected and planned-for activity in many pornography parlors–is an exceptionally potent reinforcer.

(2) Increasing Males' Self-Generated Rape Fantasies

Further evidence that exposure to pornography can create in men a predisposition to rape where none existed before is provided by an experiment conducted by Malamuth. Malamuth classified 29 male students as sexually force-oriented or non-force-oriented on the basis of their responses to a questionnaire (1981a). These students were then randomly assigned to view either a rape version or a mutually consenting version of a slide-audio presentation. The presentation was based on a rape story and pictorials in a recent popular pornographic magazine.

> The man in this story finds an attractive woman on a deserted road. When he approaches her, she faints with fear. In the rape version, the man ties her up and forcibly undresses her. The accompanying narrative is as follows: "You take her into the car. Though this experience is new to you, there is a temptation too powerful to resist. When she awakens, you tell her she had better do exactly as you say or she'll be sorry. With terrified eyes she agrees. She is undressed and she is willing to succumb to whatever you want. You kiss her and she returns the kiss." Portrayal of the man and woman in sexual acts follows; intercourse is implied rather than explicit. (1981a, p. 38)

In the mutually consenting version, there is no tying up or threats; instead, on her awakening in the car, the man tells the woman that "she is safe and that no one will do her any harm. She seems to like you and you begin to kiss." The rest of the story is identical to the rape version (Malamuth, 1981a, p. 38). All subjects were then exposed to the same audio description of a rape read by a female. This rape involved threats with a knife, beatings, and physical restraint. The victim was portrayed as pleading, crying, screaming, and fighting against the rapist (Abel, Barlow, & Blanchard, 1977, p. 898). Malamuth reports that measures of penile tumescence as well as self-reported arousal "indicated that relatively high levels of sexual arousal were generated by all the experimental stimuli" (1981a, p. 33).

After the 29 male students had been exposed to the rape audio tape, they were asked to try to reach as high a level of sexual arousal as possible by fantasizing about whatever they wanted but without any direct stimulation of the penis (1981a, p. 40). Self-reported sexual arousal during the fantasy period indicated that those students who had been exposed to the rape version of the first slide-audio presentation, created more violent sexual fantasies than those exposed to the mutually consenting version *irrespective of whether they had been classified as force-oriented or non-force-oriented* (1981a, p. 33).

Since the rape version of the slide-audio presentation is typical of what is seen in pornography, the results of this experiment suggest that such pornographic depictions are likely to generate rape fantasies even in previously non-force-oriented consumers. And, as Edna Einsiedel points out: "Current evidence suggests a high correlation between deviant fantasies and deviant behaviors. . . . Some treatment methods are also predicated on the link between fantasies and behavior by attempting to alter fantasy patterns in order to change the deviant behaviors" (1986, p. 60).

This assumption is supported by Malamuth's experimental findings (described above), since both the previously non-force-oriented male subjects and the force-oriented ones became aroused by self-generated rape fantasies after viewing violent pornography.

Case studies such as the rapist interviewed by Timothy Beneke (1982) and quoted at the beginning of this section, also provide dramatic examples of how pornography can generate rape fantasies in males who did not have them before.

People who are committed to the idea that pornography cannot predispose males to rape might respond to this kind of case study evidence by maintaining that the man interviewed by Beneke must have been predisposed to rape despite his lack of awareness of such a desire. This inference may be correct in this particular case. But the experimental data cited earlier indicate that at least 60% of male students–not the most violent sub-population in the United States culture–admit that there is some likelihood that they would rape or sexually assault a woman if they could be assured of getting away with it.

This suggests that *most men have at least some predisposition to rape women*. We cannot know if the rapist quoted by Beneke became *more* predisposed or *developed* a predisposition to rape. However, if pornography can intensify the desire to rape in 60% of the male population that admits to harboring such a desire, this is obviously an extremely serious state of affairs. Being totally preoccupied with whether or not pornography can predispose a male who was not previously disposed to it, ignores the fact that a majority of men *are* so predisposed. Furthermore, there is no good scientific reason to assume that people cannot develop new ideas or desires from the media. Would billions of dollars be spent on advertising or propaganda if it had no effect?

Because so many people resist the idea that a desire to rape may develop as a result of viewing pornography, let us focus for a moment on behavior other than rape. There is abundant testimonial evidence that at least some men decide they would like to try certain sex acts on women after seeing pornography portraying the same acts being performed on women. For example, one of the men who answered Shere Hite's question on pornography wrote: "It's great for me. *It gives me new ideas to try and see*, and it's always sexually exciting" (1981, p. 780; italics mine). Of course, there's nothing wrong with getting new ideas from pornography or other media, nor with trying them out, as long as they are not actions that subordinate or violate other human beings. Unfortunately, many of the behaviors modeled in pornography *do* subordinate and violate women, sometimes viciously.

The following three quotes of respondents in my probability sample of 930 San Francisco women suggest that pornography may have played a role in their experiences of men wanting to be violent toward them, or in one case, in proposing she participate in bestiality (Russell, 1980):

> He'd read something in a pornographic book, and then he wanted to live it out. It was too violent for me to do something like that. It was basically getting dressed up and spanking. Him spanking me. I refused to do it.
>
> –Respondent 43

> This guy had seen a movie where a woman was being made love to by dogs. He suggested that some of his friends had a dog and we should have a party and set the dog loose on the women. He wanted me to put a muzzle on the dog and put some sort of stuff on my vagina so that the dog would lick there.
>
> –Respondent 44

> I was staying at this guy's house. He tried to make me have oral sex with him. He said he'd seen far-out stuff in movies, and it would be

fun to mentally and physically torture a woman. (Did he use force?) No, he didn't succeed.

–Respondent 51

When someone engages in a particularly unusual act that he had previously encountered in pornography, it becomes even more plausible that the decision to do so was inspired by the pornography. For example, one woman testified to the Attorney General's Commission on Pornography about the pornography-related death of her son:

> My son, Troy Daniel Dunaway, was murdered on August 6, 1981, by the greed and avarice of the publishers of *Hustler* magazine. My son read the article "Orgasm of Death," set up the sexual experiment depicted therein, followed the explicit instructions of the article, and ended up dead. He would still be alive today were he not enticed and incited into this action by *Hustler* magazine's "How to Do" August 1981 article, an article which was found at his feet and which directly caused his death. (1986, p. 797)

When children do what they see in pornography, it is more difficult than in the case of adults to attribute their behavior entirely to their predispositions. The mother of two girls testified to the Commission on Pornography as follows:

> (My daughters) also had an experience with an eleven year old boy neighbor. . . . Porno pictures that (he) had were shown to the girls and to the other children on the block. Later that day, (he) invited (my daughters) into his house to play video games, but then tried to imitate the sex acts in the photos with (my) eleven year old (daughter) as his partner; (my other daughter) witnessed the incident. (1986, p. 785)

Psychologist Jennings Bryant also testified to the Pornography Commission about a survey he had conducted involving 600 telephone interviews with males and females who were evenly divided into three age groups: students in junior high school, students in high school, and adults aged 19 to 39 years (1985, p. 133). Respondents were asked if "exposure to X-rated materials had made them want to try anything they saw" (1985, p. 140). Two-thirds of the males reported "wanting to try some of the behavior depicted" (1985, p. 140). Bryant reports that the desire to imitate what is seen in pornography "progressively increases as age of respondents *decreases*" (1985, p. 140; italics mine). Among the junior high school students, 72% of the males reported that "they wanted to try some sexual experiment or sexual behavior that they had seen in their initial exposure to X-rated material" (1985, p. 140).

In trying to ascertain if imitation had occurred, the respondents were asked: "Did you actually experiment with or try any of the behaviors depicted" within a few days of seeing the materials (1985, p. 140)? A quarter of the males answered that they had. A number of adult men answered no but said that some years later they had experimented with the behaviors portrayed. However, only imitations within a few days of seeing the materials were counted (1985, p. 140). Male high school students were the most likely to report imitating what they had seen in pornography: 31% of them reported experimenting with the behaviors portrayed (1985, p. 141).

Unfortunately, no information is available on the behaviors imitated by these males. How many imitated rape, for example? Imitating pornography is only cause for concern if the behavior imitated is violent or abusive, or if the behavior is not wanted by the recipient. Despite the unavailability of this information, Bryant's study is valuable in showing how common it is for males to *want* to imitate what they see in pornography, and for revealing that many *do* imitate it within a few days of viewing it. Furthermore, given the degrading and often violent content of pornography, as well as the youthfulness and presumable susceptibility of many of the viewers, how likely is it that these males only imitated or wished to imitate the nonsexist, non-degrading, and nonviolent sexual behavior?

Almost all the research on pornography to date has been conducted on men and women who were at least 18 years old. But as Malamuth points out, there is "a research basis for expecting that children would be more susceptible to the influences of mass media, including violent pornography if they are exposed to it" than adults (1985, p. 107). Bryant's telephone interviews show that very large numbers of children now have access to both hard-core and soft-core materials. For example:

- The average age at which male respondents saw their first issue of *Playboy* or a similar magazine was 11 years (1985, p. 135).
- All of the high school age males surveyed reported having read or looked at *Playboy, Playgirl,* or some other soft-core magazine (1985, p. 134).
- High school males reported having seen an average of 16.1 issues, and junior high males said they had seen an average of 2.5 issues.
- In spite of being legally underage, junior high students reported having seen an average of 16.3 "unedited sexy R-rated films" (1985, p. 135). (Although R-rated movies are not usually considered pornographic, many of them meet the definition of pornography cited earlier.)

- The average age of first exposure to sexually oriented R-rated films for all respondents was 12.5 years (1985, p. 135).
- Nearly 70% of the junior high students surveyed reported that they had seen their first R-rated film before they were 13 (1985, p. 135).
- The vast majority of the respondents reported exposure to hard-core, X-rated, sexually explicit material (1985, p. 135). Furthermore, "a larger proportion of high school students had seen X-rated films than any other age group, including adults": 84%, with the average age of first exposure being 16 years, 11 months (1985, p. 136).

In a more recent anonymous survey of 247 Canadian junior high school students whose average age was 14 years, James Check and Kirstin Maxwell reported that 87% of the boys and 61% of the girls said they had viewed video pornography (1992).

> The average age of first exposure was just under 12 years old. A total of 33% of the boys versus only 2% of the girls reported watching pornography once a month or more often. As well, 29% of the boys versus 1% of the girls reported that pornography was the source that had provided them with the most useful information about sex (i.e., more than parents, school, friends, etc.). Finally, boys who were frequent consumers of pornography and/or reported learning a lot from pornography were also more likely to say that it was "OK" to hold a girl down and force her to have intercourse. (1992)

Clearly, more research is needed on the effects of pornography on young male viewers, particularly in view of the fact that recent studies suggest that "over 50% of various categories of paraphiliacs (sex offenders) had developed their deviant arousal patterns prior to age 18" (Einsiedel, 1986, p. 53). Einsiedel further observes that "it is clear that the age-of-first-exposure variable and the nature of that exposure needs to be examined more carefully. There is also evidence that the longer the duration of the paraphilia, the more significant the association with use of pornography" (Abel, Mittelman, & Becker, 1985) (Einsiedel, 1986, p. 53).

The first two items listed under Factor I in my theoretical model (some males becoming predisposed to rape women [1] by the pairing of sexually arousing stimuli with portrayals of rape, and [2] by becoming sexually aroused by self-generated rape fantasies after viewing pornography) both relate to the viewing of *violent* pornography. But sexualizing dominance and submission is a way in which nonviolent pornography can also predispose some males to want to rape women.

(3) Sexualizing Dominance and Submission

Like Senn and Radtke, James Check and Ted Guloien–also Canadian psychologists–conducted an experiment in which they distinguished between degrading nonviolent pornography and erotica and compared their effects (1989). Check and Guloien's experiment is rare not only for making this distinction but also for including non-students as subjects. Four hundred and thirty-six Toronto residents and college students were exposed to one of three types of sexual material over three viewing sessions, or to no material. The sexual materials were constructed from existing commercially available videos and validated by measuring subjects' perceptions of them. The contents of the sexual materials were as follows:

1. The *sexual violence* material portrayed scenes of sexual intercourse involving a woman strapped to a table and being penetrated by a large plastic penis.
2. The *sexually explicit dehumanizing but nonviolent* material portrayed scenes of sexual activity which included a man sitting on top of a woman and masturbating into her face.
3. The *sexually explicit non-degrading* material portrayed sexual activities leading up to heterosexual intercourse (Check & Guloien, 1989).

The viewing of both the violent and the nonviolent dehumanizing materials resulted in male subjects reporting a significantly greater likelihood of engaging in rape or other coercive sex acts than the control group.[9]

Although self-reported likelihood of raping is not a proper measure of *desire* to rape, since it also indicates that the internal inhibitions against acting out rape desires have been undermined to some extent, Check and Guloien's experiment does offer tentative support for the third category in Factor I: sexualizing dominance and submission. In addition, it makes theoretical sense that sexualizing dominance and submission would likely be generalized to include eroticizing rape for some men. Further research is needed on this issue, and more researchers need to follow the lead of the Canadian researchers in going beyond the distinction between violent and nonviolent pornography, and distinguishing also between nonviolent degrading pornography and erotica.

(4) Creating an Appetite for Increasingly Stronger Material

Dolf Zillmann and Jennings Bryant have studied the effects of what they refer to as "massive exposure" to pornography (1984). (In fact, it was not that massive: four hours and 48 minutes over a period of six weeks.) These researchers, unlike Malamuth and Donnerstein, focus on trying to ascertain the effects of *nonviolent* pornography and, in the study to be described, they use a sample drawn from a non-student adult population.

Subjects in the *massive exposure* condition saw 36 nonviolent pornographic films, six per session per week; subjects in the *intermediate* condition saw 18 such movies, three per session per week. Subjects in the control group saw 36 nonpornographic movies. Various measures were taken after one week, two weeks, and three weeks of exposure. In the third week the subjects believed they were participating in an American Bar Association study in which they were asked to recommend the prison term they thought most fair in the case of a rape of a female hitch-hiker.

Zillmann and Bryant (1984, 1985) found that an appetite for stronger material was fostered in their subjects, presumably, Zillmann suggests, "because familiar material becomes unexciting as a result of habituation" (1985, p. 127). Hence, "consumers graduate from common to less common forms of pornography," that is, to more violent and more degrading materials (1985, p. 127).

According to this research, then, pornography can transform someone who was not previously interested in the more abusive types of pornography, into someone who is turned on by such material. In turn, Malamuth has shown that men who did not previously find rape sexually arousing, generate such fantasies after being exposed to a typical example of violent pornography (described in (2) above). And men who have rape fantasies are more likely to act them out than men who do not.

I have argued that the laws of social learning apply to pornography, just as they apply to other media. As Donnerstein testified at the hearings in Minneapolis: "If you assume that your child can learn from Sesame Street how to count one, two, three, four, five, believe me, they can learn how to pick up a gun" (Donnerstein, 1983, p. 11). Presumably, males can learn equally well how to rape, beat, sexually abuse, and degrade females. Bryant found that many men and boys say they want to imitate sexual acts they have seen in pornography, and admit to having done so. However, as already stressed, learning how to do something, and wanting to do it, are not the same as doing it.

Evidence will be presented in the next section to show that pornography not only contributes to the number of males who would like to rape and otherwise abuse girls and women. It also plays a role in undermining their internal inhibitions against acting on these desires.

II. The Role of Pornography in Undermining Some Males' Internal Inhibitions Against Acting Out the Desire to Rape

> The movie was just like a big picture stand with words on it saying "go out and do it, everybody's doin' it, even the movies."

> –Rapist interviewed by Beneke, 1982, p. 74

The rapist interviewed by Timothy Beneke was cited earlier because of his claim that it was only after viewing a rape scene in a pornographic movie that he started having rape fantasies. This man's account–cited in the epigraph above–also provides a dramatic example of how pornography may undermine a man's internal inhibitions against committing rape.

Evidence has been cited showing that many males would like to rape a woman, but some unknown percentage of these males have internal inhibitions against doing so. Some males' internal inhibitions are likely to be very weak, others very strong. Presumably, they may also vary in the same individual from time to time. Seven ways in which pornography undermines some males' internal inhibitions against acting out rape desires are listed in Figure 1. Research evidence about these processes will be presented in this section.

(1) Objectifying Women

The first way in which pornography undermines some males' internal inhibitions against acting out their desires to rape is by objectifying women. Feminists have been emphasizing the role of objectification in the occurrence of rape for years (e.g., Medea & Thompson, 1974; Russell, 1975). Some men in this culture literally do not see women as human beings but as body parts. They are tits, cunts, and asses. This makes it easier to rape them.

> "It was difficult for me to admit that I was dealing with a human being when I was talking to a woman," one rapist reported, "because, if you read men's magazines, you hear about your stereo, your car, your chick" (Russell, 1975, pp. 249-250). After this rapist had hit his victim several times in the face, she stopped resisting and begged, "All right, just don't hurt me." "When she said that," he reported, "all of a sudden it came into my head, 'My God, this is a human being!' I came to my senses and saw that I was hurting this person." Another rapist said of his victim, "I wanted this beautiful fine *thing* and I got it." (Russell, 1975, p. 245)

Dehumanizing oppressed groups or enemy nations in times of war is an important mechanism for facilitating brutal behavior toward members of those groups. However, the dehumanization of women that occurs in pornography is often not recognized, because of its sexual guise and its pervasiveness. And it is important to note that the objectification of women is as common in nonviolent pornography as it is in violent pornography.

Doug McKenzie-Mohr and Mark Zanna conducted an experiment to test whether certain types of males would be more likely to sexually objectify a woman after viewing 15 minutes of nonviolent pornography. They selected 60 male students who they classified into one of two categories: masculine sex-typed or gender schematic–individuals who "encode all cross-sex interactions in sexual terms and all members of the opposite sex in terms of sexual attractiveness" (Bem, 1981, p. 361); and androgynous or gender aschematic–men who do not encode cross-sex interactions and women in these ways (McKenzie-Mohr & Zanna, 1990, p. 297, 299). McKenzie-Mohr and Zanna found that after exposure to nonviolent pornography, the masculine sex-typed males "treated our female experimenter who was interacting with them in a professional setting, in a manner that was both cognitively and behaviorally sexist" (1990, p. 305). For example, in comparison with the androgynous males, the masculine sex-typed males positioned themselves closer to the female experimenter, had "greater recall for information about her physical appearance" and less about the survey she was conducting (1990, p. 305). She also rated these men as more sexually motivated based on her answers to questions such as, "How much did you feel he was looking at your body?" "How sexually motivated did you find the subject?" (1990, p. 301).

This experiment confirmed McKenzie-Mohr and Zanna's hypothesis that exposure to nonviolent pornography would cause masculine sex-typed men, in contrast to androgynous men, to view and treat a woman as a sex object.

(2) Rape Myths

If males believe that women enjoy rape and find it sexually exciting, this belief is likely to undermine the inhibitions of some of those who would like to rape women. Sociologists Diana Scully and Martha Burt have reported that rapists are particularly apt to believe rape myths (Burt, 1980; Scully, 1985). For example, Scully found that 65% of the rapists in her study believed that "women cause their own rape by the way they act and the clothes they wear"; and 69% agreed that "most men accused of rape are really innocent." However, as Scully points out, it is not possible to know if their beliefs preceded their behavior or constitute an attempt to rationalize it. Hence, findings from the experimental data are more telling for our purposes than these interviews with rapists.

Since the myth that women enjoy rape is a widely held one, the argument that consumers of pornography realize that such portrayals are false is totally unconvincing (Brownmiller, 1975; Burt, 1980; Russell, 1975). Indeed, several studies have shown that portrayals of women enjoying rape and other kinds of sexual violence can lead to increased acceptance of rape myths in both men and women. For example, in an experiment conducted by Neil Malamuth and James Check, one group of college students saw a pornographic depiction in which a woman was portrayed as sexually aroused by sexual violence, and a second group was exposed to control materials. Subsequently, all subjects were shown a second rape portrayal. The students who had been exposed to the pornographic depiction of rape were significantly more likely than the students in the control group (1) to perceive the second rape victim as suffering less trauma; (2) to believe that she actually enjoyed it; and (3) to believe that women in general enjoy rape and forced sexual acts (Check & Malamuth, 1985, p. 419).

Other examples of the rape myths that male subjects in these studies are more apt to believe after viewing pornography are as follows: "A woman who goes to the home or the apartment of a man on their first date implies that she is willing to have sex"; "Any healthy woman can successfully resist a rapist if she really wants to"; "Many women have an unconscious wish to be raped, and may then unconsciously set up a situation in which they are likely to be attacked"; "If a girl engages in necking or petting and she lets things get out of hand, it is her own fault if her partner forces sex on her" (Briere, Malamuth, & Check, 1985, p. 400).

In Maxwell and Check's 1992 study of 247 high school students described above, they found very high rates of rape supportive beliefs. The boys who were the most frequent consumers of pornography and/or who reported learning a lot from it, were more accepting of rape myths and violence against women than their peers, who were less frequent consumers and/or who said they had not learned as much from it. As already mentioned, the higher consumers were also more likely to say that it was "OK" to force intercourse on a girl in several common dating situations:

> A full 25% of girls and 57% of boys indicated belief that in one or more situations, it was at least "maybe okay" for a boy to hold a girl down and force her to have intercourse. Further, only 21% of the boys and 57% of the girls believed that forced intercourse was "definitely not okay" in any of the situations. The situation in which intercourse was most accepted, was that in which the girl had sexu-

ally excited her date. In this case 43% of the boys and 16% of the girls stated that it was at least "maybe okay" for the boy to force intercourse. (1992)

According to Donnerstein, "After only 10 minutes of exposure to aggressive pornography, particularly material in which women are shown being aggressed against, you find male subjects are much more willing to accept these particular myths" (1983, p. 6). These men are also more inclined to believe that 25% of the women they know would enjoy being raped (1983, p. 6).

(3) Acceptance of Interpersonal Violence

Men's internal inhibitions against acting out their desire to rape can also be undermined if they consider male violence against women to be acceptable behavior. Studies have shown that viewing portrayals of sexual violence as having positive consequences increases male subjects' acceptance of violence against women. Examples of some of these items include "Being roughed up is sexually stimulating to many women"; "Sometimes the only way a man can get a cold woman turned on is to use force"; "Many times a woman will pretend she doesn't want to have intercourse because she doesn't want to seem loose, but she's really hoping the man will force her" (Briere, Malamuth, & Check, 1985, p. 401).

Malamuth and Check conducted an experiment of particular interest because the movies shown were part of the regular campus film program. Students were randomly assigned to view either a feature-length film that portrayed violence against women as being justifiable and having positive consequences (*Swept Away* or *The Getaway*) or a film without sexual violence. The experiment showed that exposure to the sexually violent movies increased the male subjects' acceptance of interpersonal violence against women (1981). (This effect did not occur with the female subjects.) These effects were measured several days after the films had been seen.

Malamuth suggests several processes "by which media sexual violence might lead to attitudes that are more accepting of violence against women" (1986, p. 4). Some of these processes also probably facilitate the undermining of pornography consumers' internal inhibitions against acting out rape desires.

1. Labeling sexual violence more as a sexual rather than a violent act.
2. Adding to perceptions that sexual aggression is normative and culturally acceptable.

3. Changing attributions of responsibility to place more blame on the victim.
4. Elevating the positive value of sexual aggression by associating it with sexual pleasure and a sense of conquest.
5. Reducing negative emotional reactions to sexually aggressive acts (1986, p. 5).

According to Donnerstein, in most studies "subjects have been exposed to only a few minutes of pornographic material" (1985, p. 341).

(4) Trivializing Rape
(5) Sex-Callous Attitudes
(6) Acceptance of Male Dominance in Intimate Relationships

The methodology of the Zillmann and Bryant experiment on the effects of "massive exposure" to pornography was described above (in Factor I, 4). As well as creating an appetite for increasingly stronger material, Zillmann and Bryant found that:

- "Heavy exposure to common nonviolent pornography trivialized rape as a criminal offense" (1985, p. 117). In addition, sexual aggression and abuse were perceived as causing less suffering for the victims, for example, an adult male having sexual intercourse with a 12-year-old girl (1985, p. 132).
- "Males' sexual callousness toward women was significantly enhanced" (1985, p. 117). For example, there was an increased acceptance of statements such as "A woman doesn't mean 'no' until she slaps you"; "A man should find them, fool them, fuck them, and forget them"; and "If they are old enough to bleed, they are old enough to butcher." Judging by these items, it is difficult to distinguish sexual callousness from a general hostility to women.
- The acceptance of male dominance in intimate relationships was greatly increased (1985, p. 121), and the notion that women are or ought to be equal in intimate relationships was more likely to be abandoned (1985, p. 122). Support of the women's liberation movement also sharply declined (1985, p. 134).

All these effects–both separately and together–are likely to contribute to undermining some males' inhibitions against acting out their desires to rape.

(7) Desensitizing Men to Rape

In an experiment specifically designed to study desensitization, Linz, Donnerstein, and Penrod showed ten hours of R-rated or X-rated movies over a period of five days to male subjects (Donnerstein & Linz, 1985, p. 34A). Some students saw X-rated movies depicting sexual assault; others saw X-rated movies depicting only consenting sex; and a third group saw R-rated sexually violent movies–for example, *I Spit on Your Grave, Toolbox Murders, Texas Chainsaw Massacre.* Donnerstein describes *Toolbox Murders* as follows: There is an erotic bathtub scene in which a woman massages herself. A beautiful song is played. Then a psychotic killer enters with a nail gun. The music stops. He chases the woman around the room, then shoots her through the stomach with the nail gun. She falls across a chair. The song comes back on as he puts the nail gun to her forehead and blows her brains out (1983). According to Donnerstein, many young males become sexually aroused by this movie (1983, p. 10).

R-rated films are made for audiences of 15- to 18-year-olds, but the subjects in Donnerstein and Linz's experiment were all at least 18 years old and had been preselected to make sure that they were not psychotic, hostile, or anxious. As Donnerstein and Linz point out, "It has always been suggested by critics of media violence research that only those who are *already* predisposed toward violence are influenced by exposure to media violence. In this study, all those individuals have already been eliminated" (1985, p. 34F).

Donnerstein and Linz described the impact of the R-rated movies on their subjects as follows: "Initially, after the first day of viewing, the men rated themselves as significantly above the norm for depression, anxiety, and annoyance on a mood adjective checklist. After each subsequent day of viewing, these scores dropped until, on the fourth day of viewing, the males' levels of anxiety, depression, and annoyance were indistinguishable from baseline norms" (1985, p. 34F).

By the fifth day, the subjects rated the movies as less graphic and less gory and estimated fewer violent or offensive scenes than after the first day of viewing. They also rated the films as significantly less debasing and degrading to women, more humorous, and more enjoyable, and reported a greater willingness to see this type of film again (1985, p. 34F). However, their sexual arousal by this material did *not* decrease over this five-day period (1983, p. 10).

On the last day, the subjects went to a law school where they saw a documentary reenactment of a real rape trial. A control group of subjects who had never seen the film also participated in this part of the experiment. Subjects who had seen the R-rated movies: (1) rated the rape victim as significantly more worthless, (2) rated her injury as significantly less severe, and (3) assigned greater blame to her for being raped than did the subjects who had not seen the film. In contrast, these effects were not observed for the X-rated nonviolent films.[10] However, the results were much the same for the violent X-rated films, despite the fact that the R-rated material was "much more graphically violent" (Donnerstein, 1985, pp. 12-13).[11]

In summary, I have presented a small fraction of the research evidence for seven different effects of pornography, all of which likely contribute to the undermining of some males' internal inhibitions against acting out rape desires. This list is not intended to be comprehensive. Indeed, I now have several additions to make, but space precludes my including them here.

III. The Role of Pornography in Undermining Some Males' Social Inhibitions Against Acting Out Their Desire to Rape

> I have often thought about it (rape), fantasized about it. I might like it because of having a feeling of power over a woman. But I never actually wanted to through *fear of being caught and publicly ruined.*

> –Hite, 1981, emphasis added

A man may want to rape a woman *and* his internal inhibitions against rape may be undermined by his hostility to women or by his belief in the myths that women really enjoy being raped and/or that they deserve it, but he may still not act out his desire to rape because of his *social* inhibitions. Fear of being caught and convicted for the crime is the most obvious example of a social inhibition. A second man's answer to Shere Hite's question on whether he had ever wanted to rape a woman illustrates this form of inhibition:

> I have never raped a woman, but have at times felt a desire to–for the struggle and final victory. I'm a person, though, who always thinks before he acts, and *the consequences wouldn't be worth it. Besides I don't want to be known as a pervert.* (1981, p. 715, emphasis added)

(1) Diminishing Fear of Social Sanctions

Malamuth and his colleagues, Haber and Feshbach, reported that after reading the account of a violent stranger rape, 17% of their male student subjects admitted that there was some likelihood that they might behave in a similar fashion in the same circumstances (1980). However, *53% of the same male students said there was some likelihood that they might act as* the rapist did *if they could be sure of getting away with it.*

The difference between 17 and 53% reveals the significant role that can be played by social inhibitions against acting out rape desires. My hypothesis is that pornography also plays a role in undermining some males' social inhibitions against acting out their desire to rape.

In his content analysis of 150 pornographic home videos, Palys investigated "whether aggressive perpetrators ever received any negative consequences for their aggressive activity–if charges were laid, or the person felt personal trauma, or had some form of 'just desserts' " (1986, p. 32). The answer was no in 73% of the cases in which a clear-cut answer was ascertainable. As previously mentioned, Don Smith found that fewer than 3% of the rapists portrayed in the 428 pornographic books he analyzed experienced any negative consequences as a result of their behavior (1976). Indeed, many of them were rewarded. The common portrayal in pornography of rape as easy to get away with likely contributes to the undermining of some males' social inhibitions against the acting out of their rape desires.

(2) Diminishing Fear of Disapproval by Peers

Fear of disapproval by one's peers is another social inhibition that may be undermined by pornography. For example, Zillmann found that "massive" exposure to nonviolent pornography produced overestimates by the subjects of uncommon sexual practices, such as anal intercourse, group sexual activities, sadomasochism and bestiality (1985, p. 118). Rape is portrayed as a very common male practice in much violent pornography, and the actors themselves may serve as a kind of pseudo-peer group and/or role models for consumers. Further research is needed to evaluate these hypotheses.

In general, I hypothesize the following disinhibiting effects of viewing violent pornography–particularly "massive" amounts of it: (1) Viewers' estimates of the percentage of other men who have raped women would likely increase, (2) Viewers would likely consider rape a much easier crime to commit than they had previously believed, (3) Viewers would be less likely to believe that rape victims would report their rapes to the police, and (4) Viewers would be more likely to expect rapists would avoid arrest, prosecution and conviction in those cases that are reported.

Since we already know that viewing pornography results in an increase in the trivialization of rape by males, as well as in acceptance of interpersonal violence, I would also anticipate consumers becoming less disapproving of rapists, and less likely to expect disapproval from others if they decide to rape. I hope that future researchers will test these hypotheses.

IV. The Role of Pornography in Undermining Potential Victims' Abilities to Avoid or Resist Rape

He . . . told me it was not wrong because they were doing it in the magazines and that made it O.K.

–Attorney General's Commission, 1986, p. 786

Once the first three conditions of my causal model have been met–a male not only wants to rape a woman but is willing to do so because his inhibitions, both internal and social, have been undermined–he may use pornography to try to weaken his victim's resistance or to get her to do what he wants her to do. Obviously, this step is not necessary for rape to occur, and it is more likely to be used to rape intimates than strangers.

(1) Encouraging Females to Get into High Rape-Risk Situations

Most adult rape victims are not shown pornography in the course of being raped, although the testimony of some prostitutes reveals that this is quite a common experience for them when they are raped (*Everywoman*, 1988). Pornography is more often used to try to persuade a woman or child to engage in certain acts, to legitimize the acts, and to undermine their resistance, refusal, or disclosure of these acts. For example, Donald Mosher reported in his 1971 study that 16% of the "sex calloused" male students had attempted to obtain intercourse by showing pornography to a woman, or by taking her to a "sexy" movie. To the extent that this strategy succeeds in manipulating some women into sexual engagements that do not include intercourse, it can result in women being very vulnerable to date rape.

In a more recent study conducted in Canada, Charlene Senn found that "the more pornography women were exposed to, the more likely they were to have been forced or coerced into sexual activity they did not want" (1992). In addition, a male pornography consumer was present in most of the cases in which women were exposed to pornography. This means that most women who consume pornography are not "self-directed"; they are doing it because a man wants them to (1992). This is a particularly important finding because the media have made much of the alleged fact that increasing numbers of women are renting pornographic videos.

The positive correlation between the quantity of pornography to which women are exposed and their experiences of forced or coerced sex suggests that women who cooperate with men's requests for them to see it, are more likely to be sexually assaulted. This, in turn, implies that viewing pornography somehow undermines their ability to avoid being sexually assaulted.

Here are some illustrative statements about how men have used pornography to undermine resistance to their sexual desires. Although they do not involve rape, the first two cases make it easy to see how being shown pornography can increase a child's vulnerability to rape.

> I was sexually abused by my foster father from the time I was seven until I was thirteen. He had stacks and stacks of *Playboys.* He would take me to his bedroom or his workshop, show me the pictures, and say, "This is what big girls do. If you want to be a big girl, you have to do this, but you can never tell anybody." Then I would have to pose like the woman in the pictures. I also remember being shown a *Playboy* cartoon of a man having sex with a child. (*Attorney General's Commission*, 1986, p. 783)

> He encouraged me by showing me pornographic magazines which they kept in the bathroom and told me it was not wrong because they were doing it in the magazines and that made it O.K. He told me all fathers do it to their daughters and said even pastors do it to their daughters. The magazines were to help me learn more about sex. (*Attorney General's Commission*, 1986, p. 786)

Zillmann and Bryant found that, "Massive exposure (to pornography) . . . can be said to distort the perception of many aspects of sexuality by producing the lasting impression that relatively uncommon sexual practices are more common than they actually are" (1984, pp. 132-33). Examples of such uncommon sex practices include, "intercourse with more than one partner at a time, sadomasochistic actions, and animal contacts" (1984, p. 132). When women are shown such materials, they probably feel more obliged to engage in unwanted sex acts that they mistakenly believe are normative. Following are two statements by adult women about how their husbands used pornography for this purpose. If women in this situation try to stop the sex acts before their partners' desires are met, they are at high risk of being raped.

> Once we saw an X-rated film that showed anal intercourse. After that he insisted that I try anal intercourse. I agreed to do so, trying to be the available, willing creature that I thought I was supposed to be. I found the experience very painful, and I told him so. But he kept

insisting that we try it again and again. (*Attorney General's Commission*, 1986, p. 778)

He told me if I loved him I would do this. And that, as I could see from the things that he read me in the magazines initially, a lot of times women didn't like it, but if I tried it enough I would probably like it and I would learn to like it. (*Everywoman*, 1988, p. 68)

More systematic research is needed to establish how frequently males use pornography to try to undermine the ability of potential victims to avoid or resist rape and other sexual abuse, and how effective this strategy is. Even if it were true that pornography cannot predispose men to want to rape women if they are not previously so disposed, and that it cannot intensify the desires of men who are already so predisposed, and that it cannot undermine men's internal and external inhibitions against acting out their desires to rape, if pornography can undermine potential victims' capacity to avoid rape, this alone would be cause enough to be deeply concerned about its harmfulness.

(2) A Pornography Industry That Requires Female Participation

Since the portrayal of rape is one of the favorite themes of pornography, a large and ever changing supply of girls and women have to be found to provide it. Clearly, some women are voluntary participants in simulated acts of rape. But many of the rapes that are photographed are real (Russell, 1993).

In summary, a significant amount of research supports my theory that pornography can, and does, cause rape. Nevertheless, much of the research undertaken to date does not adequately examine the four key variables in my theory. For example, Malamuth's self-reported likelihood-of-raping construct merges the desire to rape with the undermining of internal inhibitions against acting out this desire. I hope that more research will be guided in the future by the theoretical distinctions required by my model.

Some of the research findings of Malamuth and his colleagues will be described in the next section.

FURTHER EMPIRICAL FINDINGS ON THE CAUSATIVE ROLE OF PORNOGRAPHY IN RAPE

As Donnerstein points out, "One cannot, for obvious reasons, experimentally examine the relationship between pornography and *actual* sexual aggression" (1984, p. 53). However, Donnerstein has conducted a series of experiments on the effects of pornography on aggressive behavior in the laboratory. The delivery of a phoney electric shock to a confederate of the experimenter constituted the measure of aggressive behavior.

These experiments showed that when male subjects are exposed to violent pornography in which a female is the victim, there is an increase in their aggression toward females, but not toward males (Donnerstein, 1984). Violent films that were nonpornographic (depicting, for example, a man hitting a woman) also increased the levels of aggression in male subjects, but not to the same extent as violent pornographic films.

Levels of aggression were higher when subjects were first angered by the confederate. In fact, when the victim in the pornographic movie was portrayed as distressed throughout its duration by the sexual assault, only subjects who had been first angered by the confederate showed higher levels of aggression than those subjects who had not been exposed to the pornographic movie. However, when the victim was portrayed as becoming sexually aroused at the end of the movie, there was a marked increase in aggressive behavior for both the angered and the nonangered male subjects (Donnerstein, 1984).

To explain these findings, Malamuth suggests that: "positive victim reactions . . . may act to justify aggression and to reduce general inhibitions against aggression" (1984, p. 36). This interpretation is consistent with my causal model's emphasis on the important role pornographic depictions play in undermining males' inhibitions against acting out hostile behavior toward women.

Malamuth also undertook an experiment to test whether men's attitudes and sexual arousal to depictions of rape could predict aggression in the laboratory. A week after measuring male subjects' attitudes and sexual arousal to rape, they were angered by a female confederate of the experimenter. When the subjects were given an opportunity to behave aggressively toward her by administering an unpleasant noise as punishment for errors she made in an alleged extrasensory perception experiment, men who had higher levels of sexual arousal to rape and who had attitudes that condoned aggression "were more aggressive against the woman and wanted to hurt her to a greater extent" (1986, p. 16).

On the basis of this experiment, as well as two others, Malamuth concluded that "attitudes condoning aggression against women related to objectively observable behavior–laboratory aggression against women" (1986, p. 16). Considerable evidence has already been presented showing that exposure to pornography is one of the factors that increases acceptance of attitudes that condone aggression, with or without intervening anger.

Both Donnerstein and Malamuth emphasize that their findings on the relationship between pornography and aggression toward women relate to aggressive or violent, not to nonviolent, pornography. For example, Donnerstein maintains that "nonaggressive materials only affect aggression when inhibitions to aggress are quite low, or with long-term and massive exposure. With a single exposure and normal aggressing conditions, there is little evidence that nonviolent pornography has any negative effects" (1984, pp. 78-79). In the real world, however, inhibitions to aggress are often very low, and long-term and massive exposure to nonviolent material is also quite common. Furthermore, there is a lot of evidence of harm from nonaggressive pornography, aside from its impact on aggressive behavior (for example, see my earlier discussion of some of Zillmann's findings).

Finally, given how saturated our culture is with pornographic images and how much exposure many of the male subjects being tested have already had, the task of trying to design experiments that can show effects on the basis of one more exposure is challenging indeed. Because of this methodological problem, when no measurable effects result, it would be wrong to interpret the experiment as proving that there are no effects in general. We should therefore focus on the effects that *do* show up, rather than being overly impressed by the effects that do not.

Some people are critical of the fact that most of the experimental research on pornography has been conducted on college students who are not representative of men in the general population. Hence, the research of Richard Frost and John Stauffer comparing the responses to filmed violence of college students and residents of an inner-city housing project is of particular interest (1987).

In five of the ten violent films shown to these two groups the violence was directed at females. Frost and Stauffer evaluated these men's sexual arousal to these films by applying both self-report and physiological measures. They found that "there was no single form of violence for which the responses of the college sample exceeded those of the inner-city sample on either measure" (1987, p. 36). Four of the five most physiologically arousing categories of violence were the same for both groups: a female killing another female; a male killing a female; rape/murder; and a female killing a male (1987, p. 37). Interestingly, depictions of male-female assault were the least exciting of all ten types of violence measured to all subjects (1987, p. 39). Have men become bored by such a mundane form of violence in movies?

The greatest disparity between the two groups in both physiological and self-reported sexual arousal was to depictions of rape, which "caused the highest response by inner-city subjects but only the fifth highest by the college sample" (1987, p. 38). Although it is not acceptable to infer action from arousal, nevertheless, men who are aroused by depictions of violence toward women are more likely to act violently toward them than men who are not aroused by such depictions.

Hence, Frost and Stauffer's study suggests that college students are less prone to sexual violence than some other groups of men. While this is hardly surprising for many people, since inner-city environments are more violent than colleges or than the places in which most college students grew up, it does invalidate attempts to discount the pornography researchers' high figures for self-reported likelihood to rape reported by college males.

It may be remembered that Malamuth and his colleagues found that from 25 to 30% of male students admit that there is some likelihood that they would rape a woman if they could be assured of getting away with it. According to Donnerstein, after exposure to sexually violent images, particularly sexually violent images depicting women enjoying rape, up to 57% of male subjects indicate some likelihood that they would commit a rape if assured they would not be caught (1983, p. 7). This means that *as a result of one brief exposure to pornography, the number of men who are willing to consider rape as a plausible act for them to commit actually doubles.*

One such brief exposure to pornography also increases male subjects' acceptance of rape myths and interpersonal violence against women. Given the hypothesis that such increased acceptance would serve to lower viewers' inhibitions against acting out violent desires, one would expect pornography consumption to be related to rape rates. This is what one ingenious study found.

Larry Baron and Murray Straus (1984) undertook a fifty-state correlational analysis of rape rates and the circulation rates of eight pornographic magazines: *Chic, Club, Forum, Gallery, Genesis, Hustler, Oui,* and *Playboy.* A significant correlation (+ 0.64) was found between rape rates and circulation rates. Baron and Straus attempted to ascertain what other factors might possibly explain this correlation. Their statistical analysis revealed that the proliferation of pornographic magazines and the level of urbanization explained more of the variance in rape rates than the other variables investigated (for example, social disorganization, economic inequality, unemployment, sexual inequality).

In another important study, Mary Ross (1986) conducted a large national survey of over 6,000 college students from a probability sample of institutions of higher education. She found that college men who reported behavior that meets common legal definitions of rape were significantly more likely than college men who denied such behavior to be frequent readers of at least one of the following magazines: *Playboy, Penthouse, Chic, Club, Forum, Gallery, Genesis, Oui,* or *Hustler.*

Several other studies have assessed the correlation between the degree of men's exposure to pornography and attitudes supportive of violence against women. Malamuth reports that in three out of four of these studies "higher levels of reported exposure to sexually explicit media correlated with higher levels of attitudes supportive of violence against women" (1986, p. 8). In a sample of college men, Malamuth and Check (1985) found that higher readership of sexually explicit magazines was correlated with more beliefs that women enjoy forced sex. Similarly, Check (1984) found that the more exposure to pornography a diverse sample of Canadian men had, the higher their acceptance of rape myths, violence against women, and general sexual callousness. Briere, Corne, Runtz and Malamuth (1984) reported similar correlations in a sample of college males.

In her study of male sexuality, Shere Hite found that 67% of the men who admitted that they had wanted to rape a woman reported reading men's magazines, compared to only 19% of those who said that they had never wanted to rape a woman (1981, p. 1123). (With regard to the frequency of exposure to pornography of the 7,000 men she surveyed, Hite [1981] reports that only 11% said that they did not look at pornography, and never had. Thirty six percent said they viewed it regularly, 21%, sometimes, 26%, infrequently, and 6% simply acknowledged that they used to look at it.) While correlation does not prove causation, and it therefore cannot be concluded from these studies that it was the consumption of the pornography that was responsible for the men's higher acceptance of violence against women, their findings are consistent with a theory that a causal connection exists.

If the rape rate was very low in the United States, or if it had declined over the past few decades, these facts would likely be cited to support the view that pornography does not play a causative role in rape. While drawing such a conclusion would not be warranted, it is also of interest to note that my probability sample survey in San Francisco shows that a dramatic increase in the rape rate has occurred in the United States over the last several decades (Russell, 1984). Unlike the rapes studied by Baron and Straus (1984), 90% of the rapes and attempted rapes described in my survey were never reported to the police. Once again, positive correlation does not prove causation, but it is highly suggestive in this case.

Finally, it is significant that many sex offenders claim that viewing pornography affects their criminal behavior. Ted Bundy is perhaps the most notorious of these men. Although the studies in which such testimonies are reported do not permit a distinction to be made between the first three factors in my causal theory, they are relevant to the notion that a cause-and-effect relationship exists between pornography and sex offenses.

For example, in one study of 89 non-incarcerated sex offenders conducted by William Marshall, "slightly more than one-third of the child molesters and rapists reported at least occasionally being incited to commit an offense by exposure to forced or consenting pornography" (Einsiedel, 1986, p. 62). Exactly a third of the rapists who reported being incited by pornography to commit an offense said that they deliberately used pornography in their preparation for committing the rape. The comparable figure for child molesters was much higher--53% versus 33% (Einsiedel, 1986, p. 62). Pornography may also have undermined the offenders' inhibitions against acting out their desires; high sexual arousal probably has this effect on some men.

However, since these sex offenders appear to have used the pornography to arouse themselves after they had already decided to commit an offense, it could be argued that it was not the pornography that incited them. To what extent they actually required the pornography in order to commit their offenses, like some perpetrators require alcohol, we do not know. But even if these perpetrators were eliminated from the data analysis, that still leaves 66% of the rapists and 47% of the child molesters who claimed that they were at least sometimes incited by pornography to commit an offense.

Gene Abel, Mary Mittelman, and Judith Becker evaluated the use of pornography by 256 perpetrators of sexual offenses, all of whom were undergoing assessment and treatment (Einsiedel, 1986, p. 62). Like Marshall's sample, these men were outpatients, not incarcerated offenders. This is important because there is evidence that the data provided by incarcerated and non-incarcerated offenders differ (Einsiedel, 1986, p. 47). It is also likely that incarcerated offenders might be substantially less willing to be entirely frank about their anti-social histories than non-incarcerated offenders, for fear that such information might be used against them.

Abel and his colleagues reported that 56% of the rapists and 42% of the child molesters "implicated pornography in the commission of their offenses" (Einsiedel, 1986, p. 62). Edna Einsiedel, in her review of the social science research for the Pornography Commission, concluded that these studies "are suggestive of the implication of pornography in the commission of sex crimes among *some* rapists and child molesters"[12] (emphasis in original, p. 63).

In another study, Michael Goldstein and Harold Kant found that incarcerated rapists had been exposed to hard-core pornography at an earlier age than men presumed to be non-rapists. Specifically, 30% of the rapists in their sexual offender sample said that they had encountered hard-core pornographic photos in their pre-adolescence (i.e., before the age of 11) (1973, p. 55). This 30% figure compares with only 2% of the control group subjects exposed to hard-core pornography as pre-adolescents. The control group was obtained by a random household sample that was matched with the offender group for age, race, religion and educational level (1973, p. 50). Could it be that this early exposure of the offenders to hard-core pornography played a role in their becoming rapists? Further research should address this question.

CONCLUSION

This chapter describes my theory about how pornography–both violent and nonviolent–can cause rape and other forms of sexual assault. I have drawn on the findings of recent research to support my theory. Since most of this research pertains to rape rather than to child sexual abuse or non-sexual violence against women, my discussion has focused on rape. But I believe that my theory can be adapted to apply to other forms of sexual abuse and violence against women. I have done the preliminary work on such an adaptation to the causal relationship between pornography and child sexual abuse (see Figure 2), but have not found the time to record it.

In ending I want to note once more that I believe that the rich and varied data now available to us from all kinds of sources, when considered together, strongly support this theory.

- A high percentage of non-incarcerated rapists and child molesters have said that they have been incited by pornography to commit crimes;
- Pre-selected normal healthy male students say they are more likely to rape a woman after just one exposure to violent pornography;
- Large percentages of male junior high school students, high school students, and adults in a non-laboratory survey report imitating X-rated movies within a few days of exposure;
- Hundreds of women have testified in public about how they have been victimized by pornography;
- Ten percent of a probability sample of 930 women in San Francisco and 25% of female subjects in an experiment on pornography in

FIGURE 2. Theoretical Model of Pornography as a Cause of Child Sexual Abuse

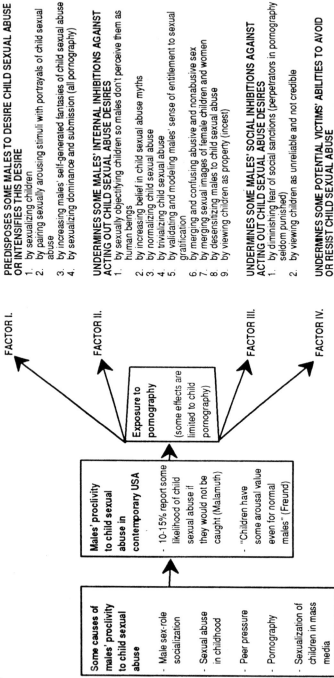

FACTOR I.

PREDISPOSES SOME MALES TO DESIRE CHILD SEXUAL ABUSE OR INTENSIFIES THIS DESIRE
1. by sexualizing children
2. by pairing sexually arousing stimuli with portrayals of child sexual abuse
3. by increasing males' self-generated fantasies of child sexual abuse
4. by sexualizing dominance and submission (all pornography)

FACTOR II.

UNDERMINES SOME MALES' INTERNAL INHIBITIONS AGAINST ACTING OUT CHILD SEXUAL ABUSE DESIRES
1. by sexually objectifying children so males don't perceive them as human beings
2. by increasing belief in child sexual abuse myths
3. by normalizing child sexual abuse
4. by trivializing child sexual abuse
5. by validating and modeling males' sense of entitlement to sexual gratification
6. by merging and confusing abusive and nonabusive sex
7. by merging sexual images of female children and women
8. by desensitizing males to child sexual abuse
9. by viewing children as property (incest)

FACTOR III.

UNDERMINES SOME MALES' SOCIAL INHIBITIONS AGAINST ACTING OUT CHILD SEXUAL ABUSE DESIRES
1. by diminishing fear of social sanctions (perpetrators in pornography seldom punished)
2. by viewing children as unreliable and not credible

FACTOR IV.

UNDERMINES SOME POTENTIAL VICTIMS' ABILITIES TO AVOID OR RESIST CHILD SEXUAL ABUSE
1. by fostering confusion between child sex and child sexual abuse
2. by legitimizing child sexual abuse
3. by modeling child sexual abuse
4. by creating an industry built on the commercialization of child sexual abuse

Exposure to pornography

(some effects are limited to child pornography)

Males' proclivity to child sexual abuse in contemporary USA

- 10-15% report some likelihood of child sexual abuse if they would not be caught (Malamuth)

- "Children have some arousal value even for normal males" (Freund)

Some causes of males' proclivity to child sexual abuse

- Male sex-role socialization

- Sexual abuse in childhood

- Peer pressure

- Pornography

- Sexualization of children in mass media

Canada reported having been upset by requests to enact pornography (Russell, 1980; Senn & Radtke, 1986);
- Many prostitutes report that pornography-related abuse has become an almost daily experience (Silbert & Pines, 1984);
- The laws of social learning must surely apply to pornography at least as much as to the mass media in general. Indeed, I–and others–have argued that sexual arousal and orgasm likely serve as unusually potent reinforcers of the messages conveyed by pornography;
- A large body of experimental research has shown that the viewing of violent pornography results in higher rates of aggression against women by male subjects.

No wonder Donnerstein stated that the relationship between pornography and violence against women is stronger than the relationship between smoking and lung cancer (see epigraph at beginning of this chapter). Just as smoking is not the only cause of lung cancer, neither is pornography the only cause of rape. I believe there are many factors that play a causal role in this crime (see Russell, 1984, for a multi-causal theory of rape). I have not attempted here to evaluate the relative importance of these different causal factors, but merely to show the overwhelming evidence that pornography is a major one.

NOTES

1. This article has undergone two fairly minor revisions since it was first published under this same title in *Political Psychology*, Vol. 9, No. 1, 1988; the first time for Catherine Itzin, Ed., *The Case Against Pornography* (London: Oxford University Press, 1992), and the second time for this volume.

2. This woman was a victim of incest through pornography who testified at the Minneapolis Hearings (Catharine MacKinnon, personal communication, 1986).

3. I often use the term *males* rather than *men* because many rapists are juveniles. Even more victims are girls–sometimes baby girls–not women.

4. As recently as 1984 Malamuth reported that in several studies an average of about 35% of male students indicated some likelihood of raping a woman (1984, p. 22). However, he says this figure has decreased to 25 to 30% since then for reasons he does not know (personal communication, July 1986).

5. This is an FBI euphemism for the frequent practice by the police of discounting rape cases reported to them as valid.

6. The fact that a sizable proportion of the killing is womanslaughter is essentially obliterated by this term.

7. This example was suggested by Robert Brannon (personal communication, October 27, 1991).

8. This way of clarifying the different elements of my definitions was suggested by Suzanne Popkin.

9. However, "those exposed to the 'erotica' stimulus did not differ significantly from either the control or both pornography conditions" (Einsiedel, 1986, p. 93). But this is not the most salient comparison for the point being made here. Another finding that relates to the broader issue of the effects of pornography, rather than the specific issue of rape, is that both the nonviolent dehumanizing and the violent materials elicited stronger feelings of depression, hostility, and anxiety than the nonviolent nondehumanizing material.

10. Why Donnerstein finds no effects for nonviolent pornographic movies while Zillmann reports many significant effects is not known.

11. In their written testimony to the Attorney General's Commission on Pornography, Donnerstein and Linz failed to even mention the effects of violent X-rated films (1985). And, in his spoken testimony to the Commission, Donnerstein gave this topic only a cursory mention. This is particularly odd since they were testifying to a commission whose only objective was to evaluate pornography, yet by their definition, the R-rated slasher movies do not constitute pornography.

12. Einsiedel also pointed out, however, that Abel and his colleagues (1985) found no difference between those offenders who used pornography and those who did not in the "frequency of sex crimes committed, number of victims, ability to control deviant urges, and degree of violence used during commission of the sex crime. The longer the duration of paraphiliac arousal, however, the greater the use of erotica."

REFERENCES

Abel, G. G., Barlow, D. H., Blanchard, E. B., & Guild, D. (1977). The components of rapists' sexual arousal. *Archives of General Psychiatry, 34*, 895-903.

Abel, G. G., Mittelman, M., & Becker, J., (1985). Sexual offenders: Results of assessment and recommendations for treatment. In M. H. Ben-Aron, S. J. Hucker, & C. D. Webster (Eds.), *Clinical criminology*. Toronto: Clarke Institute of Psychiatry.

Attorney General's Commission on Pornography: Final report. (1986). Vols. I and II. Washington, DC: U.S. Department of Justice.

Baron, L., & Straus, M. A. (1984). Sexual stratification, pornography, and rape in the United States. In N. M. Malamuth & E. Donnerstein (Eds.), *Pornography and sexual aggression*. New York: Academic Press.

Beneke, T. (1982). *Men on rape*. New York: St. Martin's Press.

Bogdanovich, P. (1984). *The killing of the unicorn: Dorothy Stratten 1960-1980*. New York: William Morrow.

Briere, J., Corne, S., Runtz, M., & Malamuth, N. (1984). *The rape arousal inventory: Predicting actual and potential sexual aggression in a university population*. Paper presented at the American Psychological Association Meeting, Toronto.

Briere, J., & Malamuth, N. (1983). Self-reported likelihood of sexually aggressive behavior: Attitudinal versus sexual explanations. *Journal of Research in Personality, 17*, 315-323.

Briere, J., Malamuth, N., & Check, J. (1985). Sexuality and rape-supportive beliefs. *International Journal of Women's Studies, 8,* 398-403.

Brownmiller, S. (1975). *Against our will: Men, women and rape.* New York: Simon and Schuster.

Bryant, J. (1985). *Unpublished transcript,* pp. 128-157. Testimony to the Attorney General's Commission on Pornography, Houston, Texas.

Burt, M. R. (1980). Cultural myths and supports for rape. *Journal of Personality and Social Psychology, 38,* 217-230.

Caputi, J. (1987). *The age of sex crime.* Bowling Green, Ohio: Bowling Green State University Popular Press.

Check, J. (1984). *The effects of violent and nonviolent pornography.* Ottawa, Canada: Canadian Department of Justice.

Check, J., & Malamuth, N. (1985). An empirical assessment of some feminist hypotheses about rape. *International Journal of Women's Studies, 8,* 414-423.

Check, J., & Guloien, T. H. (in press). The effects of repeated exposure to sexually violent pornography, nonviolent dehumanizing pornography, and erotica. In D. Zillmann & J. Bryant (Eds.), *Pornography: Recent research, interpretations, and policy considerations.* Hillside, NJ: Erlbaum.

Check, J., & Maxwell, K. (1992). *Children's consumption of pornography and their attitudes regarding sexual violence.* Paper presented at the Canadian Psychological Association Meeting, Quebec, Canada, June 11-13.

Cline, V. (Ed.). (1974). *Where do you draw the line?* Provo, UT: Brigham Young University Press.

Dietz, P., & Evans, B. (1982). Pornographic imagery and prevalence of paraphilia. *American Journal of Psychiatry, 139,* 1493-1495.

Donnerstein, E. (1983). *Public Hearings on ordinances to add pornography as discrimination against women.* Committee on Government Operations, City Council, Minneapolis, Minnesota.

Donnerstein, E. (1984). Pornography: Its effects on violence against women. In N. Malamuth & E. Donnerstein (Eds.), *Pornography and sexual aggression.* New York: Academic Press.

Donnerstein, E. (1985). *Unpublished transcript,* pp. 5-33. Testimony to the Attorney General's Commission on Pornography, Houston, Texas.

Donnerstein, E., & Linz, D. (1985). *Unpublished paper.* Prepared for the Attorney General's Commission on Pornography, Houston, Texas.

Donnerstein, E., Linz, D., & Penrod, S. (1987). *The question of pornography: Research findings and policy implications.* New York: Free Press.

Ebert, R., & Siskel, G. (1980). Unpublished manuscript. *Sneak Previews,* #304, PBS Television.

Einsiedel, E. F. (1986). *Social science report.* Prepared for the Attorney General's Commission on Pornography, U.S. Department of Justice, Washington, D.C.

Everywoman. (1988). *Pornography and sexual violence: Evidence of the links.* London: Everywoman.

Finkelhor, D. (1984). *Child sexual abuse: New theory and practice.* New York: Free Press.

Frost, R., & Stauffer, J. (1987, Spring). The effects of social class, gender, and personality on physiological responses to filmed violence. *Journal of Communication.*

Goodchilds, J., & Zellman, G. (1984). Sexual signaling and sexual aggression in adolescent relationships. In N. Malamuth & E. Donnerstein (Eds.), *Pornography and sexual aggression.* New York: Academic Press.

Hite, S. (1981). *The Hite report on male sexuality.* New York: Knopf.

Koss, M. (1986). *Hidden rape: Survey of psychopathological consequences.* Report to the National Institute of Mental Health.

Lederer, L. (1980). *Take back the night.* New York: William Morrow.

Longino, H. (1980). What is pornography? In L. Lederer (Ed.), *Take back the night.* New York: William Morrow.

Lovelace, L. (1980). *Ordeal.* New York: Berkeley Books.

Lovelace, L. (1986). *Out of bondage.* Secaucus, NJ: Lyle Stuart.

MacKinnon, C. (1987). *Feminism unmodified: Discourses on life and law.* Cambridge, MA: Harvard University Press.

Malamuth, N. (1981a). Rape fantasies as a function of exposure to violent sexual stimuli. *Archives of Sexual Behavior, 10.*

Malamuth, N. (1981b). Rape proclivity among males. *Journal of Social Issues, 37,* 138-157.

Malamuth, N. (1984). Aggression against women: Cultural and individual causes. In N. Malamuth & E. Donnerstein (Eds.), *Pornography and sexual aggression.* New York: Academic Press.

Malamuth, N. (1985). *Unpublished transcript,* pp. 68-110. Testimony to the Attorney General's Commission on Pornography, Houston, Texas.

Malamuth, N. (1986). *Do sexually violent media indirectly contribute to anti-social behavior?* Paper prepared for the Surgeon General's Workshop on Pornography and Public Health, Arlington, Virginia.

Malamuth, N., & Check, J. (1981). The effects of mass media exposure on acceptance of violence against women: A field experiment. *Journal of Research in Personality, 15.*

Malamuth, N., & Check, J. (1985). The effects of aggressive pornography on beliefs in rape myths: Individual differences. *Journal of Research in Personality, 19,* 299-320.

Malamuth, N., & Donnerstein, E. (Eds.). (1984). *Pornography and sexual aggression.* New York: Academic Press.

Malamuth, N., Haber, S., & Feshbach, S. (1980). Testing hypotheses regarding rape: Exposure to sexual violence, sex differences, and the "normality" of rapists. *Journal of Research in Personality, 14,* 121-137.

Malamuth, N., & Spinner, B. (1980). A longitudinal content analysis of sexual violence in the best-selling erotic magazines. *Journal of Sexual Research, 16,* 226-237.

Maxwell, K., & Check, J. (1992). *Adolescents' rape myth attitudes and acceptance of forced sexual intercourse.* Paper presented at the Canadian Psychological Association Meeting, Quebec, Canada, June 11-13.

McKenzie-Mohr, D., & Zanna, M. (1990). Treating women as sexual objects: Look to the (gender schematic) male who has viewed pornography. *Personality and Social Psychology Bulletin, 16*(2), 296-308.

Medea, A., & Thompson, K. (1974). *Against rape.* New York: Farrar, Straus, and Giroux.

Mosher, D. (1971). Sex callousness toward women. *Technical reports of the Commission on Obscenity and Pornography,* Vol 8. Washington, DC: Government Printing Office.

Palys, T. S. (1986). Testing the common wisdom: The social content of video pornography. *Canadian Psychology, 27,* 22-35.

Public hearings on ordinances to add pornography as discrimination against women. (1983). Committee on Government Operations, City Council, Minneapolis, Minnesota.

Russell, D. E. H. (1975). *The politics of rape: The victim's perspective.* Chelsea, MI: Scarborough House.

Russell, D. E. H. (1980). Pornography and violence: What does the new research say? In L. Lederer (Ed.), *Take back the night: Women on pornography.* New York: William Morrow.

Russell, D. E. H. (1984). *Sexual exploitation: Rape, child sexual abuse, and workplace harassment.* Beverly Hills, CA: Sage.

Russell, D. E. H. (Ed.). (1993). *Making violence sexy.* New York: Pergamon.

Scully, D. (1985). *The role of violent pornography in justifying rape.* Paper prepared for the Attorney General's Commission on Pornography, Houston, Texas.

Senn, C. (1992). *Women's contact with male consumers: One link between pornography and women's experiences of male violence.* Paper presented at the Canadian Psychological Association Meeting, Quebec, Canada, June 11-13.

Senn, C. (1993). Women's responses to pornography. In D. E. H. Russell (Ed.), *Making violence sexy.* New York: Pergamon.

Senn, C., & Radtke, H. L. (1986). *A comparison of women's reactions to violent pornography, non-violent pornography, and erotica.* Paper presented at the Canadian Psychological Association Meeting, Toronto, Canada.

Silbert, M. H., & Pines, A. M. (1984). Pornography and sexual abuse of women. *Sex Roles, 10,* 861-868.

Smith, D. (1976). *Sexual aggression in American pornography: The stereotype of rape.* Paper presented at the American Sociological Association Meeting.

Theodorson, G., & Theodorson, A. (1979). *A modern dictionary of sociology.* New York: Barnes & Noble.

Zillmann, D. (1985). *Unpublished transcript,* pp. 110-128. Testimony to the Attorney General's Commission on Pornography, Houston, Texas.

Zillmann, D., & Bryant, J. (1984). Effects of massive exposure to pornography. In N. Malamuth & E. Donnerstein (Eds.), *Pornography and sexual aggression.* New York: Academic Press.

Social Science and Public Policy: Constraints on the Linkage

Edna F. Einsiedel

University of Calgary

SUMMARY. This paper analyzes the debates over the last two decades surrounding the work of United States pornography commissions as a vehicle for exploring the political context of public policy decision-making in one area of sexual abuse prevention. Many attempts have been made to implicate pornography in the sexual exploitation of women and children, and inherent in the moves to regulate is the assumption that the linkage–between exposure to pornography and antisocial behavior–exists and is demonstrable. The United States 1970 and 1986 commissions on pornography are contrasted in terms of their staff structure, fiscal resources, use of social science research, and public policy recommendations. *[Article copies available from The Haworth Document Delivery Service: 1-800-342-9678.]*

This essay analyzes the debates over the last two decades surrounding the work of United States pornography commissions as a vehicle for exploring the political context of public policy decision-making in one

Correspondence may be addressed to Edna Einsiedel, Graduate Program in Communication Studies, University of Calgary, 2500 University Drive NW, Calgary, Alberta, Canada T2N 1N4.

This article is a revised and updated version of a chapter entitled, "Social Science and Public Policy: Looking at the 1986 Commission on Pornography" in Susan Gruber and Joan Hoff (Eds.) (1989), *For adult users only: The dilemma of violent pornography.* Bloomington, IN: Indiana University Press.

[Haworth co-indexing entry note]: "Social Science and Public Policy: Constraints on the Linkage." Einsiedel, Edna F. Co-published simultaneously in *Prevention in Human Services* (The Haworth Press, Inc.) Vol. 12, No. 2, 1995, pp. 93-110; and: *Sexual Assault and Abuse: Sociocultural Context of Prevention* (ed: Carolyn F. Swift) The Haworth Press, Inc., 1995, pp. 93-110. Single or multiple copies of this article are available from The Haworth Document Delivery Service [1-800-342-9678, 9:00 a.m.-5:00 p.m. (EST)].

93

area of sexual abuse prevention. Many attempts have been made to implicate pornography in the sexual exploitation of women and children and inherent in the moves to regulate is the assumption that the linkage (between exposure to pornography and antisocial behavior) exists and is demonstrable.

A review of the experience of pornography commissions and regulatory activities in their wake is critical in assessing the importance one might attribute to public policy efforts in the prevention of sexual abuse. Particularly for those carrying the assumption that the relationship between research findings and policy efforts is a fairly straightforward and direct link, an understanding of the complexities of such ventures might be useful. It is instructive to compare the 1970 and 1986 commissions in terms of their mode of operation and research findings to illustrate the vagaries of policy-making on such a controversial area.

The role that social science findings were to play for the 1970 pornography commission was a significant one. This was reflected in the structure of the commission staff which was headed by a behavioral scientist; the hiring of staff members, most of whom had behavioral science training (not one was a law enforcement officer); the allocation of the bulk of the commission budget to social science studies; and the ultimate decision to base much of its recommendations on social science findings. Fueled by a $2 million budget, the 1970 commission sponsored much of the seminal research on the effects of exposure to sexually explicit materials. The impetus for further research that these early studies provided was in itself one of the significant contributions of the commission. As its Effects Panel noted, these early efforts "helped to legitimate systematic inquiry into an area that heretofore has either been ignored or feared" (Report of the 1970 Commission on Obscenity and Pornography, p. 171).

The use of social science research by the 1986 commission was entirely different. To begin with, the context had changed significantly from 1970. The commission's mandate specifically precluded sponsorship of original research and, as a creature of the then Attorney-General Edwin Meese's office, it was inevitable that a law-enforcement approach would predominate. The staff consisted of four lawyers, four law enforcement officers, and one social scientist. Its budget was $500,000, or one-sixteenth of the 1970 commission's budget, after taking into account the changed value of the dollar ($.31 in 1984, using 1967, the year the 1970 commission was created, as the base year).

While the 1970 commission put all its eggs in the social science basket with the recommendations of its working panels based primarily on the research findings of the studies commissioned, the 1986 commission's format of choice was the public hearing, featuring testimony from a variety of sources. The usefulness of this format was limited to the fact that it allowed a diversity of *political* viewpoints among social scientists to be heard. Thus, social scientists advocating sexual freedom were heard from as well as those warning of potential harms from exposure to pornography. On balance, the social science hearing accomplished little in terms of providing commissioners a basic understanding of what the research was saying. Indeed, the welter of conflicting opinions only served to confuse rather than enlighten most of them. Public hearings in the end tend to be a form of theater, a way of representing viewpoints and special interests as well as a way of manipulating public opinion rather than an effective means of educating a commission about social science research.

RESEARCH CONCLUSIONS OF THE 1970 AND 1986 COMMISSIONS

The conclusions drawn from the research by the 1970 and 1986 commissions could not have been more diametrically opposed. The 1970 commission concluded that "empirical research designed to clarify the question has found no reliable evidence to date that exposure to explicit sexual materials plays a significant role in the causation of delinquent or criminal sexual behavior among youth and adults" (p. 169). The first commission thus concluded that "greater latitude can safely be given to adults in deciding for themselves what they will or will not read or view" (p. 171). The 1986 commission, on the other hand, concluded that exposure to sexually violent material as well as to nonviolent but degrading sexually explicit material led to the perpetuation of attitudes that condoned sexual violence and, more importantly, led to the commission of acts of sexual violence against women (Attorney-General's Commission on Pornography, 1986). In attempting to understand the divergence in these conclusions, it might help to put these research findings within the perspective of their socio-political contexts.

THE SOCIO-POLITICAL ENVIRONMENT OF PORNOGRAPHY COMMISSIONS

Four factors appear to differentiate the setting within which the 1970 and 1986 commissions operated, all of which had direct or indirect impacts on the research.

First, the nature and amount of pornography had changed. The 1970 report described adult men's magazines as substantially depicting partially nude females with breast and buttock exposure and "a self-imposed taboo against the depiction of female genitalia [that was] rigidly observed," a description that was almost archaic by 1986. In 1970, *Playboy* was the only widely circulated magazine of this genre. By 1975, there were eight other titles competing for a somewhat larger audience, and by 1985, there were some 14 titles dominated by *Playboy*, *Penthouse*, and *Hustler*. By this time, the distribution of sexually explicit materials had also expanded in concert with the development of new technologies (Attorney-General's Commission on Pornography, 1986).[1]

Public tolerance was also much in evidence in opinion polls, with increasing numbers reporting exposure to sexually explicit materials. Gallup poll figures from 1985 showed that it was a small minority–about one in ten–that had not seen or read *Playboy* or *Penthouse*. Alongside greater exposure, however, appeared to be heightened public concern, especially among women, who expressed greater willingness to ban outright materials featuring sexual violence.

The political climate had also changed significantly. A conservative administration was at the helm, with a Department of Justice that was particularly noted for its lack of support for civil rights. Fueled by a constituency from the right that had consistently attempted to push pornography onto the public agenda, the public debate by the mid-eighties had now taken on a new twist, with a segment of the feminist movement sharing a similar objective of restraints on pornography. While these interest groups were often portrayed as political bedfellows, the gulf between their rationales of "harm" versus "morality and family values" was immense.

The feminist assumptions that causally implicated pornography in sexual violence had an important impact on research efforts; indeed, they provided some rationale for testing hypotheses linking pornography to sexual violence. For example, Baron and Straus' work (1984, 1985) on the relationship between circulation rates of adult men's magazines and rape rates posited a theory of rape that drew on four aspects of social culture: the proliferation of pornography, sexual inequality, culturally legitimate violence, and social disorganization. Malamuth and Billings (1986) compared research on pornography in the context of the sexual communication model (i.e., pornography is communication about sexuality with no untoward effects and some beneficial ones) and the feminist model, suggesting pornography as reflective of male subjugation of women. Noting limitations with the former, they recommended greater research attention to the feminist model.

Finally, there were important differences in the research strategies employed in the early studies compared to subsequent ones. While 1970 findings suggested that no significant behavioral changes, other than slight increases in behaviors already within one's repertoire, occurred as a result of exposure to sexually explicit materials, subsequent research was demonstrating effects on attitudes, perceptions, and behaviors, particularly for certain classes of materials.[2]

THE 1986 COMMISSION'S RESEARCH FINDINGS AND POLICY RECOMMENDATIONS

The concerted attention focused on violent pornography produced results that offered some convergent validation for social scientists wary of weaknesses inherent in individual measurement approaches or single populations. These findings can be summarized as follows:

- Exposure to a sexually violent depiction in the laboratory has resulted in more aggressive sexual fantasies among those exposed.
- Rapists are aroused by depictions of both forced and nonforced sex. College males tend to be more aroused by these depictions than females.
- Depictions of forced sex in which the victim has an orgasm, or does not exhibit pain or disgust have been shown to result in arousal among college males.
- Depictions of sexual violence among college males have been shown to result in significant increases in the acceptance of rape myths and sexual violence toward women.
- Such depictions have also been shown to affect perceptions: victims of rape tend to be seen as more worthless, more responsible for the assault, while perpetrators tend to be absolved of responsibility and to be viewed less negatively.
- Sexually violent depictions have been found to lead to laboratory aggression against women.
- Such laboratory aggression toward women has also been found to correlate significantly with self-reported sexually aggressive behaviors.

The major conclusion of the 1986 commission with regard to the research findings can be found in a chapter entitled "Harms." It is here that the commission suggests that there can be harmful effects from exposure to different classes of pornography. Several aspects about this section are striking:

First, there was a recognition that not all sexually explicit materials are alike in their effects. Like the Fraser Commission in Canada (see *Report of the Special Committee on Pornography and Prostitution*, 1985), the United States commission categorized sexually explicit materials into classes or tiers. These categories included violent sexually explicit materials, nonviolent and degrading sexually explicit materials, nonviolent and nondegrading materials, and nudity.

Second, the discussion of effects, particularly for the first two categories, was based on the notion of harm. It was a notion that was clearly akin to that promoted by feminist anti-pornography supporters (see, for example, MacKinnon, 1985). Third, the findings of harm turned on the idea of either explicit sexual aggression or images of degradation. The *Final Report* (Attorney-General's Commission on Pornography, 1986) maintained that there was no evidence of harm for simple sexual explicitness or nudity.

How did the social science evidence stack up? In terms of the evidence on sexually violent material, the convergence of a variety of findings is difficult to quarrel with. Neal Malamuth's programmatic studies, for example, attempted to examine effects from a variety of angles: he compared responses of "normal" males with offender populations, correlated laboratory measures with measures of "naturalistic aggression," varied content cues, used physiological measures of arousal, and investigated correlations between arousal patterns and attitudinal as well as behavioral indicators (see reviews in Check & Malamuth, 1985; Malamuth, 1984).

The data for nonviolent pornography, on the other hand, did not offer the same kind of "neat" convergent validation. There was thus a problem in terms of attempting to explain an apparent contradiction between the nonviolent and violent pornography data. Furthermore, while there was much speculation that the stimulus materials for those studies finding negative effects in fact employed highly degrading images of women, and those with null effects were simply sexually explicit, it remained speculation at that point in time. In this instance, while the research review suggested that the data were hardly conclusive, the commission, on the other hand, suggested that attitudinal changes among those exposed to materials considered degrading to women could also promote sexual violence:

Because the causal link is less the subject of experimental studies, we have been required to think more carefully here about the assumptions necessary to causally connect increased acceptance of rape myths and other attitudinal changes with increased sexual aggression and sexual violence. And on the basis of all the evidence we have considered, from all sources, and on the basis of our own insights and experiences, we believe we are justified in drawing the following conclusion: over a large enough sample, a population that believes many women like to be raped, that believes that sexual violence or sexual coercion is often desired or appropriate, and that believes that sex offenders are less responsible for their acts, will commit more acts of sexual violence or sexual coercion than would a population holding these beliefs to a lesser extent. (Attorney-General's Commission on Pornography, 1986, p. 333)

It was notable that the observation of a likelihood of sexual violence based on holding certain attitudes was specifically couched in terms of a probabilistic outcome in the population; there was no suggestion that a particular individual, exposed to such material and holding certain attitudes, was likely to commit sexual aggression. Based on its categorization of four classes of materials and its conclusions regarding such classes, the commission recommended more vigorous prosecution of obscenity laws, particularly for sexually violent material. A major problem with this approach was that current obscenity law is based on sexual explicitness (of the prurient variety or with no literary, artistic, political or scientific value). The notion of pornography as "harm" as outlined by the commission, on the other hand, suggested that certain sexually violent materials would fall outside the rubric of the "obscene," a point conceded by the commissioners (p. 394). Recognizing that not all materials considered "pornographic," especially vis-à-vis the first two classes, might be legally obscene, it was nevertheless argued that obscenity laws were sufficient instruments to deal with the classes of materials that raised the greatest amount of concern.

Reaction from the Social Science Community

Even during the commission's tenure, the strongly politicized atmosphere saw social scientists lining up on policy sides. During its deliberation period, calls mainly against censorship were made to the commission publicly and privately. Thus, it was perhaps not so surprising that when the *Final Report* was made public, there were immediate cries of outrage and severe criticisms of the findings (*New York Times*, May 17, 1986). A second and later critical reaction appeared in journals (see Paletz, 1988; Wilcox, 1987). The debates between researchers opposed to censorship and those whose studies demonstrated negative effects (and were perceived to be aligned with proponents of restrictions) were played out in the journal pages and sometimes reached a level of acrimony rarely seen on other issues (see Christensen, 1986, 1987). A third type of reaction came from some of the social scientists prominent in the pornography research field who claimed misrepresentation of their data (Donnerstein, Linz & Penrod, 1987; Linz & Donnerstein, 1988). Researchers were harsh on their own methodological shortcomings, humble about their validity, headlining their pleas to limit effects to indirect ones (see Byrne & Kelley, 1989; Donnerstein, Linz & Penrod, 1987; Malamuth, 1986).

Finally, considerable space was devoted to what were offered as *alternative* responses to censorship, for a problem whose significance was considered to have rested on rather tenuous evidence. There were calls for sex education (Fisher & Barak, 1989), mass media campaigns with individualized skills training sessions (Linz & Donnerstein, 1989), educational briefings before and after exposure (Intons-Peterson & Roskos-Ewoldson, 1989), warning labels à la cigarette packs, and media self-censorship (Byrne & Kelley, 1989). There were also calls for an approach that separated policy exploration, research evaluation and policy recommendation (Zillmann, 1989).

SOCIAL SCIENCE AND PUBLIC POLICY: A POLITICAL INTERACTION

The proper "fit" between social science findings and the making of public policy is always difficult to establish. In discussing this interphase, I make two assumptions:

First, social science evidence can make a significant contribution to policy making, but it is not the sole foundation of policy making. As many analysts of public policy have observed, policy making is as much an expression of values, of the aggregation of competing interests, of intuition, as it is an interpretation of social science (see Cater & Strickland, 1975; Weiss, 1977). Second, if policy-making is as much a value-laden enterprise as it is a process that could be "rational," i.e., based on empirical procedures, so is social science research. The kinds of questions we consider, the way we frame those questions, the variables we select for examination–or those that we ignore–the interpretations we give to our findings, reflect our interests, the influence of our peers, and our normative preferences. To view the social science research process as an objective, value-free enterprise is itself as much a distorted view of social science.

That said, what can be gleaned from the use of social science research by the 1986 commission? I will limit discussion here to three areas: how a social problem is defined, the process of interpreting social science findings, and the policy recommendations that might flow directly from the social science evidence. Three vital contributions of social science research to policy-making lie in the areas of conceptualization and problem definition, the obtaining of systematic data, and the recommendation of alternative strategies that stem directly from the data. How did social science fare on these three levels?

Problem Definition

As Wildavsky (1984) has argued, political context determines how people identify problems. Problem definition circumscribes two questions: (1) is *it* (i.e., the concept at hand) a "problem" and (2) what is the nature of the problem? Of course, the appointment of a commission to look into "the problem" of pornography suggests the first question was moot. This did not belie the fact that there was disagreement about the first question. The American Civil Liberties Union, in the company of that group of feminists more concerned about the pernicious effects of censorship, and, of course, the sex industry as a whole, variously argued (a) that pornography could and did have positive effects; (b) that the problem, if there was one, was insufficient to warrant any restrictions on free expression; or (c) that "pornography" could not be defined satisfactorily and therefore, could not be regulated satisfactorily (see, for example, Nobile & Nadler, 1986).

The opposing viewpoint, on the other hand, argued that there was a significant societal problem. This camp found anti-pornography feminists and conservatives allied, although with different frameworks for defining the pornography problem. The latter, of course, defined pornography as a moral and aesthetic problem. Society, they argued, should regulate obscene displays because they corrupt the social fabric (Berns, 1976; Herson, 1984). Feminists' definition of the problem revolved around pornography as inherently harmful to women's physical and mental well-being, to their social status, to their collectivity. Its restriction was thus necessary if social equality between genders was to be maintained (MacKinnon, 1985).

It is revealing that the commission appeared to adopt this latter feminist position in its report, although individual statements by commissioners reflected the preference among some for the problem definition provided by the conservative camp. Father Bruce Ritter, for example, noted that "a much larger issue is at stake here than the individual harm or degradation of a particular man or woman. . . . society itself suffers a grave harm." (Attorney-General's Commission on Pornography, 1986, p. 95).

The focus on pornography as a problem was also complemented on the social science side by researchers' increased attention to the issue in the seventies and early eighties, for theoretical and practical reasons. The focus on pornography by some social scientists–in much the same way others have zeroed in on television to help explain antisocial behaviors–suggests the attribution of some significance to the concept's capacity to explain behaviors or social problems of interest. It also suggests that social values or political assumptions, such as the harm or harmlessness of certain materials, is worthy of testing.

Conceptualizing the Problem

In her analysis of the influence of social science on policy, Weiss (1982) has argued that social science plays an important role in affecting the shape and content of policy discourse. "Because research provides powerful labels for previously inchoate and unorganized experience, it helps to mould officials' thinking into categories derived from social science" (p. 291). She maintains that the ideas derived from research provide "organizing perspectives" that help to make sense of information and experience, or frameworks to help interpret problems and suggest policy alternatives.

In looking to social science for such a perspective, the 1986 commission found current research wanting. Dissatisfied with the violent-non-violent classes commonly found in the literature, the commission noted:

> We have unanimously agreed that looking at all sexually explicit materials, or even all pornographic materials, as one undifferentiated whole is unjustified by common sense, unwarranted on the evidence, and an altogether oversimplifying way of looking at a complex phenomenon. In many respects, we consider this one of our most important conclusions. Our subdivisions are not intended to be definitive, and particularly with respect to the subdivision between non-violent and degrading, we recognize that some researchers have usually employed broader or different groupings. Further research or thinking, or just changes in the world, may suggest finer or different divisions. To us, it is embarking on the process of subdivision that is most important, and we strongly urge that further research and thinking about the question of pornography recognize initially the way in

which different varieties of material may produce different consequences. (Attorney-General's Commission on Pornography, 1986,
pp. 320-21)

From a policy perspective, this categorization was an amalgam of logic,
social science, values and politics. Logic because it was indeed based on
the presence or absence of certain attributes–violence and degradation, for
instance; social science because there was a partial meshing with the two
classes used by a number of researchers (violent and nonviolent pornography); values because it appeared to have "bought into" the feminist distinction between erotica and pornography (see, for example, Steinem,
1980); and politics because the separation between the degrading and the
merely sexually explicit allowed some terrain for compromise. For liber-
als, it was important not to condemn the sexually explicit, and, for conservatives, if most pornography could be called "degrading," then the sexually explicit was an elusive class that might encompass sex education
materials but no more.

Beyond such considerations, the argument for "subdivisions" was not
that far afield from what common sense–or theory–would suggest, regardless of whether one agreed or disagreed with the commission's categorization scheme: that different attributes in the stimulus material might have
different effects. This proposition raises the issue of whether the research
findings supported the policy conclusions drawn.

Strictly speaking, the answer was no. There were hardly any studies
dealing with "non-violent degrading" material but, while recognizing this
inconclusive status in the research, the report nevertheless took the position that absence of evidence on behavioral effects *did not preclude that
negative effects could occur.* Relying more on "experience" and "common sense," the commission argued that "degrading materials" could
also result in attitudinal changes supportive of the acceptance of sexual
coercion.

While it is tempting to argue in favor of strict reliance on social science
evidence for policy decisions, and to suggest that "good" policy recommendations will result from a "neutral" evaluation of the research (see
Zillmann, 1989), it is doubtful that the research questions on nonviolent
pornography will be resolved in the context of the normal strictures of the
research process. For many social scientists, the class of nonviolent pornography represents that nightmarish terrain, the slippery slope, where
visions abound of trigger-happy prosecutors unleashed to do duty for
vocal minorities, where specific media (a number of men's magazines,
cable programs) are implicated, and where findings of negative effects

project unseemly images of Victorian prudery. For some researchers, the nonviolent class evokes an arm's length response.

As an ironical footnote to the use of categories of sexually explicit materials, the Supreme Court of Canada delivered a landmark ruling in 1992 (R. v. Butler, 1992, S.C.J. No. 15) that essentially adopted the *harms* approach of anti-pornography feminists and the United States pornography commission. This was based on the categories of sexually explicit materials approach, with the Canadian court agreeing that sexually explicit materials with violent content and sexually explicit materials with non-violent but *degrading and dehumanizing* elements would be considered obscene and therefore legally actionable. The highest court of Canada thus essentially agreed with the United States commission's social science findings, disagreed with its own commission's internal research evaluation (which summarily dismissed most of the pornography research; see Einsiedel, 1988), and based its ruling on the notion that harmful sexually explicit material (i.e., the two classes mentioned above) "predisposed persons to act in an antisocial manner."

The Interpretation of Data

Unfortunately for policy-makers, it is quite often the case that social science research fails to produce clear-cut findings. These findings must be interpreted by both social scientists and policy makers, and interpretation is as much politics as it is the logic of the findings. It is a value-laden process where "truth" is oftentimes a matter of which side of the political spectrum the interpreter is on.

For the social scientist, his or her interpretations are already normally cautious, laden with caveats and calls for further research. These qualifiers easily become fact when there is fear of restrictions or regulations. For example, "some-effects-but-more-research-is-needed" can easily be represented as "no-effects, period." For the policy-maker, the question becomes what the research says to date, what is sufficient evidence to justify action, and what alternatives to research evidence exist to justify action?

McLeod and Reeves (1981) suggested two apt metaphorical labels for the two extremes among those who interpret social science findings:

> Type One worriers fear the possibility of making too strong inferences and, consequently, tend to accept a position of no media effects. The evidence they cite tends to be from field studies of persuasion using gross measures of both media exposure and attitude change.

Type Two worriers hold a diametrically opposing set of concerns in making research inferences. They worry most about overlooking any media effect and frequently cite the difficulties that beset attempts to find even "obvious" effects. . . . They worry less about the proportion of effect that media variables account for, noting that even a small effect–say, 2 percent in an election campaign–can make a very great difference. (p. 262)

Among the commissioners, these two viewpoints were much in evidence. In his personal statement on the issue of pornography, one commissioner argued:

It appears extremely naive to assume that the river of obscenity which has inundated the American landscape has not invaded the world of children. This seven billion dollar industry pervades every dimension of our lives. There are more stores selling pornographic videos than there are McDonald hamburger stands. . . . It is my belief that the behavior of an entire generation of teenagers is being adversely affected by the current emphasis on premarital sexuality and general eroticism seen nightly on television, in movies, and other sources of pornography. (Dobson, 1986, p. 78)

Beyond the polemic, this statement was a classic argument of assuming effects from pervasiveness of certain media content.

On the other side of the continuum, two commissioners argued:

First, it is essential to state that the social science research has not been designed to evaluate the relationship between exposure to pornography and the commission of sex crimes; therefore, efforts to tease the current data into proof of a causal link between these acts simply cannot be accepted. . . .

Human behavior is complex and multi-causal. To say that exposure to pornography in and of itself causes an individual to commit a sexual crime is simplistic, not supported by the social science data, and overlooks many of the other variables that may be contributing causes. (Levine & Becker, 1986, p. 204)

That the same body of data generated such widely divergent conclusions among policy makers is hardly unexpected. Indeed, the Canadian pornography commission (*Report of the Special Committee on Pornography and Prostitution,* 1985) quite astutely observed:

Those who see freedom of speech as the highest value argue that the data must demonstrate that concrete harm to *individuals* [emphasis added] is caused by pornography in order to support controls on it. They reject the idea that controls can be justified by a showing of some generalized harm, or by showing . . . that pornography impairs the realization of other social values. . . .

The proponents of the equality approach are, of course, more tolerant of existing shortcomings of empirical research about the actual harms to individuals of pornographic material. They point out that the momentum of such research is in the direction of being able to show harms. . . . The difference between these two approaches is quite striking. The egalitarian approach does not require that the whole burden of justifying legislation should fall upon the research data; the libertarian approach does. Moreover, the libertarian approach imposes, in effect, a very high burden of proof before the data will be taken . . . demonstrably to justify incursions on freedom of expression. (p. 98)

This debate among social scientists about the interpretation of social science data and the debate between social scientists and policy makers is one that, interestingly enough, is not unique to the present situation. Sixteen years earlier, the same conundrum was recognized by some social scientists and policy makers.

In 1970, the issue was the contradiction in the findings between the President's Commission on the Causes and Prevention of Violence and the Commission on Obscenity and Pornography. While the former reported undesirable effects from the portrayal of violence on TV, the latter maintained short-lived effects, none of them worrisome ("behaviors already in one's repertoire"). A prominent social psychologist asked then: "Can it be that these seemingly different conclusions were affected to some extent at least by a prevailing liberal ideology and its attitudes toward aggression and sex?" (Berkowitz, 1971). A policy analyst similarly observed that the difference in recommendations was the result "not of different empirical findings, but of different judgments about similar findings" (Wilson, 1971, p. 47). Indeed, this differential judgment about the same issue has been documented in the case of three countries' varying responses to social science research on pornography (Einsiedel, 1988).

Sixteen years later, the 1986 commission was basically in a similar dilemma, only worsened by the following occurrences: (a) the ongoing violence research had become more rigorous and more definitive (see National Institute of Mental Health, 1982); (b) the violence research had been instrumental in making inoperative the catharsis hypothesis, which had provided a convenient rationale for the notion of pornography as "safety valve"; (c) the pornography research results had been coming up with "negative effects" that did not conform with 1970 findings; and (d) the policy effort, on the other hand, was spearheaded by an administration whose politics most social scientists loved to hate.

It is not at all clear how this dilemma will ever be satisfactorily resolved, particularly in the context of an issue that arouses such extreme passions. The larger questions are often ones of politics and values for which social science is not the sole, or perhaps even the most important arbiter. In the larger scheme of things, the polity has to address the question of how much importance to attach to pornography as a social problem. There is further the additional issue of what to do if indeed it is defined as a major problem.

In terms of the social science–public policy relationship, there is much to be learned from this particular case. For policy makers, having social science data hardly guarantees their use, much less their "proper" use. From the research point of view, the probabilistic nature of research findings sometimes leads to a range of interpretations, with choices made just as often on the basis of ideological preferences as on the nature of the data themselves. Perhaps in the end, the lessons learned result as much from having raised these issues.

NOTES

1. The availability and type of material on the market had a direct bearing on the stimulus materials used in the research. In 1970, many of the experimental studies utilized sexually explicit materials from sex research institutes (the Kinsey Institute in Bloomington, Indiana, and its counterpart in Hamburg, West Germany) because of the difficulty of obtaining materials from the open market. One study had to rely on confiscated items from the Bureau of Customs collection while another had to use materials created by the researcher himself—a film of "a female sensuously disrobing" (Tannenbaum, 1970). It is as much an indication of changing times that subsequent researchers used material that commonly depicted oral sex, group sex, in some cases, bestiality, and anal intercourse, in addition to garden-variety heterosexual intercourse. Many of these materials were easily obtainable from the local video outlet or the corner periodical outlet (see, for example, descriptions of stimulus materials in Linz, 1985; Zillmann & Bryant, 1984; Donnerstein, 1980).

2. The differences were mainly in the following areas: first, most of the 1970 studies involved one-time exposures to the stimulus materials while a number of subsequent studies had subjects exposed up to several weeks in duration. Second, the 1970 studies examined sexually explicit materials as one class of stimuli,

perhaps reflecting the predominant material of this period. This was rectified in later studies which attempted to differentiate between sexually explicit materials with and without violent content. Third, the catharsis model (suggesting inhibition of aggressive tendencies after viewing violence), which provided the framework for some of the 1970 studies had, by the second commission's tenure, become obsolete as an explanatory model for media effects (National Institute of Mental Health, 1982; Comstock, 1987). The majority of studies subsequent to 1970 tended to be grounded on models that predicted some type of effect from the media. Fourth, subsequent studies were characterized by a more diverse array of dependent variable measures, or measures of effects, including a range of attitudinal and perceptual measures, refinements in physiological measures of arousal, and a diversity in behavioral change measures.

REFERENCES

Attorney-General's Commission on Pornography (1986). *Final Report.* Washington, DC: U.S. Government Printing Office.

Baron, L. & Straus, M. (1984). Sexual stratification, pornography, and rape in the United States. In N. Malamuth & E. Donnerstein (Eds.), *Pornography and sexual aggression* (pp. 186-210). Orlando, FL: Academic Press.

Baron, L. & Straus, M. (1985, August). *Legitimate violence and rape: A test of the cultural spillover theory.* Paper presented at the Eastern Sociological Society meeting, Philadelphia.

Berkowitz, L. (1971, December). Sex and violence: We can't have it both ways. *Psychology Today,* 17-23.

Berns, W. (1976). *The first amendment and the future of American democracy.* New York: Basic Books.

Byrne, D. & Kelley, K. (1989). Basing legislative action on research data: Prejudice, prudence, and empirical limitations. In D. Zillmann & J. Bryant (Eds.), *Pornography: Research advances and policy considerations* (pp. 363-386). NJ: Lawrence Erlbaum.

Cater, D. & Strickland, S. (1975). *TV violence and the child.* New York: Russell Sage Foundation.

Check, J. & Malamuth, N. (1985). Pornography and sexual aggression: A social learning theory analysis. In M.L. McLaughlin (Ed.), *Communication yearbook, v. 9* (pp. 210-238). Beverly Hills, CA: Sage.

Christensen, F. (1986). Sexual callousness re-examined. *Journal of Communication, 36:*1, 174-188.

Christensen, F. (1987). Effects of pornography: The debate continues. *Journal of Communication, 37*(1), 186-188.

Comstock, G. (1987). Violence. In E. Barnouw (Ed.), *The international encyclopedia of communications* (pp. 460-472). New York: Oxford University Press.

Dobson, J. (1986). Personal statement. In Attorney-General's Commission on Pornography, *Final Report* (pp. 71-88). Washington, DC: U.S. Government Printing Office.

Donnerstein, E. (1980). Aggressive erotica and violence against women. *Journal of Personality and Social Psychology, 39*, 269-277.

Donnerstein, E., Linz. D., & Penrod, S. (1987). *The question of pornography: Research findings and policy implications.* New York: Free Press.

Einsiedel, E. (1988). The British, Canadian and U.S. Pornography Commissions and their use of social science research. *Journal of Communication, 38*(2), 108-121.

Fisher, W. & Barak, A. (1989). Sex education as a corrective: Immunizing against possible effects of pornography. In D. Zillmann & J. Bryant (Eds.), *Pornography: Research advances and policy considerations* (pp. 289-322). NJ: Lawrence Erlbaum.

Herson, L. (1984). *The politics of ideas: Political theory and American public policy.* Homewood, IL: Dorsey.

Intons-Peterson, M. & Roskos-Ewoldson, B. (1989). Mitigating the effects of violent pornography. In S. Gubar & J. Hoff (Eds.), *For adult users only: The dilemma of violent pornography* (pp. 218-239). Bloomington: Indiana University Press.

Levine, E. & Becker, J. (1986). Personal statement. In Attorney-General's Commission on Pornography, *Final Report* (pp. 195-212). Washington, DC: U.S. Government Printing Office.

Linz, D. (1985). *Sexual violence in the mass media: Effects on male viewers and implications for society.* Unpublished Ph.D. dissertation. Madison: University of Wisconsin.

Linz, D.& Donnerstein, E. (1988). The methods and merits of pornography research. *Journal of Communication, 38*(2), 180-192.

Linz, D. & Donnerstein, E. (1989). The effects of counter-information on the acceptance of rape myths. In D. Zillmann & J. Bryant (Eds.), *Pornography: Research advances and policy considerations* (pp. 259-288). NJ: Lawrence Erlbaum.

MacKinnon, C. (1985). Pornography, civil rights, and speech. *Harvard Civil Rights–Civil Liberties Law Review, 20*, 1-70.

Malamuth, N. (1984). Aggression against women: Cultural and individual causes. In N. Malamuth & E. Donnerstein (Eds.), *Pornography and sexual aggression* (pp. 19-52). Orlando, FL: Academic Press.

Malamuth, N. (1986). Do sexually violent media indirectly contribute to antisocial behavior? In E. Mulvey & J. Haugaard (Eds.), *Report of the Surgeon-General's workshop on pornography and public health* (pp. 86-100). Washington, D.C: U.S. Dept. of Health and Human Services, Office of the Surgeon General.

Malamuth, N. & Billings, V. (1986). The functions and effects of pornography: Sexual communication versus the feminist models in light of research findings. In J. Bryant & D. Zillmann (Eds.), *Perspectives on media effects.* Hillsdale, NJ: Lawrence Erlbaum.

McLeod, J. & Reeves, B. (1981). On the nature of mass media effects. In G.Wilhoit & H. DeBock (Eds.), *Mass communications yearbook* (pp. 250-271). Beverly Hills, CA: Sage.

National Institute of Mental Health (1982). *Television and behavior: Ten years of scientific progress and implications for the eighties.* Baltimore, MD: U.S. Dept. of Public Health.

New York Times (1986, May 17). p. A1.

Nobile, P. & Nadler, E. (1986). *United States of America vs. sex.* New York: Minotaur.

Paletz, D. (1988). Pornography, politics and the press. *Journal of Communication,* *38*(2), 122-137.

Report of the Special Committee on Pornography and Prostitution (1985). Ottawa, Canada: Minister of Supply and Services.

Ritter, Fr. Bruce (1986). Personal Statement. In Attorney-General's Commission on Pornography, *Final Report* (pp. 89-114). Washington, DC: U.S. Government Printing Office.

Steinem, G. (1980). Erotica and pornography: A clear and present difference. In L. Lederer (Ed.), *Take back the night: Women on pornography.* New York: Morrow.

Tannenbaum, P. (1970). Emotional arousal as a mediator of erotic communication effects. In *Technical Report of the Commission on Obscenity and Pornography, vol. 8* (pp. 326-356). Washington, D.C: U.S. government printing office.

United States President's Commission on Obscenity and Pornography (1970). *Report.* New York: Random House.

Weiss, C. (1977). *Using social research in public policy making.* Lexington, MA: D.C. Heath.

Weiss, C. (1982). Policy research in the context of diffuse decision-making. *Journal of Higher Education, 53*(6), 280-296.

Wilcox, B. (1987). Pornography, social science and politics: When research and ideology collide. *American Psychologist, 42,* 941-943.

Wildavsky, A. (1984). *Speaking truth to power: The art and craft of policy analysis.* Boston: Little, Brown.

Wilson, J. (1971). Violence, pornography, and social science. *The public interest, 22:* Winter, 45-61.

Zillmann, D. (1989). Pornography research and public policy. In D. Zillmann & J. Bryant, (Eds.), *Pornography: Research advances and policy considerations* (pp. 387-403). NJ: Lawrence Erlbaum.

Zillmann, D. & Bryant, J. (1984). Effects of massive exposure to pornography. In N. Malamuth & E. Donnerstein (Eds.), *Pornography and sexual aggression* (pp. 115-138). Orlando, FL: Academic Press.

The Effects of African American Women's Sexual Revictimization: Strategies for Prevention

Gail Elizabeth Wyatt
Cindy M. Notgrass
Gwen Gordon

University of California, Los Angeles

SUMMARY. This paper presents a study of African American women's sexual revictimization experiences in the context of historical and sociocultural factors. African American and White American women have been socialized differently about the history of rape in America and stereotypes about who meets the societal criteria for rape victims today. In order to better understand the cumulative impact of African American women's sexual revictimization, and to

Address correspondence to Gail Elizabeth Wyatt, Neuropsychiatric Institute, University of California, Los Angeles, 760 Westwood Plaza, Los Angeles, CA 90024.

This research was funded by National Institute of Mental Health Grant RO1 NH33603; Research Scientist Career Development Award KO1 MH00269; an award from the Southern California Injury Prevention Research Center under the auspices of the Public Health Service Centers for Disease Control Center Grant #R49/CCR903622 to Gail Elizabeth Wyatt. Portions of this article were extracted from: Wyatt, G. (1992). The sociocultural context of African American and White American women's rape, *Journal of Social Issues, 48,* 77-91 and reprinted with permission from The Society for the Psychological Study of Social Issues. The authors wish to thank Carolyn Swift for her editorial suggestions and Sarah Lowery for manuscript preparation.

[Haworth co-indexing entry note]: "The Effects of African American Women's Sexual Revictimization: Strategies for Prevention." Wyatt, Gail Elizabeth, Cindy M. Notgrass, and Gwen Gordon Co-published simultaneously in *Prevention in Human Services* (The Haworth Press, Inc.) Vol. 12, No. 2, 1995, pp. 111-134; and: *Sexual Assault and Abuse: Sociocultural Context of Prevention* (ed: Carolyn F. Swift) The Haworth Press, Inc., 1995, pp. 111-134. Single or multiple copies of this article are available from The Haworth Document Delivery Service [1-800-342-9678, 9:00 a.m.-5:00 p.m. (EST)].

111

develop strategies for prevention, this study examines different aspects of sexual revictimization in the population. A community sample of 126 African American women were interviewed about their consensual and nonconsensual sexual histories over the life-course. The results identified the influence of a variety of types of sexual abuse experiences prior to and since age 18 that were associated with aspects of their sexual behaviors and contraceptive use. Strategies for the prevention of sexual assault on a societal, community, and individual level are described. These strategies can hopefully begin to reduce the cycle of sexual revictimization among African American women. *[Article copies available from The Haworth Document Delivery Service: 1-800-342-9678.]*

In formulating an approach to the prevention of sexual revictimization of African American women, this paper has three objectives: (1) to demonstrate the necessity of integrating the history of rape in colonial America with the current knowledge base in the field of sexual assault, (2) to better understand the ethnic and cultural factors associated with disclosure and consequences of rape among African American and White women, and (3) to examine the influence of sexual revictimization on the subsequent sexual experiences and behavior of African American women.

EFFECTS OF RAPE AMONG AFRICAN AMERICAN WOMEN

In American culture, rape and sexual vulnerability have a unique history because of the sexual exploitation of slaves for over 250 years. Economic and legal factors have influenced cultural definitions of sexual assault for American women, and especially for women of African descent.

Because of the historical context of rape, African American women may be somewhat cautious about accepting changes in societal attitudes about their right to be protected from rape. This may complicate their post assault adjustment, help seeking behaviors, and attitudes about those who attempt to control their sexual behavior. Reasons for nondisclosure may differ by racial and ethnic group. In some cases women may not perceive the assault as "real rape" by societal standards; in others they may perceive themselves as unlikely rape victims, though well aware of current definitions of rape (Williams & Holmes, 1981).

Research has also not taken into consideration the historical factors related to African American women's rape and disclosure patterns. Attitudes about rape and the effects of these experiences upon women's adjustment years later may still be influenced by the sociocultural context in which the type of sexual abuse was initially defined. If African American women perceive that society does not consider that they can be raped nor would they be believed if they disclosed their assault, the chances are minimal that they will disclose or seek help from authorities that represent societal views of "real rape."

SEXUALITY AND RAPE IN COLONIAL AMERICA

As early as the 15th century, even before the African slave trade began, the sexual practices of Africans were described by Christian missionaries who dramatized the need for some control over their "sexual appetites" (Getman, 1984). These descriptions also reinforced assumptions that African sexual behavior could be brought under control if Africans were enslaved. Concomitantly, there were also a variety of economic factors that created a need for a more cost effective labor force than White servitude.

Consequently, laws were enacted to institutionalize access to this labor force and discourage racial mixing that would allow for future generations of slave descendants to be free (Getman, 1984). Sexual oppression was viewed as a means of enhancing the labor force. By 1660, there were laws that encouraged sex between Black women and White men, but sex between White women and Black men was strongly discouraged, in order to ensure that children from interracial unions would produce children who were also slaves (Getman, 1984; Wriggins, 1983). Historically, children were thought to be the property of their fathers (La Free, 1989) but during slavery, they were the property of their mothers, who, in turn belonged to slave masters.

It became apparent that there were differences in the consequences of sexual assault of White versus Black women, especially when the alleged assailant was a Black male. For example, free or enslaved Black men convicted of an incident of attempted or completed rape of a White woman were often castrated or sentenced to death (Jordan, 1968). However, regardless of fornication statutes and anti-miscegenation laws, there were no penalties for the rape of Black women by White men. The reasons are apparent in the following quote: "Abuse had only positive economic and social ramifications for the slave owners–an increase in the slave population and the further subjugation of the Black community through the sexual tyranny of White men over slaves" (Getman, 1984, p. 126).

In spite of the wealth of literature written by Black female slaves about the deleterious effects of not being considered worthy of being protected, prevalent stereotypes held that Black women, because of their sexual "nature" could be raped by a man, regardless of the perpetrator's race (Getman, 1984). Little attention was given to the sexual oppression of women of African descent, because legal sanctions were unavailable to them (Hines, 1989). Furthermore, throughout American history, the legal system has overlooked or has considered the rape of Black women less seriously than it has similar assaults on their White peers (Wriggins, 1983).

As a result of this period in American history, the sexualization of men and women of African descent has been fostered in our culture and has remained as a component of racial oppression (Williams, 1984). While stereotypes about the sexual abilities of African American men often enhance assumptions of their male prowess, stereotypes about African American women continue to stress negative expectations of their sexual promiscuity (Wyatt, 1982). This brief review is a reminder that sexual assault for African American women has been perceived and treated differently in our society. Although there is no evidence to believe that all African American women today may be aware of their ancestors' maltreatment, there is reason to believe that some African American women may not be convinced that rape is treated any differently today than it was in the past.

RAPE AS A HIDDEN CRIME: BARRIERS TO DISCLOSURE

In spite of increasingly sophisticated research on sexual assault, and improvement in the treatment of sexual abuse victims by legal and health professionals, there are a variety of reasons victims/survivors still tend not to disclose their assaults. Rape that is unacknowledged or hidden continues to be influenced by societal definitions and the circumstances under which sexual assault occurs (Koss & Burkhardt, 1989). However, nondisclosure is a multi-faceted issue: there are other reasons that contribute to the nondisclosure of rape. Less attention has been directed to the influence of racial/ethnic group membership on societal definitions of rape. Because many victims/survivors do not perceive that their experience meets the criteria for a "real rape" (Burt, 1980; Estrich, 1987), they tend not to disclose assaults, even to police, and to blame themselves for the incidents' occurrence. Although open discussions of sexual victimization have been described as important to the recovery process (Davis & Friedman, 1985; Wyatt, Newcomb, & Notgrass, 1990), victims/survivors often experience emotional and physical problems that are not only untreated but are not understood by those around them (Pennebaker & Herron, 1984; Wyatt, Newcomb, & Notgrass, 1990).

Long established patterns of nondisclosure of rape have often been reinforced by historical, societal, and legal attitudes about racial and ethnic group identity of victims/survivors. Ironically, given our history, research has not focused upon the effects of rape on Black women (Williams & Holmes, 1981), nor have studies examined women's perceptions of the likelihood of their rape incidents being considered "real" if they are members of an ethnic group at high risk for rape (Hines, 1989). Furthermore, little attention has been given to knowledge of ethnic or racial stereotypes concerning African American women's sexual practices that are thought to disqualify them as rape victims (Williams, 1979). There is evidence to suggest that minorities are more likely to agree that "a girl's reputation is ruined if she is raped" than are nonminorities (Williams, 1979). It is possible that American minority groups may perceive and experience consequences of rape and other forms of sexual abuse for their group differently than do nonminorities (Borque, 1989).

Many of these historical and societal perceptions contribute to the dearth of information about a range of African American women's consensual and nonconsensual sexual experiences (Wyatt, 1985). However, sexual abuse persists today. For some African American women, sexual abuse begins in childhood and extends throughout adolescence. The effects on women's sexual and psychological functioning are captured in this vignette:

> I sit on my couch trying to bring to memory the tragedy of my childhood . . . It was me and my Dad in [my parents'] bed . . . I hated the things I felt when he touched me. I was a very quiet and shy girl. I would not talk for hours. Most people thought there was something wrong with me. My Dad would continue his . . . fondling . . . I went to three different junior high schools. My father stopped fondling me and began penetrating [me] during this time . . . I asked him why he hurt me this way and his response was "before a boy touches [me] I had to do that". . . .

> It was my first year of college . . . this was the beginning of my sexual permissiveness . . . I became pregnant at 17, but had to abort because I did not know who the father was. My second child was born when I was 20. My other two children were fathered by the same man since my first son . . . I experienced more heartache and pain as a child and that has transferred to my adulthood.

Other African American women experience sexual victimization during childhood and again in adulthood with other perpetrators. For example, in our study of a variety of sexual experiences of African American women in Los Angeles County, one woman reported 10 incidents with different perpetrators before age 18 and six since age 18. Other women report repeated incidents of observing perpetrators exhibiting themselves as well as abuse incidents during childhood or adulthood. These are examples of sexual revictimization, about which we know very little.

Existing research does confirm that women who have experienced sexual abuse at some time in their lives are at risk for future victimization experiences (Atkeson, Calhoun, & Morris, 1989; Dvorak-Marhoefer et al., 1988; Mandoki & Burkhart, 1989; Miller, 1978; Russell, 1986; Sorenson, Siegel, Golding, & Stein, 1991; Wyatt, Guthrie, & Notgrass, 1992).

Studies that examine revictimization specifically have described women with strong dependency needs (Miller et al., 1978), an inability to prevent future attacks (Atkeson et al., 1989), and a greater number of sexual partners (Mandoki & Burkhart, 1989; Wyatt, Guthrie, & Notgrass, 1992; Wyatt, Newcomb, Riederle, Notgrass, & Lawrence, in press). However, when African American women exhibit patterns of high risk sexual activity such as frequent intercourse with multiple sex partners, unintended pregnancies or the non-use of contraceptives, their sexual permissiveness and lack of responsibility as childbearers are far too often identified as the sole contributing factors. In spite of the history of sexual abuse of women of African descent, sexually victimizing experiences are rarely examined for their influence on sexual decision making that result in frequent sexual contact or unintended pregnancies (Wyatt, 1992; Wyatt, Guthrie, & Notgrass, 1992).

Although the effects of sexual abuse in childhood and in adulthood have been well documented (see Browne & Finkelhor, 1986; Russell, 1986; Wyatt, 1985; Wyatt, Newcomb, & Notgrass, 1990 for further discussion), the effects on women who have experienced single versus multiple incidents of sexual abuse have yet to be explored. Most of these studies have examined current incidents of abuse, but have not assessed the cumulative effects of abusive experiences years later (Atkeson et al., 1989; Dvorak-Marhoefer et al., 1988; Mandoki & Burkhart, 1989; Miller et al., 1978; Russell, 1986). Similarly, few studies examine the cumulative impact of both noncontact and contact abuse experiences on later sexual and psychological outcomes (Russell, 1984; Wyatt, 1986). The paucity of research raises many questions. Do women with multiple incidents in both childhood and adulthood have more severe effects than women with multiple incidents only before age 18, or only as adults? Other studies are currently emphasizing other vulnerability factors that may have a cumulative impact on risks for psychological outcomes such as depression (Dohrenwend, 1981).

This paper presents a study of African American women's sexual revictimization experiences in the context of historical and sociocultural factors in an attempt to broaden our understanding of why rape is hidden, especially for African American women. African American and White American women have been socialized differently about the history of rape in America and stereotypes about who meets the societal criteria for rape victims today. In order to better understand the cumulative impact of African American women's sexual revictimization, and to develop strategies for prevention, this study examines different aspects of sexual revictimization for this population. Incidents of sexual abuse involving body contact among women before and after age 18, the legal age of adulthood; incidents of both less severe (noncontact) and severe types of abuse (contact) in women before and since age 18; and the total number of incidents reported are assessed. Hopefully, these dimensions of abuse will identify the influence of single versus multiple incidents and their cumulative effects on women's relationship problems, their sexual satisfaction, the type and frequency of their sexual behavior patterns, contraceptive use and their psychological well being. Unlike most other research that typically employs small samples of ethnic minorities of lower socioeconomic status, this study utilizes a community sample of African American women who ranged in educational and financial status, some of whom reported abuse over their lifetime.

METHOD

Sample Selection

Multi-stage stratified probability sampling with quotas was used to recruit comparable samples of African American and White American women 18 to 36 years of age in Los Angeles County, for a larger study of women's sexual experiences. The age criteria excluded minors, who could not participate without parental consent, but included women who had an opportunity to develop a number of adult, heterosexual relationships. The actual quotas used for the study were based upon the Los Angeles County population of African American women 18 to 36 years of age, with differing levels of education, marital status, and numbers of children. The inclusion of African American and White American women in the sample was based upon their own ethnic identification[1] (see Wyatt, 1985, for further discussion).

The participants were located by random-digit dialing of 11,834 telephone prefixes in Los Angeles County, combined with four randomly generated numbers. The specific procedures for recruiting the sample have been described elsewhere (Wyatt, 1985). Random digit telephone dialing procedures identified 1,348 households in which a woman resided. Of those who met the demographic criteria, 709 agreed to participate and 266 refused, resulting in a 27 percent refusal rate.[2] The first 248 women meeting the desired quotas were interviewed: 126 African American women and 122 White American women. The victimization experiences of African American women were selected for this study.

Table 1 describes the demographic characteristics of the abused and non-abused women in the sample. Of the 126 African American women, 85 had experienced sexual abuse at some time in their lives. The remaining 41 women served as non-abused controls.

TABLE 1. Demographic Characteristics of African American Women (N = 126)

	Number	Percent
Age range (in years)		
18-26	58	46
27-36	68	54
Education		
Less than high school	19	15
High school graduate	43	34
Some college	47	37
College graduate	10	8
Graduate education	7	6
Children		
None	38	30
1 or more	88	70
Marital status		
Ever married	73	57
Never married	53	42

Procedure

Each participant was interviewed face to face at the location of her choice by a trained female interviewer of the same ethnicity. Participants were reimbursed $20 for their time and up to $2.50 for expenses. Interviews were usually conducted in two sessions and ranged in total from three to eight hours. At the completion of the interview, referrals for mental health services were provided upon request (for fewer than five percent of the sample).

Instrumentation

In an effort to obtain more specific information regarding a range of women's sexual experiences and the effects on their intimate relationships, psychological and sexual functioning, the Wyatt Sex History Questionnaire (WSHQ), a 478-item structured interview, was used to obtain retrospective and current data regarding women's consensual and abusive sexual experiences from childhood to adulthood, and the lasting effects of these experiences. Before its use in research, it was initially pretested on two multi-ethnic groups (77 female volunteers and 16 pilot subjects). Questions were arranged chronologically from childhood to adulthood so that inconsistencies in data would be apparent. If inconsistencies were noted, immediate clarification from the participant was possible. For example, if a woman reported first intercourse at age 19 and a sexual assault at the same age, a series of questions were asked about the circumstances of each event to ensure that they were not identical.

Reliability was established for certain portions of the questionnaire. Interrater reliability, established on a weekly basis among the four interviewers, averaged .90. When 10 audio tapes were randomly selected to be examined for accuracy of interviewers' written transcriptions of participants' responses, only two responses out of 4,780 items were noted to have been in error.

Several additional analyses were conducted to examine the reliability of the data. Since data were collected retrospectively, subjects were asked about their demographic characteristics during telephone recruitment and again during the interview between one to nine months later. Pearson correlations ranged from .82 to 1.0.

Finally, 119 respondents were re-interviewed about current and past demographic characteristics one month to two years after the initial interview (Peters, 1984). Pearson correlations ranged from .65 to .98. Overall, participants' responses over time were consistent, strengthening the probability that the responses to other questions were consistent, as well. At the end of the interview that covered a range of sex-related topics, participants were asked a series of questions about whether they had experienced any of several types of sexual abuse most commonly reported over the life-span. If the participant answered "yes" to any of these questions, she was asked more detailed questions about each incident.

Definition of Child Sexual Abuse

Sexual abuse was initially defined as unwanted or coercive incidents prior to age 18 by someone of any age or relationship to the subject (Wyatt, 1985). To separate women's child sexual victimization from exploratory sexual experimentation before age 12 or consensual sexual activity with peers, two additional exclusion criteria were used. If the perpetrator was more than four years older than the subject, the incident was considered sexual abuse. If the age difference was less than five years, only contact that was not desired or involved coercion was included. Sexual abuse included incidents of non-body contact as well as those involving body contact, ranging from breast or genital fondling to attempted or completed vaginal or oral intercourse.

The specific questions used in the analyses were:

- During childhood and adolescence, did anyone ever expose themselves (their sexual organs) to you?
- During childhood and adolescence, did anyone masturbate in front of you?
- Did a relative, family friend or stranger ever touch or fondle your body, including your breasts or genitals, or attempt to arouse you sexually?
- During childhood and adolescence, did anyone try to have *you* arouse them, or touch *their* body in a sexual way?
- Did anyone rub their genitals against your body in a sexual way?
- During childhood and adolescence, did anyone attempt to have intercourse with you?
- Did you have any other sexual experiences involving a relative, family friend, or stranger?

Definition of Sexual Assault in Adulthood

Sexual assault since age 18 included observing a male exhibiting his genitals, or masturbating as well as incidents of attempted or completed involuntary penetration of the vagina or anus by the penis or another object. After this definition was read to each person, they were asked about sexual experiences that may have occurred without their consent. These experiences may have involved a friend, relative, or stranger. The specific questions of interest to this study were:

- Since age 18 did anyone ever expose themselves (their sexual organs) to you?
- Since age 18 did anyone masturbate in front of you?
- Since the age of 18, have you ever been raped?
- Since the age of 18, has anyone ever tried to rape you?

Regardless of a woman's uncertainty about whether a particular experience constituted sexual abuse, she was encouraged to describe the incident. Some women were particularly hesitant about identifying cases of attempted or completed rapes committed by persons known to them and may not have included incidents such as these in reports of sexual assault. They were, nevertheless, included in this study.

The approach used to assess the prevalence of types of sexual assault since age 18 differs from studies that use behavioral descriptions and exclude the term "rape" (Koss & Gidycz, 1985). This study also defined incidents of attempted and completed rape and asked about the circumstance of each incident. Rape related information was sought after rapport was well established, one to two hours into the structured interview. Discrepancies between the women's and research definitions of rape and terms such as "anus" (a word about which 9% were unfamiliar), "vagina," and, "other objects used for penetration" were clarified. We found it particularly useful to discuss the definition of sexual assault before and since age 18 prior to women's descriptions of their experiences. After the completion of the interview, it was not uncommon for women to recontact the interviewer and report additional incidents that they had not previously considered as sexual abuse.

Definition of Sexual Revictimization

Revictimization was defined as women's reports of at least one incident of sexual abuse in childhood before age 18 that occurred again in adulthood since age 18 or incidents of one versus more than one incident of sexual victimization.

Outcome Variables

The outcome variables included the following behaviors: masturbation, cunnilingus, fellatio, vaginal intercourse, anal intercourse, group sex, and exchanging primary partners (partner swapping). Numbers of sexual partners and the length of relationships since age 18, use of barrier methods of birth control, number of unintended pregnancies and abortions during the lifecourse were also included. These variables were reduced by factor analyses, principal component solution with orthogonal rotations, using .25 or above as the absolute factor loading (SAS, 1982). Four factors were extracted accounting for 36% of the common variance. Factor 1 included the frequency of sexual behaviors including masturbation, cunnilingus, fellatio, vaginal intercourse, anal intercourse, group sex, and exchanging primary partners (partner swapping). Factor 2 included effective use of barrier methods of birth control. Factor 3 included numbers of sexual partners and length of relationship. Factor 4 included unintended pregnancies and abortions. Total scores from the Rosenberg Self-Esteem Scale, the General Well-Being Scale, and the Mosher Sex Guilt Scale were used to assess psychological variables. A measure of sexual satisfaction was derived from 25 WSHQ items involving the respondent's initiation of sexual contact, positive and negative feelings about sex, and their overall sexual satisfaction with the primary partner. The items were entered into a principal component solution with orthogonal rotation using .25 as absolute factor loadings and yielded two factors. They were: Factor 1, involving dissatisfaction with vaginal intercourse and negative feelings about the primary partner and Factor 2, sexual dysfunctions with the primary partner.

A series of analyses of variance was used with three methods of assessing women's revictimization experiences: (1) incidents of abuse involving contact and noncontact experiences were compared to assess the cumulative influence of a range of incidents on later effects; (2) incidents involving contact sexual abuse in childhood and rape experiences in adulthood were compared to determine if the point at which abuse occurred was significantly associated with later effects; and (3) single versus multiple (two or more) experiences of contact and noncontact abuse were examined to determine if repeated abuse contributed to a greater severity of later effects. Factor loadings from factor analyses or total scores were used as outcome variables in the analyses.

RESULTS

As previously reported, overall, 57% of African American women reported at least one incident of child sexual abuse prior to age 18. Specifically, 43% reported no abuse, 17% experienced only noncontact abuse, and 40% experienced contact abuse (Wyatt, 1985).

Two thirds (64%) of African American women reported no incidents of sexual abuse since age 18, 11% reported noncontact abuse and 25% reported an incident of attempted or completed rape (Wyatt, Newcomb, & Notgrass, 1990). Overall, 36% reported at least one incident of sexual abuse since age 18.

The frequency of sexual behaviors women engage in is described in Table 2.

Frequency of Sexual Behaviors

There are two findings of note regarding the frequency of sexual behaviors. First, women who reported incidents of contact and noncontact sexual abuse in childhood or in adulthood significantly differed from women who were abused in childhood and adulthood [$F(3, 122) = 4.37, p < .006$]. Specifically, women who reported abuse before or after age 18 were significantly more likely to engage in masturbation, vaginal intercourse, oral sex, anal sex, group sex, and partner swapping with more frequency than women who experienced sexual victimization beginning in childhood and recurring years later [$F(1, 125) = 4.31, p < .04$] and [$F(1, 125) = 4.12, p < .05$], respectively. When least square means were considered using the Bonferroni Test (Miller, 1966), women abused only in childhood and those abused in childhood and adulthood were also more likely to engage in these sexual behaviors more frequently than women who did not report abuse.

Likewise, women with incidents of attempted or completed rape after age 18 reported different patterns of sexual behavior than women without these experiences [$F(3, 92) = 3.73, p < .02$]. Women who reported sexual assault since age 18 were more likely to report higher frequencies of sexual behaviors, as defined above [$F(1, 92) = 3.91, p = .05$].

Frequency of Unintended Pregnancies and Abortions

African American women with histories of abuse were also likely to report greater numbers of unintended and aborted pregnancies.

Contact and noncontact sexual abuse. Women who reported incidents of contact and noncontact sexual abuse, before *or* since age 18 significantly differed from women who experienced abuse before *and* since age 18 [$F(3, 122) = 4.11, p < .009$]. Women who reported abuse before or since age 18 were significantly more likely to have unintended and aborted pregnancies [$F(1, 125) = 4.24, p < .05$] and [$F(1, 125) = 7.20, p < .009$], respectively. When least square means were considered using the Bonfer-

TABLE 2. Sexual Behaviors of African American Women[1]

Behavior	Number	Percent
Masturbation–Per Month		
Never	67	53
One time	16	13
Two times	8	6
Three times	35	28
Cunnilingus–Per Month		
Never	46	37
One to four times	42	34
Five to eight times	17	14
Nine to 12 times	14	11
14 to 60 times	6	5
Fellatio–Per Month		
Never	57	46
One to four times	31	25
Five to eight times	16	13
Nine to 12 times	8	6
14 or more times	13	10
Vaginal Intercourse–Per Week		
None	15	12
Once	17	14
Two or more times	94	75
Anal Sex–Ever		
Never	100	80
One time	19	15
One to ten times	6	5
Group Sex–Ever		
Never	115	92
One or more times	6	5

Percentages may not total 100 due to rounding.

[1]Some behavior groups may not equal N = 126 due to missing data.

roni Test (Miller, 1966), women who were victimized before and since age 18 were more likely to have unintended and aborted pregnancies than women who were sexually abused only in one period of their lives, or women who did not report abuse.

Contact sexual abuse. Turning to more invasive incidents of abuse, women who reported incidents of contact sexual abuse only in childhood significantly differed from women who reported contact sexual abuse only in adulthood or were abused in childhood and adulthood [$F(3, 89) = 5.26, p < .003$]. Specifically, women who were abused only in childhood were significantly more likely to have unintended and aborted pregnancies than women who were abused in childhood and in adulthood [$F(1, 92) = 7.70, p < .007$]. When least square means were considered using the Bonferroni Test (Miller, 1966), women who were abused only in adulthood and women who were abused in childhood and adulthood were also significantly more likely to have unintended and aborted pregnancies than women who did not report abuse.

Dimensions of Sexual Satisfaction

Multiple incidents of abuse were associated with African American women reporting dysfunctional partners later in life. Women with multiple incidents in childhood differed from women with multiple incidents in adulthood or those who were abused in childhood and adulthood or women who reported no abuse histories [$F(8, 117) = 2.38, p < .03$]. Specifically, women with multiple incidents of contact and noncontact abuse in childhood were significantly more likely to report having sexually dysfunctional male partners later in life than women who were abused only in adulthood or those who were abused in childhood and adulthood [$F(2, 125) = 5.01, p < .009$]. When least square means were considered using the Scheffe Test (Miller, 1966), women with two or more incidents of abuse in childhood reported significantly more dysfunctions in their partners than women with one or no incidents.

Women with Multiple Sex Partners and Brief Relationships

Three patterns of abuse were associated with multiple partners and brief relationships as the outcomes. Regardless of the type of abuse (contact or noncontact), women who reported incidents of sexual abuse since age 18 significantly differed from women who reported abuse only in childhood and women reporting child and adult abuse [$F(3, 122) = 5.94, p < .0009$]. Women with abuse since age 18 were significantly more likely to have greater numbers of sexual partners and brief sexual relationships with men $[F(1, 125) = 13.17, p < .0005]$. When least square means were considered using the Bonferroni Test (Miller, 1966), women abused since age 18 were significantly more likely to have greater numbers of partners and brief sexual relationships with men than women who reported no sexual abuse. Similarly, women who were abused in childhood and adulthood were more likely to have significantly more partners and brief sexual relationships with men than women with no reported abuse histories.

Women who were abused since age 18 and reported incidents of contact sexual abuse in adulthood also differed from women who reported contact sexual abuse only in childhood or contact sexual abuse in childhood and adulthood $[F(3, 89) = 8.61, p < .0002]$. Specifically, they were more likely to have multiple sexual partners and brief sexual relationships than women who were abused only in childhood or who were abused in childhood and adulthood $[F(1, 92) = 18.98, p < .0002]$. When least square means were considered using the Bonferroni Test (Miller, 1966), women who were sexually abused since age 18 or those who were abused in childhood and adulthood were significantly more likely to have multiple sexual partners and brief sexual relationships than women who were abused only in childhood or those who did not report abuse.

In terms of repeated incidents, women reporting two or more experiences of contact and noncontact abuse in childhood differed from women with other abuse patterns only in adulthood or those who were abused in childhood and adulthood $[F(8,117) = 4.35, p < .0002]$. Specifically, women with two or more abuse incidents either before age 18 or after age 18 were significantly more likely to have a greater number of multiple sexual partners and brief sexual relationships than women who were abused in childhood and adulthood $[F(2, 125) = 7.06, p < .002]$ and $[F(2, 125) = 4.88, p < .01]$, respectively. When least square means were considered using the Scheffe Test (Miller, 1966), women with two incidents of abuse were significantly more likely to have greater numbers of multiple male sexual partners and brief sexual relationships compared to women with one or no incidents.

DISCUSSION

In an effort to better understand the dimensions of sexual revictimization and its effects, this paper places sexual revictimization within the context of historical and societal perceptions of African American women's sexuality. This historical perspective serves to illustrate that knowledge of the possibility of sexual victimization has existed for African descended women long before research documented the prevalence of these experiences in America. While we have no empirical documentation about how perceptions of being a likely victim of assault can influence the effects of actual incidents, there is evidence that perceived susceptibility of health risks do influence health beliefs (Lau & Ware, 1981).

This perspective is important to consider when examining the effects of sexual revictimization. If a woman does not perceive herself as a believable victim of sexual abuse, due to historical and societal criteria that question whether her experiences are "real," she may be less motivated to disclose such incidents. Research has documented that African American women are less likely than their White peers both before and since age 18 to disclose abuse incidents to police (Wyatt, 1991; Wyatt, 1992). Furthermore, nondisclosure of abuse was found to be a predictor of negative lasting effects of sexual victimization (Wyatt & Mickey, 1988). Thus, the cumulative impact of these undisclosed incidents may increase African American women's risk of sexual revictimization.

The findings suggest that the cumulative impact of incidents ranging from least (noncontact abuse) to more severe (fondling to oral sex) in childhood or adulthood were significantly associated with an increased frequency of a variety of sexual practices, many of which are at risk for the transmission of disease. Furthermore, the cumulative impact of incidents in childhood or adulthood was also associated with unintended and aborted pregnancies. These behaviors are characteristic of individuals who appear to exhibit compulsive sexual patterns and who may not anticipate sexual encounters by using contraceptives that prevent disease transmission or unintended pregnancy. Consequently, they may choose to terminate pregnancies because as one Black woman explained:

> I don't think about when I will have sex, so I don't use contraceptives. I did not intend to become pregnant, I would never want to have a child with [him] and I didn't want to bring a child in this world under those circumstances. However, whenever he asked me, I would have sex.

The rationale for unprotected sexual activity appears to be associated with difficulties in acknowledging one's own sexual needs, and being intimidated by the perceived power and sexual desires of a male sexual partner. This finding is consistent with other studies describing the dependency needs of survivors (Miller et al., 1978), the dynamics of their accommodation to the perpetrators' wishes (Summit, 1983) and their feelings of being powerless to express their own desires (Finkelhor & Browne, 1985). There is another dimension that contributes to decision making around sex. In this study, African American women also reported that they received little sex education at home and that sex was rarely discussed (Wyatt, 1990). If women are socialized not to discuss sex, it is difficult for them to learn about what and with whom these discussions should take place, how to make decisions about contraceptive use or the selection of sexual partners prior to adulthood. Consequently, even without a sexual abuse history, these women may not have been adequately prepared for sexual decision making.

Abuse occurring during only one of the two periods studied, such as adulthood, was associated with compulsive sexual practices. Abuse occurring during childhood was also associated with increased patterns of unintended and aborted pregnancies. Thus, it does not appear to be the number of repeated incidents alone that contributes to high risk patterns. Sexual abuse during one developmental period such as prior to or since age 18 may also contribute to similar outcomes, as well as more than one type of abuse during these periods. Two out of three dimensions of revictimization were associated with multiple partners and brief relationships: The cumulative impact of a range of less severe and severe incidents since age 18; and women reporting more than one incident of abuse since age 18. Similarly, women reporting attempted or completed incidents of rape were also likely to have multiple partners and brief relationships. These findings highlight the impact of repeated abuse incidents, even those that were less severe, that may complicate the process of women learning adequate coping strategies to prevent these abuse incidents from occurring (Koss & Burkhart, 1989). However, the cycle of multiple partners can increase women's risks for being in relationships where both physical and sexual coercion may occur.

Descriptions of sexual dysfunction were associated with abuse prior to age 18. Child sexual victimization appears to have a significant impact on African American women's early perceptions of self and their feelings about themselves as sexual beings. These misperceptions appear to develop early in life and may influence the selection of sexual partners years later. Women in primary relationships reported their partners as having erectile problems. It is difficult, however, to attribute sexual problems solely to one partner. Other research has suggested that incest survivors tend not to initiate sex and consequently, their partners may suffer from lack of sexual arousal (Maltz, 1988). It is possible that women in these relationships may also perceive sexual problems as being their partner's fault and may not become aware of how their attitudes and behaviors influence their partner's sexual difficulties. More research including African American women is needed to explore their sexual functioning within the relationship context.

There is a clear need for clinicians and researchers to define and clarify the nature of abuse and repeated incidents ranging from noncontact to contact abuse throughout the lifecourse, in order to understand the effects of these experiences on women's sexual functioning. It should be noted that none of the psychological outcome variables were significantly associated with women's abuse histories. In a community sample where the average time spanning the age of most recent abuse was 15 1/2 years for child abuse and 5 1/2 years for incidents occurring since age 18, women's more severe psychological difficulties may have been resolved, to some extent. Other methods of examining psychological outcomes as moderators of sexual abuse are forthcoming (Wyatt, Newcomb, Riederle, & Notgrass, in press). Nevertheless, the findings regarding sexual outcomes help to better understand the cumulative nature of sexual revictimization.

Strategies for Prevention and Intervention

There are two approaches that can be taken to both prevent the sexual victimization of African American women and intervene in the cycle of revictimization to prevent multiple occurrences of incidents. Efforts at prevention should begin on a societal level.

Stereotypes of African American women are still being conveyed through the media (Wyatt, 1982). The American public and the African American community, as well, need to become more aware of the impact of damaging stereotypes of African American women as sexually permissive. The stereotypes tend to convey the message that African American women are available targets for any type of sexual activity and that young girls are sexually active at early ages.

The process of re-education regarding African American women's sexuality should not end with the general public. Professionals in health related fields also tend to have very little information about African American family life and socialization or the impact of poverty on sexual behavior. Consequently, they often tend to overlook factors that contribute to high risk sexual patterns, contraceptive use or family planning. Too much emphasis is placed on the reasons for behaviors or patterns themselves being influenced by African American cultural values rather than a full understanding of the influences of poverty or other family related problems. For example, if an African American adolescent female comes to a health facility to confirm a pregnancy, there is no certainty that the professionals involved would obtain a sexual and socialization history to identify the nature of coercive sexual contact both within and outside of her family.

Consequently, risk factors that have been identified for early sexual activity (Wyatt, 1988) may not be discussed with the adolescent or her parents which may not only increase the likelihood of revictimization, but also of future difficulties in sexual decision making.

Rape crisis treatment centers, clinics and hospitals need to develop intervention strategies especially for African American women regarding rape, why it occurs and its effects. This information needs to be ethnic group specific because of the preponderance of African American women living in high crime areas. They face a variety of different realities that are seldom included in the treatment of rape. As stated earlier, previous studies indicated that African American women are more likely not to report rape to police or other agencies (Wyatt, 1992). Consequently, the disclosure of sexual assault may not go beyond family members. Many times, a more in-depth understanding of the effects of sexual abuse and revictimization are needed to aid the survivor in the healing process. Family members and other supportive persons can be included in therapy to help survivors feel that their dependence upon familiar rather than legal authorities is understandable. The option to press charges and to testify in court should always be discussed. If survivors choose not to follow this course, however, then alternative family support becomes even more critical (Wyatt, Newcomb, & Notgrass, 1990).

Similarly, we should use the information available about sexual abuse and the cycle of revictimization to educate the African American community. This information could include strategies to improve neighborhood and individual safety. Neighborhood safety tips could range from awareness of high risk areas of neighborhoods and methods to ensure safety (i.e., use the buddy system–never walk outside at night alone) to encouraging police to meet with community groups or churches and to discuss how to lower the crime and rape rates in areas at risk or how rape victims are treated if they report an assault.

African American family members need to learn how to identify those families who are at risk for problems, including sexual abuse, and to understand that denial of abuse simply creates an environment where victimization can continue. Some families are reluctant to acknowledge sex related problems because of concern that they will be perceived as having no morals about sex or not acknowledging the incest taboo. Their nondisclosure may partly be an effort to downplay stereotypes of black sexuality and assumptions that black families socialize their children to be sexually permissive. Efforts to change societal and community perceptions of African American women as targets of sexual victimization will require a long range commitment from those who are concerned about prevention. The same sources that support women's issues and rights could be directed toward African American women. Educational programs in schools and churches are good strategies that can be easily implemented at the community level. These programs could receive funding through federal and private agencies, and women's groups, as well as African American civic and religious organizations. The need to prevent the sexual abuse of African American women will have to assume some priority, however, in order to achieve long range goals of educating the general public.

Likewise, individual behavior change is necessary. African American women need to be re-educated about the effects of sexual abuse and the likelihood of revictimization. They should become aware of high risk behaviors such as having multiple partners, and the long term health consequences. The resistance to using effective contraceptives may place them at risk for sexually transmitted diseases, and limit their abilities to plan family size. There is still too little educational information about the choices that African American women need to make as responsible sexual beings. However, suggestions about behavior change should always be made within the context of their relationships as well as the social and economic environment in which they live.

These strategies are a beginning attempt to target a group of women who are not always perceived by societal norms as likely victims of rape and other coercive sexual experiences (Wyatt, 1992). However, if each African American woman can be encouraged to obtain sexual knowledge and to understand the factors that can negatively impact sexual choices, we may begin to lessen the chances of sexual victimization and its reoccurrence for African American women. If our communities and society can acknowledge and reaffirm their right to make choices as sexual beings, the likelihood of their seeking help to enhance sexual decision making will be greatly increased.

NOTES

1. The term "African American" refers to women of African descent whose parentage also includes a variety of other ethnic and racial groups found in America. Caucasian women additionally included women of Jewish heritage. These women spent at least 6 of the first 12 years of their childhood in the United States.

2. The 27% refusal rate excludes 335 women who terminated telephone contact before information regarding their demographic characteristics could be obtained. The estimated rate of refusal, including those who terminated phone contact before their eligibility could be assessed, as well as those who did not answer when called but who might have been eligible, was 33%. However, if the 335 women who terminated contact were considered, the refusal rate would increase to 45%.

REFERENCES

Atkeson, B.M., Calhoun, K. S., & Morris, K.T. (1989). Victim resistance to rape: The relationship of previous victimization, demographics, and situational factors. *Archives of Sexual Behavior, 18*, 497-507.

Borque, L.B. (1989). *Defining rape.* Durham, NC: Duke University Press.

Browne, A., & Finkelhor, D. (1986). Impact of child sexual abuse: A review of the research. *Psychological Bulletin, 99*, 66-77.

Burt, M.R. (1980). Cultural myths and supports of rape. *Journal of Personality and Social Psychology, 38*, 217-230.

Dohrenwend, B.X., & Dohrenwend, B.P. (1981). Life stress and illness: Formulation of the issues. In B.S. Dohrenwend & B.P. Dohrenwend (Eds.), *Stressful life events and their contexts.* New York: Watson.

Davis, R.C., & Friedman, L.N. (1985). The emotional aftermath of crime and violence. In C.R. Figley (Ed.), *Trauma and its wake: The study and treatment of post-traumatic stress disorder* (pp. 90-111). New York: Brunner/Mazel.

Dvorak-Marhoefer, S., Resick, P., Hutter, C.K., & Girelli, S.A. (1988). Single-versus multiple-incident rape victims. *Journal of Interpersonal Violence, 3,* 145-160.

Estrich, S. (1987). *Real rape.* Cambridge, MA: Harvard University Press.

Finkelhor, D., & Browne, A. (1985). The traumatic impact of child sexual abuse: A conceptualization. *American Journal of Orthopsychiatry, 55,* 4, 530-541.

Getman, K. (1984). Sexual control in the slaveholding South: The implementation and maintenance of a racial caste system. *Harvard Women's Law Review, 7,* 115-153.

Hines, D.C. (1989). Rape and the inner lives of Black women in the middle west. *Signs: Journal of Women in Society, 14,* 912-920.

Jordan, W. (1968). *White over Black: American attitudes toward the Negro* (pp. 1550-1812). Williamsburg, VA: University of North Carolina Press.

Koss, M. & Burkhart, B. (1989). A conceptual analyses of rape victimization. *Psychology of Women Quarterly, 13,* 27-40.

Koss, M.P., & Gidycz, C.A. (1985). Sexual experiences survey: Reliability and validity. *Journal of Consulting and Clinical Psychology, 42,* 162-170.

La Free, G. (1989). *Rape and criminal justice: The social construction of sexual assault.* Balmont, CA: Wadsworth Publishing Co.

Lau, R.R., & Ware, J.F. (1981). Refinements in the measurement of health specific locus-of-control beliefs. *Medical Care, 19,* 1147-1158.

Maltz, W. (1988). Identifying and treating the sexual repercussions of incest: A couples therapy approach. *Journal of Sex and Marital Therapy, 14,* 142-170.

Mandoki, C.A., & Burkhart, B.R. (1989). Sexual victimization: Is there a vicious cycle? *Violence and Victims, 4,* 179-190.

Miller, R.G., Jr. (1966). *Simultaneous Statistical Influence.* New York: McGraw-Hill.

Miller, J., Moeller, D., Kaufman, A., Divasto, P., Pathak, D., & Christy, J. (1978). Recidivism among sex assault victims. *American Journal of Psychiatry, 135,* 1103-1104.

Pennebaker, J.W., & O'Herron, R.C. (1984). Confiding in others and illness rate among spouses of suicide and accidental death victims. *Journal of Abnormal Psychology, 93,* 473-476.

Peters, S.D. (1984). *The relationship between childhood sexual victimization and adult depression among Afro American and white women.* Unpublished doctoral dissertation, University of California, Los Angeles.

Russell, D.E. (1984). *Sexual exploration: Rape, child sexual abuse and workplace harassment.* Newbury Park, CA: Sage Publication.

Russell, D. (1986). Incestuous abuse and revictimization. *Journal of Interpersonal Violence,* SAS, International (1982). *SAS User's Guide: Statistics.* Cary, NC.

Sorenson, S.B., Siegel, J.M., Golding, J.M., & Stein, J.A. (1991). Repeated sexual victimization. *Violence and Victims, 6,* 299-309.

Summit, R.C. (1983). The child sexual abuse accommodation syndrome. *Child Abuse and Neglect, 7,* 1977-1993.

Williams, J.E. (Winter 1979). Sex role stereotypes, women's liberation and rape: A cross-cultural analysis of attitudes. *Sociological Symposium,* No. 25, 61-97.

Williams, J.E. (1984). Secondary victimization: Confronting public attitudes about rape. *Victimology: An International Journal, 9,* 66-81.

Williams, J.E., & Holmes, K.A. (1981). *The second assault: Rape and public attitudes.* Westport, CT: Greenwood Press.

Wriggins, J. (1983). Rape, racism, and the law. *Harvard Women's Law Journal, 6,* 103-141.

Wyatt, G.E. (1982). Identifying stereotypes of Afro-American sexuality and their impact on sexual behavior. In D. Bass, G. Wyatt, & G. Powell (Eds.), *The Afro-American Family: Assessment, Treatment and Research Issues* (p. 333-346). New York: Grune Stratton.

Wyatt, G.E. (1985). The sexual abuse of Afro-American and White-American women in childhood. *Child Abuse and Neglect, 9,* 507-519.

Wyatt, G.E. (1986). The relationship between the cumulative impact of a range of child sexual abuse experiences and women's psychological well-being. *Victimology: An International Journal, 11*(4).

Wyatt, G.E. (1988). The relationship between child sexual abuse and adolescent sexual functioning in Afro-American and White American women. *Human Sexual Aggression: Current Perspectives, 528,* 111-122.

Wyatt, G.E., & Mickey, R. (1988). The support of parents and others as it mediates the effects of child sexual abuse: An Exploratory study. In G.E. Wyatt & G.J. Powell (Eds.), *The Lasting Effects of Child Sexual Abuse.* Newbury Park, CA: Sage Publications.

Wyatt, G.E. (1990). The aftermath of child sexual abuse: The victim's experience. *Journal of Family Violence, 5,* 61-80.

Wyatt, G.E., & Newcomb, M. (1990). Internal and external mediators of women's sexual abuse in childhood. *Journal of Consulting and Clinical Psychology, 58*(6), 758-767.

Wyatt, G.E., Newcomb, M., & Notgrass, C.M. (1990). Internal and external mediators of women's rape experiences. *Psychology of Women Quarterly, 14*, 153-176.

Wyatt, G.E. (1991). Child sexual abuse and its effects on sexual functioning. *Annual Review of Sex Research, 1*, 249-266.

Wyatt, G.E. (1992). The sociocultural context of African American and White American women's rape. *Journal of Social Issues, 48*(1), 77-91.

Wyatt, G.E., Guthrie, D., & Notgrass, C.M. (1992). Differential effects of women's child sexual abuse and subsequent sexual revictimization. *Journal of Consulting and Clinical Psychology, 60*(2), 167-173.

Wyatt, G.E., Newcomb, M., Riederle, M., & Notgrass, C.M. (In press). *The Effects of Child Sexual Abuse on Women's Sexual and Psychological Functioning*. Newbury Park: Sage Publications.

Intrafamilial Child Sexual Abuse in the Hispanic Community: A Prevention Approach

Rosina M. Becerra
Alfreda P. Iglehart

University of California, Los Angeles

SUMMARY. This paper outlines prevention strategies using marketing techniques in the area of intrafamilial child sexual abuse for the Hispanic community. Data from a study of child sexual abuse in the Hispanic community are presented. These data point out a few of the sociocultural similarities and differences between Hispanic and non-Hispanic cases. The paper suggests the use of broadcast media, Spanish language formats, targeting audiences, and the use of spokespersons as factors in prevention program development. [Article copies available from The Haworth Document Delivery Service: 1-800-342-9678.]

Virtually all cultures consider incestuous sexual relationships with children a taboo. Traditionally the forbidden nature of the behavior has restrained acknowledgement of the prevalence of the act. This has impeded the development of prevention and intervention methods for addressing child sexual abuse, particularly intrafamilial child sexual abuse.[1]

Today's freer social climate has allowed more open communication about sexuality and has increased public and professional awareness about

---

Address correspondence to Rosina Becerra, School of Social Welfare, University of California, Los Angeles, CA 90024.

[Haworth co-indexing entry note]: "Intrafamilial Child Sexual Abuse in the Hispanic Community: A Prevention Approach." Becerra, Rosina M., and Alfreda P. Iglehart. Co-published simultaneously in *Prevention in Human Services* (The Haworth Press, Inc.) Vol. 12, No. 2, 1995, pp. 135-146; and: *Sexual Assault and Abuse: Sociocultural Context of Prevention* (ed: Carolyn F. Swift) The Haworth Press, Inc., 1995, pp. 135-146. Single or multiple copies of this article are available from The Haworth Document Delivery Service [1-800-342-9678, 9:00 a.m.-5:00 p.m. (EST)].

135

this group of vulnerable children. Because of this rising public awareness more attention has turned to uncovering sexual abuse of children. Suski (1986), examining aggregate data provided by child protective service agencies nationwide to the National Center on Child Abuse and Neglect, reported that between 1976 and 1984 sexual maltreatment reports increased from six to 13 percent. Reports to the State of California Department of Social Services during a similar period (1977-1981) showed that reported cases of sexual abuse increased 228 percent (Office of the California State Attorney General, 1985, p. ES-1). These data show that the more open climate has created changes in state and local policy which have increased the emphasis on the reporting and investigating of child sexual abuse (Suski, 1986).

In response there has been a proliferation of sexual abuse prevention programs. The majority of primary prevention efforts in child sexual abuse have been undertaken in the schools. These efforts focus on teaching children to distinguish between appropriate and inappropriate touches, helping children make self-protective decisions, enabling them to refuse to do something that feels uncomfortable, and knowing where to go for help (Stilwell, Lutzker, & Greene, 1988; Vernon & Hay, 1988). While these programs have focused on the potential victim, they have given little attention to the potential adult perpetrator. Moreover, very little is known about their effectiveness (Conte, Rosen, & Saperstein, 1986; Miller-Perrin & Wurtele, 1988; Reppucci & Haugaard, 1989; Wurtele, 1987).

While child sexual abuse prevention programs have proliferated there remains a dearth of information about the causes and correlates of sexual abuse. Even with a wider recognition of the occurrence of child sexual abuse, little empirical research has been conducted to broaden the knowledge base of this problem. Because so little is known about the predictors or causes of child sexual abuse, particularly incest or intrafamilial child sexual abuse, the problem is little understood and thus difficult to prevent. Some factors discussed as possible links to intrafamilial child sexual abuse include male domination, social isolation, overcrowded conditions, external stress, divorce and remarriage, erosion of sexual prohibitions, sexual estrangement between the adult couple, and a search for nurturance through sexual means (Finkelhor, 1981, 1982, 1984; Meiselman, 1978; Mrazek & Kempe, 1981). How these factors give rise to the behavior is not clearly established. Research as yet does not explain why some families who experience the cited factors are incestuous while others are not.

The knowledge base about the psychological impact of sexual abuse and types of effective interventions for victims and families has increased during the past decade. Gaps exist, however, with respect to knowledge about prevention and intervention programming for various cultural and ethnic groups. To date, for example, there is little published information on the characteristics of Hispanic families who have been faced with or face the problem of intrafamilial child sexual abuse. No literature exists about the use of specific child sexual abuse prevention approaches with Hispanic populations.

In this paper, data gathered on Hispanic families in treatment with clinicians who are experienced in working with intrafamilial sexual abuse are presented. These data suggest some approaches for consideration when planning prevention and intervention programs for Hispanic populations.

A STUDY OF HISPANIC CASES

Fifty-nine social work clinicians in Los Angeles participated in the study (Becerra, 1983). At the time of this study they represented the majority of the approximately 80 clinicians from various settings with experience in treating intrafamilial sexual abuse cases among Hispanics. Sixty-five clinicians working in public social services (Department of Public Social Services, Department of Mental Health), three nonprofit agencies serving primarily the Hispanic population, and practitioners in private practice were identified and asked to participate. Everyone agreed to participate, however, only 59 completed client questionnaires. The final distribution of clinician settings were: Department of Mental Health (34%), Department of Public Social Services (30%), private practice (24%), and private social services (12%). Of these clinicians 31% were of Hispanic origin and 52% spoke Spanish.

Each clinician was asked to submit information on one to three of his or her cases of intrafamilial child sexual abuse. One of the submitted cases had to be Hispanic. Because of the difficulty in obtaining information on these cases and the procedures that needed to be followed to ensure confidentiality of the victims and families, the number of active cases of intrafamilial child sexual abuse in the Los Angeles area could not be determined. However, by asking the clinicians how many Hispanic cases they had, it was determined that these clinicians represented about 457 active Hispanic cases of child sexual abuse. No information was available on the distribution of cases for the other ethnic groups. No conclusions can be drawn from this study with respect to the incidence or prevalence of child sexual abuse in the Hispanic community because of numerous uncontrolled factors, including the availability of resources within the community for Hispanic families with this problem, the willingness of victims or family members to seek help through official or professional sources, and the unknown number of Hispanic cases handled by clinicians not included in the study–especially since the 80 or so clinicians in the pool did not represent all clinicians carrying these cases but rather those who were identified as having particular experience working with Hispanic families.

The research (Becerra, 1983) was based on a total of 119 families: 71 Hispanic and 48 white non-Hispanic cases of daughter-father/father figure sexual abuse. The father figures in the 119 cases were stepfathers (21%) and mothers' boyfriends (9%) who cohabited or spent a significant amount of time in the household.

The two ethnic samples differed in several demographic features–family income, family size and composition, and the presence of a father in the home. Although the majority of families from both ethnic groups were low-income, Hispanic victims tended to come from poorer and somewhat larger families. The average annual income for Hispanic families was $12,500 compared to $15,000 for white non-Hispanic families. In the Hispanic families it was more likely that older siblings, grandparents and other relatives lived in the home. The victims were female in all cases because clinicians were asked to submit, in their judgement, their most typical cases. The Hispanic victim was more likely to live with her natural father (58%) than the white non-Hispanic victim (35%).

There was a higher probability of multiple molestations in the non-Hispanic families (43% versus 24%), that is, more than one child in the family was likely to be victimized. Whether larger families guard against multiple molestations is unknown, but household size in this study suggests that some slight differences in the home infrastructures between these two groups of victims may be preventive in nature.

In general, compared with non-Hispanic mothers, Hispanic mothers had fewer years of schooling, were less likely to speak English or work outside the home, were more likely to have larger families, to be in less-skilled jobs, and to be more reliant, both financially and emotionally, on the male partner.

Among the perpetrators, Hispanics had a mean of 9.6 years of schooling while the non-Hispanics were more likely to be high school graduates. About one-half of the Hispanic perpetrators were born outside the United States–mostly in Mexico. One-third of the Hispanic perpetrators spoke only Spanish. Both the Hispanic and non-Hispanic perpetrators worked mostly in blue collar jobs, such as operatives in factories, laborers or as skilled craftsmen. Although most of the men in both samples were employed, about one-third were either unemployed or not employed full-time. In general, they were in the 30-40 year age range and had no previous psychiatric or criminal histories. While a higher proportion of non-Hispanic perpetrators in the study reported a previous history of sexual abuse with their own children, other children, and/or other sex-related crimes as well (35% versus 14%), it may be that non-Hispanic men with these types of histories may be more likely to be in treatment with these clinicians than Hispanic men.

Another difference found between Hispanic and non-Hispanic families is the sexual abuse reporting pattern. Hispanic child victims were twice as likely as the non-Hispanic victims to be the source of the report (17% versus 9%). One explanation is that many of the Hispanic mothers who did not speak English may have used their child as the means for reporting. Hispanic mothers appear to be more likely to report through channels such as hospitals and clinics, and through the use of their own children as interpreters. The intrafamilial sexual abuse of non-Hispanic children was reported more often by school authorities, relatives, friends and neighbors, possibly because non-Hispanic children are more likely than Hispanic children to talk to these sources.

Once reported, the intrafamilial child sexual abuse tended not to recur, according to clinicians' reports. Unfortunately the fact that clinicians do not get any further complaints may not mean there is no further sexual abuse. In many cases either the perpetrator or the child was removed from the home so that opportunity was decreased. In other cases, other family members may have been more watchful of the victim or the victim might have feared reprisals if she reported continuing incidents. It was the exception rather than the rule, however, that the intrafamilial sexual abuse had occurred only once or twice. In both samples the abuse had been ongoing for an average of four years at the time it was reported. The mean age for onset of the sexual abuse among these victims was nine years old. The age range of the victims extended from eight months to 17 years, showing that no age group is free from risk. The high risk ages were 7-12 for both samples in the study. Thus, the duration of the sexual abuse and the maintenance of "the secret" could only become more detrimental to the child over time because of the emotional costs to the child.

The lack of marketable skills and education interacted to produce a tenuous economic environment for these families. While Hispanic fathers in the study were more likely to be employed (71.8% versus 64.6%), they were more likely to be underemployed or employed in low paying jobs than white non-Hispanic fathers and to have larger families dependent on their wages. Discrimination and prejudice based on ethnicity and limited facility with the English language added to this environmental stressor. Hispanic fathers, then, were more likely to have experienced discrimination and to be in the lower socioeconomic strata of society.

The stress caused by discrimination, economic deficiency, and lack of opportunity is likely to produce a wide variety of symptoms and reactions among individuals (Catalano & Dooley, 1980; Snowden, 1982), even those not thought to be "at risk" by other criteria. Clinicians in this study noted that substance abuse was often associated with these stress factors and helped mask feelings of inadequacy, needs for nurturance, and feelings of being shortchanged in society. Substance abuse can also create a lack of support at home and unresponsiveness from the spouse, which compound the perpetrator's sense of alienation. These factors, taken together, suggest stressors that may lead to dysfunctional behavior as a coping mechanism. Whether the incidence of intrafamilial child sexual abuse increases with such stress factors has not been empirically established. Environmental conditions such as poverty, racial and ethnic discrimination and economic turmoil contribute to the stress. These are not characteristics unique to child sexual abuse, but rather present a challenge to society at large. Resolution of these issues is included as one effort that will enhance all prevention strategies.

What can we learn from these data to prevent maladaptive coping patterns and to intervene effectively with families at risk for intrafamilial sexual abuse, especially those of Hispanic origin?

Preventive Intervention Strategies

Four frameworks for primary prevention in the field of mental health, adapted from Goldston (1977), are identified below:

- primary prevention of problems of known etiology
- primary prevention of problems of unknown etiology
- primary prevention of emotional distress, maladaptation, maladjustment, needless psychopathology, and human misery
- promotion of health and well-being

Goldston states that limited resources should not be expended on the prevention of problems of unknown etiology, but rather that preventive activities should be "characterized by specific actions directed at specific populations for specific purposes" (1977, p. 26). Although little is known about the etiology of child sexual abuse, correlates of the problem include emotional distress, maladaptation, and maladjustment. In these situations Goldston advocates using psycho-socio-cultural-educational approaches. Using this framework, several areas are proposed here as possible strategies for interventions to prevent intrafamilial child sexual abuse in the Hispanic community.

A broad primary prevention goal for society-at-large is the elimination of maltreatment of children. Promoting mentally healthy children helps to prevent the development of adults with mental dysfunction and thus contributes to the well-being of society. Granted that the causes of intrafamilial sexual abuse are unknown, one strategy for reducing the incidence is to increase the level of knowledge about the problem through public information campaigns. In addition to education about child sexual abuse, these efforts could also focus on strengthening family relationships and developing coping mechanisms to deal with stressful situations.

Primary prevention of incest or intrafamilial sexual abuse begins on the community level. Topics in reference to sexuality are viewed as especially sensitive in the Hispanic community because it is believed that these are matters of a personal nature to be discussed, if at all, in the home between adults. Sex with children is particularly abhorrent because children represent the pride and future of the family; they have a place of primacy within the family constellation. Sexual behavior with children, then, can only be explained within the Hispanic community by assuming that the perpetrator is mentally ill. While many other communities may feel similarly, the Hispanic culture in particular is built around the family constellation with children as the central focus. Thus, while sexuality between adults is a sensitive topic within the Hispanic community, sex with a child is an even more sensitive and difficult topic (Mindel, Haberstein, & Wright, 1988). For this reason, much can be learned from the experience of increasing knowledge and disseminating information on AIDS to the Hispanic community, also a sensitive sexually related topic (Hu, Keller, & Fleming, 1989).

Johnson and Delgado (1989) have addressed some strategies derived from consumer marketing–with a particular focus on Hispanic markets. Their approach is adapted here to the prevention of intrafamilial child sexual abuse. A key marketing component, as private profit-oriented corporations are finding, is the use of the broadcast media, television and radio, for providing communication messages in both English and Spanish. The print media are highly reliant on literacy level and are less successful in reaching a broad audience (Hu, Keller, & Fleming, 1989). While all types of media are used today to reach the Hispanic population, such use has not been extensive nor has it been language-culture and message-sensitive to the targeted population. Approaches to reaching the Hispanic community must consider a number of areas–such as language subgroups (e.g., Spanish only, English and Spanish, English only); format preferences, appropriateness and preferences of spokespersons, message content and targeted audiences (e.g., children, mothers, fathers, parents, extended family).

Medium and Language

Hu, Keller, and Fleming (1989) found that television and radio were cited by Hispanics in the United States as their major sources of information. Radio, in particular, was a more important medium for Hispanics than for non-Hispanics. The Spanish-speaking report lower frequencies of media usage, perhaps determined by the availability of Spanish language media in their area. For example, as extensive as public education has been on the topic of AIDS, information and knowledge on AIDS decrease dramatically as Spanish-speaking dominance increases. Among the Spanish speaking, 47% reported not having received AIDS information; among those who were bilingual but with Spanish as the primary language, 33% reported not having received AIDS information; and among the English only Hispanics, 12% indicated no information on AIDS (Hu, Keller, & Fleming, 1989).

In the intrafamilial sexual abuse data presented above a large percentage of mothers and fathers were Spanish speaking only or preferred to speak Spanish in everyday life. Hispanic mothers and fathers tended to have relatively low numbers of years of schooling, which in combination with Spanish language dominance suggests that broadcast media may be preferable over print media for communicating prevention messages to parents.

Therefore, primary considerations for reaching Hispanic families are the use of broadcast media and the extent of Spanish language programming in the community to be served, factors that may be more critical in areas that do not have extensive Spanish language broadcasting such as exists in Los Angeles, New York, or Miami. Thus, Spanish language television and radio are suggested to reach the segment of the Hispanic community not served by English language media.

Audiences and Content

Prevention messages on the community level have usually been targeted at general audiences rather than at specific segments of the audience–unlike commercial advertising firms which sell their products by targeting specific audience segments. In public information campaigns with prevention goals, messages to each of the audience segments need to be tailored to address corresponding segments of the community. For example, because of the nature of the assault, the messages can be tailored to children–potential victims; fathers and other extended family members–potential perpetrators; mothers and other family members–potential witnesses; and extended family members who may be knowledgeable witnesses. Each has a role and must receive particular content from the message rather than a generalized message aimed at the broader community. Community members in high density Hispanic areas are sensitive to not being intrusive in family matters. Although heightened awareness can provide the impetus to intervene, interventions are contingent on one of the key actors reporting the sexual abuse.

Even though children are often participants in child sexual abuse prevention programs in the schools, which would suggest an opportunity for a child to reveal her own sexual molestation, our data show that revealing sexual abuse to school authorities is much lower among Hispanic children than non-Hispanic children. There are strong traditional values against discussion of personal family matters with teachers, neighbors, friends or others outside the family–a value well ingrained in Hispanic children from an early age. This value may account for some of the low rates of sexual abuse of Hispanic children reported from schools, neighbors, friends or other community sources. Thus, there is a need for media messages targeted at Hispanic children and delivered by appropriate Hispanic spokespersons in a format acceptable to children. These messages should not only convey information, but give children permission to reveal sexually abusive adult behavior to others, including those outside the immediate family.

The Hispanic community needs to understand the extent of the problem in American society today, not only in non-Hispanic communities but within the Hispanic community as well. At present we are aware of no empirical research to determine the incidence and prevalence rates of child sexual abuse in the Hispanic community (see Sorenson & Siegel, 1992, for adult interview data on sexual assault in the Los Angeles Hispanic community). Hispanic families need to understand that even in a culture that is traditionally very child focused, this type of sexual assault can and does occur. Community members, parents, family, and neighbors must be made aware of the extent of the problem, what can be done to prevent it, and everyone's responsibility to report it.

Fathers and other male family members need to be educated about the emotional, physical, and social damage done to children who are sexually abused; about their own responsibilities for safeguarding their child's welfare; and the social and legal penalties imposed on those who sexually abuse their own or other's children. In addition, programs to educate parents–particularly fathers–in ways to cope with stress and feelings of inadequacy should be disseminated through the media.

Mothers need to be aware of the resources available to them within their communities, such as avenues for reporting sexual abuse and support groups for themselves and their children. They need to be aware of programs that strengthen communication with their children, their husbands, and with the total family constellation. Educating the mother of the family constellation in a culturally appropriate manner can alert her to early warning signs of child sexual abuse and empower her to do something about the situation.

The key issue here is to focus not only on a message to the Hispanic community but to address it appropriately to the needs of each segment of the population to be reached.

Formats and Spokespersons

How a message is delivered to the community is very important if it is to be heard. Programs are needed that assist families in identifying and reporting sexual abuse. Formats and persons who are able to communicate such messages are critical components in message delivery. For example, a culturally sensitive and linguistically relevant play, developed by the Latino Sexual Abuse Prevention Program in Los Angeles, dealt with a Latino family's ordeal when they discovered that their children had been sexually abused by an uncle (Escalante, 1985). This play examines family dynamics, reflecting the family's role as a major strength in Hispanic culture. It offers lessons in communication, respect, trust, and dignity between family members since sexual abuse redefines the roles, positions, and values of the family. The program teaches families that expressions of affection are good, but that there are rules for expressing caring and respect. It utilizes a format that is very favored in the Hispanic community—one that is likely to draw interest and provide a message at the same time.

Outreach to families at risk is important. Critical to this approach to the Hispanic community are programs presented by bilingual and bicultural persons. For some messages, Hispanics well known in the entertainment field are ideal. In instances requiring a more complicated level of presentation, medical personnel or persons perceived as having expert knowledge are best. There is a high degree of respect within the Hispanic community for doctors and others perceived as knowledgeable in their areas. Obviously, bilingual bicultural individuals with whom the audience can identify should be sought for public health campaign presentations directed to the Hispanic community.

CONCLUSION

While the content of the information campaigns on child sexual abuse directed to the Hispanic community need not be significantly different than that directed to any community, the delivery and packaging of this information needs to be addressed in Spanish, in Spanish language newspapers, television stations, and radio. In particular, Spanish language television is an excellent medium for reaching the maximum number of new immigrants who are Spanish speaking only and of low socioeconomic class. Programming on identifying and reporting the sexual abuse and understanding its impact on those involved can also be developed at community centers, multipurpose service centers that specifically reach out to Hispanics, and church sponsored programs. There are many avenues within the community that can be utilized. In order to reach the Hispanic community, primary prevention programs must be presented in a culturally and linguistically acceptable format in order for the message to be received.

Environmental conditions such as poverty, racial and ethnic discrimination, and economic turmoil contribute to stress. These are not characteristics unique to child sexual abuse, but rather present a challenge to society at large. Resolution of these issues is included as one effort that will enhance all prevention strategies.

NOTE

1. *Child sexual abuse* in this paper is the generic term referring to the sexual molestation of children under the age of 18. This term is used regardless of the relationship of the perpetrator/offender to the child victim. The perpetrator/offender may be unknown to the child. *Incest* is the sexual abuse of children by a blood relative. *Intrafamilial child sexual abuse* is sexual molestation of children by someone in the family constellation who may or may not be related by blood lines. Intrafamilial child sexual abuse incorporates incest but is not limited to blood relatives and can include relatives by marriage, cohabitation, and others who make up the family constellation.

REFERENCES

Becerra, R. M. (1983). *Child sexual abuse in the Hispanic community.* Grant from Office of Child Abuse Prevention, State of California. Unpublished.

Catalano, R. & Dooley, D. (1980). Economic change in primary prevention. In R. Price, R. Ketterer, B. Bader, & J. Monahan (Eds.), *Prevention in mental health: Research, policy, and practice.* Beverly Hills, CA: Sage.

Conte, J. R., Rosen, C., & Saperstein, L. (1986). An analysis of programs to prevent the sexual victimization of children. *Journal of Primary Prevention, 6,* 141-155.

Escalante, V. (May 2, 1985). Latino play on sexual abuse moves community. Los Angeles, CA: *Los Angeles Times.*

Finkelhor, D. (1981). Removing the child–prosecuting the offender in cases of sexual abuse: Evidence. *Child Abuse and Neglect, 7,* 195-205.

Finkelhor, D. (1982). Sexual abuse: A sociological perspective. *Child Abuse and Neglect, 6,* 95-102.

Finkelhor, D. (1984). *Child sexual abuse: New theory and research.* New York: Free Press.

Goldston, S. E. (1977). An overview of primary prevention programming. In D.C. Klein & S.E. Goldston (Eds.), *Primary prevention: An idea whose time has come* (pp. 23-44). US Dept. of HEW, ADAMHA, #77-447. Washington, DC: US Government Printing Office.

Hu, D. J., Keller, R., & Fleming, D. (1989). Communicating AIDS information to Hispanics: The importance of language and media preference. *American Journal of Preventive Medicine, 5,* 196-200.

Johnson, E.M., & Delgado, J. L. (1989). Reaching Hispanics with messages to prevent alcohol and other drug abuse. *Public Health Reports, 104,* 588-594.

Meiselman, K. C. (1978). *Incest.* San Francisco: Jossey Bass.

Miller-Perrin, C. L., & Wurtele, S.K. (1988). The child abuse prevention movement: A critical analysis of primary and secondary approaches. *Clinical Psychology Review, 8,* 313-329.

Mindel, C. H., Haberstein, R.W., & Wright, R. Jr. (Eds.). (1988). *Ethnic families in America: Patterns and variations.* New York: Elsevier.

Mrazek, P. M. & Kempe, H. (Eds.). (1981). *Sexually abused children and their families.* New York: Pergamon.

Office of the California State Attorney General. (1985). *Commission on the enforcement of child abuse laws.* Sacramento, CA.

Reppucci, N. D., & Haugaard, J. J. (1989). Prevention of child sexual abuse: Myth or reality. *American Psychologist, 44,* 1266-1275.

Snowden, L. (Ed.). (1982). *Reaching the underserved: Mental health needs of neglected populations.* Beverly Hills, CA: Sage.

Sorenson, S., & Siegel, J. (1992). Gender, ethnicity, and sexual assault: Findings from a Los Angeles study. *Journal of Social Issues, 48,* 93-104.

Stilwell, S. L., Lutzker, J.R., & Greene, B.F. (1988). Evaluation of a sexual abuse prevention program for preschoolers. *Journal of Family Violence, 3,* 269-281.

Suski, L. B. (1986). Child sexual abuse–an increasingly important part of child protective service practice. *Protecting Children,* (Spring), 3-8.

Vernon, A. & Hay, J. (1988). A preventative approach to child sexual abuse. *Elementary School Guidance and Counseling, 22,* 306-312.

Wurtele, S.K. (1987). School-based sexual abuse prevention programs: A review. *Child Abuse and Neglect, 11,* 483-495.

Prevention and the Ecology of Sexual Harassment: Creating Empowering Climates

Meg A. Bond

University of Massachusetts, Lowell

SUMMARY. Sexual harassment is a pervasive form of sexual exploitation that has a devastating impact on women. Although there is an increasing literature on the development of policies and procedures to deal with sexual harassment situations, relatively little has been done either to address the diverse conditions that set the stage for harassment or to design preventive interventions. An ecological analysis of sexual harassment is used to identify individual, relationship and environmental risk factors and to formulate preventive approaches. The function of sexual harassment in organizations and the ways in which organizational climates contribute to harassment are discussed. The fostering of *empowering climates* is proposed as critical to prevention, and several dimensions of empowering climates are explored.[1] *[Article copies available from The Haworth Document Delivery Service: 1-800-342-9678.]*

Sexual harassment, the unwanted sexualization of work, academic, or other professional relationships, has been described as so pervasive in our

Address correspondence to Meg A. Bond, Department of Psychology, University of Massachusetts, Lowell, MA 01854.

The author is grateful to William C. Madsen, Charlotte Mandell, Anne Mulvey, Christopher Keys and Carolyn Swift who provided invaluable feedback on previous drafts of this article.

[Haworth co-indexing entry note]: "Prevention and the Ecology of Sexual Harassment: Creating Empowering Climates." Bond, Meg A. Co-published simultaneously in *Prevention in Human Services* (The Haworth Press, Inc.) Vol. 12, No. 2, 1995, pp. 147-173; and: *Sexual Assault and Abuse: Sociocultural Context of Prevention* (ed: Carolyn F. Swift) The Haworth Press, Inc., 1995, pp. 147-173. Single or multiple copies of this article are available from The Haworth Document Delivery Service [1-800-342-9678, 9:00 a.m.-5:00 p.m. (EST)].

147

society as to be invisible and inaudible. In her ground breaking book, MacKinnon (1979) argued that sexual harassment is based in a sexism so institutionalized that it usually goes unnoticed.

> It is not surprising . . . that women would not complain of an experience for which there has been no name. Until 1976, lacking a term to express it, sexual harassment was literally unspeakable, which made a generalized, shared, and social definition of it inaccessible. The unnamed should not be mistaken for the nonexistent. Silence often speaks of pain and degradation so thorough that the situation cannot be conceived as other than it is. (p. 27-28)

Research supports MacKinnon's claims about the pervasiveness of sexual harassment. Over 50% of the private sector working women interviewed by Gutek (1985) reported experiencing at least one incident they considered sexual harassment on the job. About 43% of the women in surveys of U.S. government workers reported some form of sexual harassment at work (U.S. Merit Systems Protection Board, 1981; 1988). On campus, it appears that approximately 30% of undergraduate women are sexually harassed by at least one professor (Benson & Thompson, 1982; Koenig & Ryan, 1986; Paludi, in press). These rates increase for women in graduate programs (Bond, 1988; Fitzgerald, Shullman, Bailey, Richards, Swecker, Gold, Ormerod, & Weitzman, 1988; Schneider, 1987) and for women of color (DeFour, 1991; Gruber & Bjorn, 1982). Fitzgerald and Ormerod (in press) indicate that, "it is reasonable (if not conservative) to estimate that one out of every two women will be harassed at some point during their work or academic lives" (p. 13). When definitions of sexual harassment include sexist comments and jokes, the incidence rate can exceed 70% (Adams, Kottke, & Padgitt, 1983; Bond, 1988). If we include secondary victims, i.e., women who are aware of the harassment of others, the percentage of women affected by sexual harassment rises even further (Bond, 1988).

The pervasive nature of sexual harassment is often attributed to the broader oppression of women in our society (e.g., MacKinnon, 1979; Benson & Thompson, 1982). There is strong support from observations in both work and academic settings that the vast majority of harassment incidents involve male harassers and female targets (Fitzgerald et al., 1988a; Gutek & Morasch, 1982; Reilly, Lott, & Gallogly, 1986). While there are occasional reports of women harassing men and men harassing men, it is generally recognized that sexual harassment is a much more pervasive and debilitating problem for women. Therefore, this paper will focus on the pattern of men harassing women.

In the last decade, institutions of work and academia have begun to take notice of sexual harassment, or, as MacKinnon (1979) puts it, "break the systematic silence." The Thomas-Hill controversy in 1991 brought national visibility to the issue when University of Oklahoma Law Professor Anita Hill alleged that Clarence Thomas sexually harassed her when she worked for him at the Department of Education and at the Equal Employment Opportunity Commission. As Hill detailed her treatment by Thomas during his nationally televised Supreme Court confirmation hearings, many women heard her describe a personally familiar scenario. She put words to experiences many women had suffered yet never before dared label (at least publicly) as sexual harassment. Following the hearings, the media was filled with different women's accounts of harassment, and reports of sexual harassment to official agencies increased dramatically. Almost 10,000 women filed reports of sexual harassment with the EEOC from October 1991 to October 1992–an increase of 44% over previous years ("Harassment charges reach record," 1992). However, even in settings with accessible reporting procedures, much sexual harassment goes unreported and unnoticed (Markunas & Joyce-Brady, 1987; Riger, 1991). After-the-fact reporting procedures are not enough to contain such a widespread problem.

There is clearly a need for an expanded focus on prevention. Effectively preventing sexual harassment requires an understanding of its multiple dimensions and hence the adoption of an ecological analysis. This article addresses the ecology of harassment and explores implications for prevention.

DIMENSIONS OF SEXUAL HARASSMENT

Sexual harassment typically occurs in the context of a relationship of unequal power. It has become broadly understood as the "inappropriate sexualization of an otherwise nonsexual relationship" (Fitzgerald & Ormerod, in press, p. 7). It involves focusing more on a woman's sexuality and gender than on her role and competencies as worker or student through behaviors that range from sexist jokes or comments to requests or pressures for sex.

In her pioneering work, MacKinnon (1979) described two different types or levels of sexual harassment: quid pro quo harassment and conditions of work harassment. Quid pro quo harassment (which means, literally, "this for that") involves subtle or overt bribery or coercion for sexual attentions as in the more widely publicized cases of sexual harassment. Conditions of work harassment (also referred to as "gender harassment") includes those behaviors that create an offensive or intimidating environment in which women feel unsafe, devalued or otherwise isolated. It is important to recognize that verbal or physical conduct which wittingly or unwittingly creates an offensive, intimidating environment for women is as much a part of the definition of sexual harassment as is forced submission to unwelcome sexual behavior.

There is both empirical (Bond, 1988; Fitzgerald et al., 1988a; Fitzgerald & Hesson-McInnis, 1989; Till, 1980) and legal support for this multidimensional definition. The distinction between forms of sexual harassment has also been incorporated into the formal legal definitions of sexual harassment. In 1980, the EEOC defined sexual harassment as, "unwelcome sexual advances, requests for sexual favors, and other verbal or physical conduct of a sexual nature" (1) when such behavior becomes a condition of employment, (2) when it affects employment decisions (i.e., quid pro quo) *and* (3) when "such conduct has the purpose or effect of unreasonably interfering with an individual's work performance or creating an intimidating, hostile, or offensive working environment" (i.e., gender harassment) (EEOC, 1980). A year later, the U.S. Education Department's Office of Civil Rights adopted a similar definition for the academic community which added learning environments to the third condition.

A recent supreme court decision (*Harris v. Forklift Systems*, 1993) has helped to further clarify the legal definition of hostile environment. The requirement that a woman must suffer demonstrable psychological harm and/or that her work performance must visibly suffer before winning damages from an employer was thrown out. The court affirmed that derogatory comments, sexual jokes, and uncouth behavior alone can amount to sexual harassment by creating an insulting environment which women, and not men, have to endure. A woman need not have a nervous breakdown to prove that the working conditions are hostile enough to constitute sexual harassment.

The distinction between quid pro quo harassment and gender harassment has clear implications for prevention. First and foremost is the need for preventive efforts to address both types of harassment situations. Although now part of the legal and empirical definition of harassment, gender harassment is less likely than quid pro quo harassment to be universally defined as sexual harassment by individuals in the work force or academy. Behavior involving direct threats of retaliation or promises of reward are clearly viewed as harassment by both men and women. However, when the quid pro quo is less explicit or when the behavior could be construed as "romantic" or "teasing," there is greater divergence of opinion about whether the behavior constitutes sexual harassment (Adams,

Kottke, & Padgitt, 1983; Konrad & Gutek, 1986; Reilly, Carpenter, Dull, & Bartlett, 1982). A starting place for prevention is to clearly communicate definitions of the different forms of sexual harassment.

The relationship between quid pro quo and gender harassment also has important implications for prevention. Gender harassment can contribute to a climate that permits quid pro quo harassment, and the way in which quid pro quo harassment is handled can contribute to whether a climate encourages or discourages gender harassment (Bond, 1992; Bond, Mulvey, & Mandell, 1993). The impact of quid pro quo harassment also affects women whose awareness of the harassment of others alerts them to their own risk status. As secondary victims of quid pro quo harassment, they become primary victims of gender harassment. An ecological analysis of sexual harassment provides a useful framework for placing the different forms of harassment into context and for better understanding the reciprocal relationship between the two types of harassment.

ECOLOGICAL ANALYSIS

An ecological analysis of sexual harassment incorporates an understanding of how individual behavior is *embedded* in the environment (Kelly, 1979; Trickett, Kelly, & Vincent, 1985; Trickett, 1984). It considers the *interactions* between people, roles, and settings, and emphasizes the necessity of analyzing the context of behavior. An ecological perspective considers relationship and environmental factors as well as individual characteristics, and as a result moves beyond focusing options for intervention on punishment of the harasser and/or on coaching for the victim. By addressing the broader context in which sexual harassment occurs, an ecological analysis sets the stage for the development of systemic solutions and thereby provides critical groundwork for prevention efforts.

Other models have been used to explain sexual harassment. Tangri, Burt, and Johnson (1982) have described the biological, sociocultural and organizational models of sexual harassment. Each of these models incorporates only one level of analysis, whereas what is needed is a multilevel analysis which considers the contributions of individual, relationship, organizational *and* societal factors simultaneously (Rappaport, 1977). An ecological model does this and considers the reciprocal interactions between levels as well (Kelly & Hess, 1986).

An ecological model requires an analysis of the conditions at each level that set the stage for harassment. The following discussion considers what types of individual and relationship factors increase the risk of harassment as well as what characteristics of the work or academic environment contribute to a climate in which harassment is likely, or even encouraged, to happen. Finally, interactions between the levels of analysis are explored by looking at what kinds of organizational climates inhibit or enhance the individual or relationship characteristics that put people at risk. An analysis addressing such issues is key to designing effective preventive efforts.

Although the strength of an ecological analysis lies in the examination of multilevel factors and their interaction, not all levels contribute equally to the problem. As Goldner, Penn, Scheinberg, & Walker (1990) argue when talking about domestic violence, we must begin any analysis of male violence against women with the recognition that gender inequality is a social reality. Our social reality, based in power/resource differences, shapes the dynamics and the outcomes of any harassment situation. Thus while we can discuss individual factors that place both the female target and the male harasser "at risk," the questions for the women and men involved are not parallel. When we ask what puts an individual woman *at risk* for harassment, the focal question is *not* how she "contributes to the problem" but rather what conditions make her more likely to become the target of sexual harassment. With respect to harassers, the question is what types of men in what types of situations are more likely to engage in harassment. Understanding such characteristics and/or situations should not imply, however, that men are helpless victims of circumstance, devoid of responsibility for changing or addressing the problem. Harassers still must be held accountable for their behavior. In work integrating feminist and systemic analyses of violence against women, Goldner and colleagues (1990) caution, "Violence may be 'explainable,' but it is not excusable, and it may or may not be forgivable. That is up to the victim" (p. 345). An ecological or systemic analysis of sexual harassment should not confuse the broad identification of risk factors with diffused responsibility for action.

Although there is still a relatively small research literature directly addressing the questions raised by an ecological analysis, a mix of research results and theoretical analyses provide a basis for exploration and will be discussed below.

At Risk Relationships

Power is clearly a significant variable in relationships at risk for sexual harassment, however, there is not a simple correlation between power differential and frequency of harassment. Power differences are emphasized in most analyses of the dynamics of sexual harassment, and definitions of sexual harassment typically include some concept of coercion or the misuse of power (Benson & Thompson, 1982; Fitzgerald, 1991;

MacKinnon, 1979). Although central to the basic dynamic, attributing sexual harassment to an abuse of power and privilege is merely a starting place. We need to consider the multiple sources of power in our society–such as gender, position, ethnicity, age and physical superiority–and how opportunities to exercise power interact with individual and environmental risk factors to produce the behavior of sexual harassment.

Power is defined only in part by one's position within an organization. To the extent that power is defined as the ability to make things happen (Kanter, 1977), we must recognize the differential access to resources between men and women. To the extent that power is defined as physical superiority, we must recognize that biology typically gives men the edge in terms of physical strength. To the extent that power is defined as the desire and ability to win, we must recognize the ways in which men are socialized to compete and believe their abilities to be superior, while women are socialized to cooperate and take care of others (Gilligan, 1982). In all of these ways, men have more power than women. Power is based not only in one's formal organizational position, but also in one's gender, resources and relationship style. In examining multiple sources of power, it becomes apparent that all sexual harassment by men of women involves a power difference–even peer harassment has an element of power abuse.

However, power alone does not seem to inevitably lead to sexual harassment, nor does the frequency of sexual harassment appear to be a function of the *size* of the power differential. When undergraduate students are harassed it tends to be by teaching and research assistants, whereas graduate and professional students name professors and instructors (Allen & Okawa, 1987). It has also been found that women with the *least power* within the organization are *not* necessarily the ones harassed most frequently. On at least one campus, junior and senior students report more harassment than freshmen and sophomores (Allen & Okawa, 1987). Graduate students typically report more harassment by faculty than undergraduates (Fitzgerald et al., 1988a). Women managers in Gutek's (1985) study were slightly more likely to be harassed than other working women. These studies point out that factors such as access and opportunities for interaction must be considered along with power differential. Undergraduates presumably have more contact with faculty as they move into upper level courses. Graduate students typically have more intensive relationships with faculty than undergraduates (Schneider, 1987). The high incidence of peer harassment (U.S. Merit Systems Board, 1988; Gutek & Morasch, 1982) is also undoubtedly related to opportunities for contact.

In at least one campus study, sexual harassment by male faculty and administrators was reported more often by faculty than by students, and more often by administrators than by staff (Fitzgerald et al., 1988a). Working on the same project or in the same sphere can both provide more opportunities for abuse *and* intensify the salience of the power difference. When McCain (1983) considered tenured and untenured faculty separately, the rates of harassment reported by *un*tenured women faculty (49%) were the highest and rates reported by tenured women (32%) were the lowest with rates falling in-between for graduate students (41%) and undergraduates (34%). It is important to avoid over-interpreting the *differences* in percentages, since to do so might distract from the fact that all groups reported considerable harassment. However, the relative vulnerability of untenured female faculty is noteworthy since it probably reflects their unique combination of dependence on other faculty to advocate for their advancement (salience of power difference) and potential for equal status (threat). Along a similar line, Gutek (1985) found that women in the work force with advanced degrees were at high risk for harassment. She suggests that the professional orientation of these women makes them more dependent upon particular positions at certain points in their careers and thus highly vulnerable to harassment. These findings raise a concern that relationships with transitory power differences may be at particular risk.

In sum, it appears as if relative power sets the stage for harassment, while other factors–such as structural opportunities for contact, shared work commitments, salience of power difference to career, potential for equal status–may interact to determine whether harassment actually occurs.

At Risk Women

The most consistent finding in sexual harassment research is that gender is the critical factor in determining risk status. Women are significantly more at risk than men (Fitzgerald et al., 1988a; Gutek, 1985; U.S. Merit Systems Protection Board, 1981; 1988). However, we are also beginning to understand what puts some women more at risk than others.

Sexual harassment is *not restricted* to a particular group of women based on age, marital status, physical appearance, race, class, occupation or pay range (e.g., Crull, 1987; Gutek, 1985). While any woman in the work force or academia is a potential victim, there is some evidence that women in *certain circumstances* are more likely to be targeted.

The vulnerability of younger women to sexual harassment (LaFontaine & Tredeau, 1986; Gruber & Bjorn, 1982) is reflected in the finding that women workers under the age of 35 report more harassment than older women

(Gutek, 1985; U.S. Merit Systems Protection Board, 1988). Youth may well interact with a woman's relative power within a system, but the impact is probably not simply additive. Given the finding that some higher status women are harassed more frequently than lower status women, it may be that it is the youthful *within* each status level who are most at risk. It may also be that the key issue is age *relative to the harasser*. Further research is needed to clarify the relationship between age and seniority in harassment situations.

A woman's marital status appears to be related to sexual harassment, although the relationship may be somewhat complicated by other factors. Some studies have shown that unmarried women (divorced, separated, never married or cohabiting) experience harassment more often than married or widowed women (Benson & Thompson, 1982; Fitzgerald & Ormerod, in press; Gruber & Bjorn, 1982; Gutek, 1985). This could, at first glance, look like an indication that sexual harassment is an extension of invitations from one "available" individual to another and perhaps supportive of the biological model. However, victims report that their harassers are typically married (Gutek, 1985; U.S. Merit Systems Protection Board, 1981; 1988), and there is some evidence that women's marital status may be less salient than relationship stress. In a survey of women in clinical psychology, Glaser and Thorpe (1986) found that women who went through a divorce or separation during graduate school were more likely than other women to have been propositioned by educators. Since these women were propositioned even more often than single women, some factor other than their perceived "availability" as sexual partners appears to be operating. Relationship dissolution involves emotional vulnerability and stress. In addition, such change often initiates the loss or realignment of social support networks and other tangible resources such as money and property. These results suggest the importance of social support and other stress-buffering resources in reducing women's risk.

DeFour (1991) has argued that women of color are at greater risk for sexual harassment due to myths about their sexual or "promiscuous" natures *and* to concerns about limited alternative job options. Gruber and Bjorn (1982) found that in their study of women in blue collar positions, black women were not only subjected to more sexual harassment, they were also more likely to face more severe forms of harassment. Although Gutek (1985) found that ethnic/minority women were *not* more likely to report sexual harassment than white women in her phone interviews, those who did report were less likely to quit their jobs when they were victims of sexual harassment. It is quite possible that women of color experience more sexual harassment than white women, yet are more likely to underreport it due to their economic vulnerability.

Lack of resources and marginality appear to be key conditions which put individual women at risk for sexual harassment. Youth and relationship loss are often associated with reduced social and economic resources. In these situations, harassers potentially have power based on position and gender as well as based on age and a stable support base. Women who are marginal by virtue of being "different" from those determining the dominant culture of the setting may also be at risk. Ethnic minority women within work and academic settings are often marginalized by not only having less influence, but also by being more alienated from the central workings of the organization (Fleming, 1983). When faced with lack of mobility and fewer alternative job options, such women would be forced to stay in alienating positions. The possibility that marginal status is associated with increased vulnerability to harassment parallels the finding that isolated women are more at risk for physical abuse by partners (Gelles, 1980; Schechter, 1982).

At Risk to Harass

What are the characteristics of men who harass? Are there differences between men who engage in gender harassment and men who make more blatant propositions and explicit threats of quid pro quo harassment? Although these questions have not been extensively researched, there are some studies that give us clues.

Pryor (1987) found that men who would initiate severe sexual harassment tend to emphasize male social and sexual dominance to a greater degree than men unlikely to harass. Likelihood of harassing was negatively related to empathy and feminist attitudes, and strongly related to acceptance of victim blaming myths about rape (e.g., women ask for it). Victims describe their harassers as white, older than themselves, married, and with reputations for repeated episodes of sexually exploitive behavior (Gutek, 1985; Perry, 1983; U.S. Merit Systems Protection Board, 1981). Inappropriate sexualization of male-female interactions by men has also been associated with lack of general social skills (Pryor, 1987) and with being relatively physically unattractive (Gutek, Nakamura, Gahart, Handschumacher, & Russell, 1980).

Another important, and somewhat more insidious, risk factor is harassers' failure to recognize and acknowledge their power (Paludi, in press; Zalk, 1991). For example, Fitzgerald, Weitzman, Gold and Ormerod (1988b) found that 25% of respondents to a survey of male faculty reported engaging in sexual relations with female students enrolled at their university. Although some men reported *frequently* initiating personal relationships with women (but not men) students, they did not typically label their behavior as sexual harassment. Some men believed that faculty-student sexual relations were ethically acceptable under certain circumstances: e.g., when there was "mutual consent," when faculty are not in a position to evaluate the student, when the student is close in age to the faculty member, when the outcome is a "successful" relationship, and when the relationship is initiated by the student. Such conditions ignore the *inherent* power differential between faculty and students, and the ways in which organizationally-defined power augments personal and psychological power. Zalk (1991) argues that there is no such thing as "informed consent" when an individual is asked to comply with a request of most any kind from someone with significantly more power. The rationalizing conditions also ignore the negative impact that faculty-student relationships can have on others not involved in the particular liaison.

Victims' perceptions of harassers corroborate findings about abuse of power, attitudes toward women, and lack of social skills. In-depth interviews of 28 victims of sexual harassment conducted by the Working Women's Institute in New York revealed that the women saw a mix of factors as the source of their harasser's behavior (Crull, 1988). The most common explanation given was that the harasser had power at work which he was often fearful of losing. The second most common explanation attributed the harassment to the man's beliefs about women–both in terms of adherence to traditional gender role expectations and with respect to a generalized derogatory attitude toward women.

The individual and relationship risk factors identified here expand the overall picture of harassment. They move us beyond simple paradigms that emphasize individual characteristics and beyond an acontextual analysis of power to a more ecological view that considers the ways power differentials *interact* with other factors. The structure of the working relationship may provide the power and opportunity for men with derogatory beliefs about women and little ability to empathize to express sexual aggression particularly toward those women with few social or concrete resources. The situation is made even more insidious when the harasser does not recognize his power and views the woman as a free and willing partner in the "negotiation." This expanded picture now needs to be explored in the context of organizational and setting factors.

At Risk Settings: Structural and Functional Issues

What kinds of organizational characteristics are related to sexual harassment? This issue will be explored by considering the ways in which the structure of the work place contributes to sexual harassment, the "function" of sexual harassment as it relates to structural issues, and finally, the relationship between harassment and organizational climate.

The gender composition of the workplace is a structural factor which is clearly related to the incidence of sexual harassment, although the relationship is a complex one. Studies have shown that blue-collar tradeswomen (Gold, 1987) and women employed in traditionally male-dominated occupations of management and engineering (LaFontaine & Tredeau, 1986) experience substantially more of all types of sexual harassment than pink or white collar women in more female-dominated settings. One survey revealed that the complaint rate within Fortune 500 companies drops by half when women make up more than 50% of a corporate population (Sandroff, 1988). In academic settings, women in typically male-populated academic disciplines are at greater risk for sexual harassment than women in other fields (Bond, Mulvey, & Mandell, 1993; Till, 1980).

Gruber and Bjorn (1982) make an observation that helps refine our understanding of how sexual harassment relates to gender ratios. They interviewed female auto workers and found that when a very small number of women were in a work area, the women received little attention. When proportional representation was less than the plant average of 10%, women were not harassed to the same extent as women in more numerically proportionate areas. That is, when women were more visible (greater than 10%) yet still in the minority, the frequency and severity of sexual harassment increased. Gruber and Bjorn speculated that increased harassment was due to the ways greater visibility of women increased male coworkers' feelings of threat.

Fitzgerald and Ormerod (in press) describe a 1989 dissertation by Baker which showed that high levels of sexual harassment of women workers are associated with their participation in male-dominated work groups. Differential rates were not attributable to type of occupation (pink vs. blue collar) or to number of men encountered in the workplace–but were related to the gender ratio of the immediate work group.

The results of work on gender ratios and previously cited work on structural predictors draw a complex picture. Consider two findings side by side: (1) women with more power within a system sometimes report higher rates of harassment by supervisors and professors than women of lower status (Fitzgerald et al., 1988b; Gutek, 1985; McCain, 1983), and (2) women who are invisible *or* in the majority of the work group are less frequently harassed than when they are in a *noticeable minority* (Gruber & Bjorn, 1982). Within an ecological framework, these observations raise the question of the *function* of the behavior within the system. In what ways might sexual harassment serve to preserve the status quo, i.e., play a homeostatic role?

Sexual harassment is effective in maintaining male privilege and power by devaluing, diverting and intimidating women into less powerful, less visible and marginal positions (MacKinnon, 1979; Russell, 1984). Gruber and Bjorn (1982) observe that sexual harassment is more frequent when male coworkers cannot effectively punish or disadvantage women by other means such as withholding work-related information or training.

Sexual harassment may serve a different function in traditionally male than in traditionally female settings (Fuehrer, Schilling, Crull, Bond, D'Ercole, & O'Connor, 1990; Gutek & Morasch, 1982). In traditionally female jobs (e.g., clerical or nursing positions), sexual harassment helps maintain the division of labor along gender lines by reinforcing the belief that men and women differ in significant ways in temperament, capabilities and interests. Sexual harassment (and the threat of sexual harassment) serves to blur the distinction between which expectations of women workers are based on gender and which are based on job requirements (Gutek & Morasch, 1982). Harassment simultaneously "reminds" women that they are organizationally, occupationally, and socially subordinate to men. In traditional male-dominated blue collar or professional positions where objective work requirements do not result in the subordination of women, sexual harassment will most likely occur when men feel their positions are threatened (Benson & Thompson, 1982; Walshok, 1978). In these positions, where work role expectations do not overlap with female gender role expectations, harassment seems to function to protect male domination of the occupation.

In male-dominated settings, it may be that sexual harassment is more likely at the particular stage of setting development when women become newly visible. At this stage, men's fear of change and the imagined loss of power and control may be far worse than any actual outcomes. Exploration of such a developmental hypothesis would prove particularly useful in the design of prevention programs since alternative ways to deal with the transitional threat could be identified and addressed.

In a manner similar to the way in which fear of rape constrains women who have never been direct victims (Brownmiller, 1975; Riger & Gordon, 1981; Russell, 1984), knowledge of sexual harassment discourages women from joining particular work groups, organizations, occupations or fields (Adams, Kottke, & Padgitt, 1983; Benson & Thompson, 1982). Sexual harassment can function to enhance the power of men and to limit women's access to status and resources in part by fear and in part by maintaining the view of women as primarily gendered and secondarily, if ever, as possessing a unique mix of competencies.

Function need not imply intent. Even though sexual harassment has the impact of keeping women "in their place," it is unlikely that sexual harassment is a "plot" deliberately designed by men to keep women down. Rather, it has become an almost automatic or unconscious process supported by the long history of the exclusion of women and by general resistance to change. Whatever the precursors or intent behind harassers' behavior, exposing the impact of sexual harassment and the function that it serves is critical to challenging the homeostatic process and pushing for systems changes (i.e., second order change, Watzlawick, Weakland, & Fisch, 1974).

At Risk Settings: Climate and Meaning of Behavior

The ecological model also needs to incorporate an understanding of the *meaning* of behavior within a system–not simply the function. What do particular behaviors mean to people within a particular context or system? Those with power in the system determine the "dominant story," i.e., determine the dominant framework for how behavior is understood, valued, and interpreted within that setting (White & Epston, 1989; 1990). The dominant story not only provides a framework for organizing and interpreting behavior, but it also constricts acknowledgment or interpretations of behavior which do not fit within the framework (Bruner, 1986). In this way, the dominant story both organizes meaning and filters out alternative meanings.

> (Storying) is relied upon for the ordering of daily lives and for the interpreting of further experiences . . . It is clear that the sense of meaning and continuity that is achieved through the storying of experience is gained at a price. A narrative can never encompass the full richness of our lived experience . . . The structuring of a narrative requires recourse to a selective process in which we prune from our experiences those events that do not fit with the dominant evolving stories that we and others have about us. (White & Epston, 1989, p. 20)

Since men are dominant in most of the organizations within which women work (Kanter, 1977), they are writing the dominant story. This organizational "authorship" is then furthered by societal support for male dominance. The meaning attached by men to certain behaviors is often different from that attached by women, yet it is through men's dominant story that sexual harassment is viewed.

Thus, it becomes important to look at the differences in how men and women define, perceive, and attribute responsibility in sexual harassment situations. Men are less likely than women to define sexual harassment to include jokes, teasing remarks of a sexual nature and unwanted suggestive looks or gestures, and women are more likely than men to disapprove of romantic relationships between faculty and students (Koenig & Ryan, 1986). Women see a wider range of men's behaviors as bothersome and harassing than men do (Gutek, 1985; Tangri, Burt, & Johnson, 1982), while men often discount women's concerns about their behavior as being exaggerated sensitivity to a simple misunderstanding (Fuehrer et al., in press).

Research on attributions about who is responsible for causing and addressing sexual harassment reflect similar themes. Men, more than women, shift the responsibility onto women victims (Koenig & Ryan, 1986; Paludi, 1988). Men view sexual harassment as a *personal* not an organizational issue. Men, more often than women, endorse the view that a man's sexual attraction to women is "only natural" and that women "have to expect sexual advances and learn how to handle them" (Koenig & Ryan, 1986). In the academic setting, Paludi and colleagues (Donovan, Grossman, Kinderman, Matula, Paludi, & Scott, 1987; Paludi, 1988) have found that women students are more likely than men to label harassment as an abuse of faculty power and to assign a central role to the college for preventing and dealing with all levels of harassment. Maypole and Skaine (1983) found that among blue collar workers, women are more likely than men to view harassment in power/dominance terms. In this study, the men also consistently viewed sexual harassment as less of a problem to women than women did.

In work and academic settings, the dominant story or framework is perpetuated by organizational socialization processes through which acceptable values and behaviors are defined (Fuehrer & Schilling, 1988). Sexual harassment occurs within a systemic context of organizational climates, structures, and authority relations which condone it. Many norms within work and educational settings contribute to sexual harassment. Gutek (1985) observed that the presence of a general unprofessional ambience and a sexualization of the workplace contribute to sexual harassment in organizational settings. In academia, department members' *visible approval* of sexual contact between educators and students is a predictor of both gender and quid pro quo harassment (Bond, 1988).

Although sexual relationships between coworkers do not always have negative consequences, an institution which condones amorous relationships between members implicitly promotes sexualized relationships between men and women. Such norms contribute to the dynamic of "sex-role spill over" where gender-role expectations overshadow work role expectations (Gutek, 1985). It is as if gender is in neon and specific competencies are in shades of gray. A focus on a woman's gender and sexuality as her predominant characteristics can block the view of the woman's competencies. It has the effect of grouping all women together and limiting appreciation of their different skills, abilities and preferences. A focus on sex both dehumanizes and deskills individual women.

Fuehrer and Schilling (1988) argue that as a result of men's traditional domination in organizations, the prevailing morality is characterized by male values for individual rights, competition, and entitlement and is based on respect for the autonomy of individuals. Women's morality, based more on responsibility for maintaining relationships (e.g., Gilligan, 1982), may put them in a position to protect and preserve the mentoring relationship through yielding to the mentor's harassing demands. The perpetuation of harassment and the dominant story that supports it are, thereby, facilitated by women's sense of responsibility for protecting others and further strengthened in academic and professional settings by explicit institutional values for "academic freedom" and "professional license" which inhibit the challenging of harassing behavior. When dealing with sexual harassment, women are guided by an "injunction to care" while the male "moral imperative appears as an injunction to protect the power differential" (Paludi, in press, p.11).

In sum, at risk climates are those that promote sexualized views of women and embrace an ethos based on individual rights and entitlement. Such climates perpetuate a constricted definition of sexual harassment, cloud the view of women's competencies, and reject the notion of collective responsibility for addressing the problem. The dominant story in such settings is invalidating of women. It approaches women as a class rather than as individuals, denies women's *experience* of harassment (treats harassment like it does not exist), and isolates women in their victimization.

Addressing Risk Factors

The ecological analysis provides a framework for looking at who and what are "at risk." Gender harassment can be an unwitting process in which the cumulative impact of comments or behaviors is that women feel devalued, excluded, or stereotyped on the basis of gender. Men who have grown up in our society are at risk for contributing to this type of harassment. Virtually *all* women are at risk for being harassed. Climates that embrace stereotypic views of women's and men's roles or structure job responsibilities by gender seem more at risk than others.

Quid pro quo harassment involves a direct link between a sexual harasser's behavior and work-related outcomes for the target of the harassment. Men who deny the dynamics of power, who are less able to empathize, who believe in traditional sex roles and who endorse victim blaming beliefs about violence against women are more likely than others to engage in sexual harassment. Women who are in marginal positions or have fewer resources are at higher risk. Settings where women are in a *visible* minority and climates that support views of women as sex objects are associated with higher risk for sexual harassment.

Preventive strategies based on the identified risk factors would work to: reduce the isolation of women, educate about the impact of men's behavior on women, increase the accountability of all organization members to one another, challenge any sexualized threats and intimidation, promote nonstereotypic views of men and women, change conditions that highlight gender over other qualities, and challenge the denial of power. Interventions addressing these risk factors, taken together, would work toward the development of climates in work and academic settings that are empowering of women.

PREVENTION THROUGH EMPOWERMENT

An ecological analysis emphasizes the embeddedness of sexual harassment within settings that promote or tolerate the sexualization and victimization of women. The prevention of sexual harassment, like other forms of violence against women, requires changes in our culture and sociocultural norms that affect gender roles in our society. The immediate context for beginning efforts is the organizational setting. To accomplish the primary prevention of sexual harassment, we need to radically change the values and processes that guide our institutions. Focusing on the organizational setting allows us to develop some manageable, short term strategies that begin to move us in the right direction.

Policies and Procedures

The most common strategy for addressing sexual harassment within organizations over the last decade has been the development of formal policies and procedures.[1] The availability of such policies is relatively new, and their impact on prevention is difficult to assess. Unfortunately there is evidence that when policies do exist, many within the organization are either unaware of them or see them as ineffective (Carlson & Tibbetts, 1988; Markunas & Joyce-Brady, 1987). Others feel that reporting bears too high a cost (e.g., loss of promotion or job, criticism and isolation from coworkers) (Robertson, Dyer, & Campbell, 1988). Such fears are not without reason. In a study by Coles (1986), one half of those who filed a formal complaint were fired and 25% resigned due to psychological pressures associated with either the harassment or the complaint process. Riger (1991) also points out that the definitions and dispute resolution processes incorporated by most policies are incompatible with female perspectives and preferred interpersonal styles. It is not surprising that many sexual harassment incidents are never reported and, even if reported, are handled informally (Markunas & Joyce-Brady, 1987; Remick, Salisbury, Stringer, & Ginorio, 1990; U.S. Merit Systems Protection Board, 1988).

Policies and procedures can in some instances play an important role. If easily accessible, they can provide crisis intervention for women who have been violated. Talking to a responsible official can help a victim feel less "crazy" and validate that she was not responsible for creating the harassment situation. Under ideal circumstances, policies will also serve as deterrents to future incidents of sexual harassment. If conveyed with conviction, they can help create an overall climate intolerant of sexual harassment.

At worst, policies and procedures support a victim-blaming stance by communicating, even if inadvertently, that it is the sole responsibility of the harassment victim to take action. Confidential, individually-focused strategies, particularly those decided on a case by case basis, may reduce the recurrence of sexual harassment by a particular man, but they rarely reduce the overall threat of harassment. The burden of action (and proof) is placed on the victim of harassment.

Primary prevention of sexual harassment requires us to look at the problem in a new way. An ecological analysis goes beyond training victims to identify, avoid, and report harassment and even beyond targeting harassers for change. This approach identifies and addresses risk factors while creating environmental and structural supports that encourage a radically different climate within organizations.

Empowering Climates

Definitions. Empowerment is a process "by which people, organizations, and communities gain mastery over their lives" (Rappaport, 1984, p. 3).

Empowerment . . . suggests both individual determination over one's life and democratic participation in one's community . . . empowerment conveys both a psychological sense of personal control or influence and a concern with actual social influence, political power, and legal rights. (Rappaport, 1987, p. 121)

Empowerment is action congruent with an ecological world view (Rappaport, 1987). The *ecological analysis* of sexual harassment highlights the need to understand how the environment shapes and constrains behavior, while *empowerment* is the process by which values are redefined and resources redistributed within the environment.

Organizational climate consists of members' collective beliefs, expectations, and values regarding how organization members should think, feel, and behave toward one another (Poole, 1985). *Empowering organizational climates* can be defined as those climates that support and maximize the potential of all members. Empowering climates are characteristic of settings which provide resources and opportunities for women and men to develop multidimensional personal, interpersonal, and work-related capacities and to gain greater control over their lives. Empowering climates permeate settings where women can make things happen and reach their goals, while also expanding their vision of what is possible–settings where women are active and equal participants in creating structures, norms, values, and ethics. This vision requires some fundamental shifts in how organizations operate.

What does an empowering climate look like? It includes an ethic of caring and responsibility, support for diversity, reduced emphasis on gender, and increased contextual thinking. Outlined below are some intervention strategies that make initial steps toward promoting empowering climates in work and academic settings.

Ethic of caring and responsibility. A work climate based on caring and responsibility acknowledges and celebrates interdependencies between members. This process involves increasing rewards based on cooperation rather than on competition, and publicly acknowledging people for their ability to cooperate and be effective team members.

An emphasis on the *impact* people have on one another is a critical element of an ethic of caring and responsibility. The male definition of what constitutes sexual harassment may predominate based on men's power to define the social norms of an organization. However, since sexual harassment is technically (and legally) defined by the *impact* of the behavior, and not by the intent behind it, women's definitions should be the more critical determinants. *Impact* can be reinforced over *intent* by making sensitivity to impact on others part of selection criteria and formal work evaluations, and by workshops on empathy and communication skills. Modeling of empathic responses by management and administration would be critical.

An ethic of responsibility is supported by mechanisms that increase the accountability of all organization members to one another. For example, an organization could design more accessible mechanisms for reporting inappropriate behavior, incorporate peer and supervisee/student reviews into performance evaluations, and make cooperation (and collaborative contributions to the work/university community) an important factor in salary reviews. An ethic of caring is also enhanced by reducing the isolation of individual women. Supportive networks can be created through more structured mentoring programs for women. Addressing the isolation of men also enhances an ethic of caring and responsibility by promoting connection and emphasizing accountability to others.

Support for diversity. An empowering climate is also supportive of diversity. Organizational processes that embrace, or at least accommodate, differences must be identified. This element of an empowering climate also involves challenging a normative view of what is appropriate behavior, e.g., the notion that there is one right way to approach a job, "act professional," or be "healthy." It requires challenging the ways women are marginalized by virtue of being outside the prevailing work or academic norms, e.g., ethnic-minority, lesbian, older, younger. In a sense, support for diversity involves incorporating the principle of equifinality (c.f., Katz & Kahn, 1978; von Bertalanffy, 1968) into the way we think about our world on a daily basis, i.e., that many different equally worthy processes can lead to the same outcome. Increased tolerance for diversity will require organizations to clarify which goals are most basic to their mission, i.e., separate out which "goals" are more related to preferred style than to preferred outcomes. Recruitment, orientation and ongoing socialization can also be oriented toward acceptance of diversity.

Reduced salience of gender. An empowering climate is also one in which people are viewed as individuals and not defined *primarily* by their gender. Achieving such a view involves uncovering sex role "spill over" (Gutek & Morasch, 1982) and exposing the de-skilling of women that occurs when generalizations based on gender obscure differentiation of individual competencies. The influence, even if unwitting, of gender stereotypes and sexist attitudes in shaping how individual women are seen and in how jobs and opportunities in the organization are defined must be challenged.

To reduce the salience of gender, organizations must address the ways in which women are constrained by sexualized threats and general intimidation which so rudely bring attention to gender over other qualities (c.f., *Harris v. Forklift Systems*, 1993). Upper management and administration can communicate clearly through policies and their behavior that sexist attitudes and behavior will not be tolerated. Education can be provided to all employees and members of academic communities about the legal and ethical requirements to provide environments free from intimidation. Both work and academic settings can make gender-fairness a group goal, and make resource distribution dependent upon success in this area. Funding for new positions or projects can be made contingent upon maintaining a record of nonsexist behavior. Advocates should be available so women can talk confidentially about their concerns, and these resource people should have direct access to top organizational policy makers.

Structural conditions that highlight gender over other qualities must also be changed. Organizations can work to eliminate the division of labor along gender lines and achieve more balanced gender ratios within all work settings. It is important to target settings where women are a relatively new minority and provide special training for all employees about issues that emerge when integrating a work unit. Organizations can challenge the notion that women entering a field inevitably displace men (e.g., publicly acknowledge that women are no more a threat to the individual man than would be the influx of new competent men), and publicize successes and advantages of work units or departments that have balanced gender ratios.

Contextual thinking. Reducing the salience of gender for job definitions or assignments goes hand in hand with the development of contextual ways of thinking. A focus on individual differences without considering context breeds a "boot strap" philosophy and can mystify discriminatory practices and lead to blaming *individuals* for unequal treatment. While the notion that different things happen under different conditions appears to be common sense, predominant institutionalized frameworks attribute success or failure to either the individual OR the context. Credit in both directions is usually beneficial, and blame in either direction can be counterproductive (Rappaport, Davidson, Wilson, & Mitchell, 1975). Understanding the ecological notion of person-environment fit is critical to creating an empowering climate. We must look at how the setting or context constrains and/or promotes the effectiveness of individuals and, conversely, how individuals contribute to or detract from an empowering climate (c.f., Keys & Frank, 1987).

Contextual thinking also involves recognizing how power affects relationships. Power provides a context for assigning meaning to behavior–the same behavior performed by a person with low status will be interpreted very differently when performed by a person of higher status. People behave differently when they have different degrees of power. Even more profound is the way in which power affects how others react. We need to increase awareness of the impact power has on others and sensitize people to the diverse sources of power. Organizations can develop ethical codes that acknowledge the way position power generalizes beyond work roles and implement procedures for holding members accountable for their impact on others.

CONCLUSION

The development of empowering climates is critical to the prevention of sexual harassment. An empowering climate is one that adopts an ethos beyond the dominant stories that support, hide, or deny sexual harassment. This process involves creating new norms where it is clear to all that harassment is unacceptable. An empowering climate needs to incorporate new stories based on caring, responsibility and empathy. The new stories need to be less linear and incorporate an understanding of how context shapes behavior. The stories also need to value individuals and confront gender stereotypes and the intolerance of differences.

Change in these basic values requires action at all ecological levels. At the individual level, the goals are to reduce isolation, increase equitable access to resources, enhance interpersonal competencies, and increase tolerance for differences. At the relationship level, it is important to recognize interdependencies, emphasize accountability for impact, increase awareness of power dynamics and begin working from a mutual and collaborative model of relationships. At the level of the work group, change should focus on balancing gender ratios, increasing cooperation, and embracing diversity. It is the responsibility of the organization as a whole to support all of these efforts and, thereby, undercut the homeostatic function sexual harassment has served, and revise and diversify the dominant stories about the meaning of interpersonal behavior. The development of empowering climates should enable women to become full participants in their work and academic lives, and thus is central to the prevention of sexual harassment.

NOTE

1. There are several excellent sources of advice regarding the development of thoughtful procedures (Biaggio, Brownell, & Watts, 1991; Fuehrer et al., 1990; Paludi & Barickman, 1992; Remick et al., 1990).

REFERENCES

Adams, J., Kottke, J., & Padgitt, J. (1983). Sexual harassment of university students. *Journal of College Student Personnel, 24*, 484-490.

Allen, D., & Okawa, J. (1987). A counseling center looks at sexual harassment. *Journal of NAWDAC, 51* (1), 9-16.

Benson, D., & Thompson, G. E. (1982). Sexual harassment on a university campus: The confluence of authority relations, sexual interest and gender stratification. *Social Problems, 29*, 236-251.

Biaggio, M.K., Brownell, A., & Watts, D. (1991). Addressing sexual harassment: Strategies for prevention and change. In M.A. Paludi (Ed.), *Ivory power: Sexual and gender harassment in the academy* (pp. 213-230). Albany: SUNY Press.

Bond, M.A. (1992, November). *The ecology of sexual harassment: Implications for campus intervention.* Invited Colloquium at Wilfrid-Laurier University in Waterloo, Canada.

Bond, M.A. (1988). Division 27 sexual harassment survey: Definition, impact and environmental context. *The Community Psychologist, 21* (2), 7-10.

Bond, M.A., Mulvey, A., & Mandell, C. (1993, August). *Sexual harassment and departmental climate on campus.* Paper in presented at the national meeting of the American Psychological Association, Toronto, Ontario, CN.

Brownmiller, S. (1975). *Against our will: Men, women and rape.* New York: Simon & Schuster.

Bruner, E. (1986). Ethnography as narrative. In V. Turner & E. Bruner (Eds.), *The Anthropology of Experience* (pp. 139-155). Chicago: University of Chicago Press.

Carlson, H., & Tibbetts, K. (1988). Sexual harassment policies: Who reads them? Who needs them? *The Community Psychologist, 21* (2), 17-18.

Coles, F. S. (1986). Forced to quit: Sexual harassment complaints and agency response. *Sex Roles, 14*, 81-95.

Crull, P. (1987). Searching for the causes of sexual harassment: An examination of two prototypes. In C. Bose, R. Feldberg, & N. Sokoloff (Eds.), *Hidden aspects of women's work* (pp. 225-244). New York: Praeger.

Crull, P. (1988). Women's explanations of their harasser's motivations. *The Community Psychologist, 21* (2), 7-10.

DeFour, D. C. (1991). The interface of racism and sexism in the academy. In M.A. Paludi (Ed.), *Ivory power: Sexual and gender harassment in the academy* (pp. 45-52). Albany: SUNY Press.

Donovan, J., Grossman, M., Kinderman, J., Matula, S., Paludi, M.A. & Scott, C. (1987, March). *College women's attitudes and attributions about sexual and gender harassment.* Paper presented at the Association for Women in Psychology Conference, Bethesda, MD.

Equal Employment Opportunity Commission. (1980). Guidelines on discrimination because of sex. *Federal Register, 45* (219), 74676-74677.

Fitzgerald, L.F. (1991) Sexual harassment: The definition and measurement of a construct. In M. Paludi (Ed.), *Ivory power: Sexual and gender harassment in academia* (pp. 21-44). New York: SUNY Press.

Fitzgerald, L.F., & Hesson-McInnis, M. (1989). The dimensions of sexual harassment: A structural analysis. *Journal of Vocational Behavior, 35,* 309-326.

Fitzgerald, L.F., & Ormerod, A. J. (in press). Breaking silence: The sexual harassment of women in academia and the workplace. In F. Denmark & M. Paludi (Eds.), *Handbook of the psychology of women.* New York: Greenwood Press.

Fitzgerald, L.F., Shullman, S.L., Bailey, N., Richards, M., Swecker, J., Gold, A., Ormerod, A. J., & Weitzman, L. (1988a). The incidence and dimensions of sexual harassment in academia and the workplace. *Journal of Vocational Behavior, 32,* 152-175.

Fitzgerald, L. F., Weitzman, L., Gold, A., & Ormerod, A. J. (1988b). Academic harassment: Sex and denial in scholarly garb. *Psychology of Women Quarterly, 12,* 329-340.

Fleming, J. (1983). Black women in black and white college environments: The making of a matriarch. *Journal of Social Issues, 39* (3), 41-54.

Fuehrer, A., & Schilling, K. (1988). Sexual harassment of women graduate students: The impact of institutional factors. *The Community Psychologist, 21* (2), 12-13.

Fuehrer, A., Schilling, K., Crull, P., Bond, M.A., D'Ercole, A., & O'Connor, P. (1990). Prevalence and types of sexual harassment in the workplace. In J. Jones, B. Steffy, & D. Bray (Eds.), *Applying psychology in business: A manager's handbook* (pp. 690-699). Lexington, MA: Lexington Books.

Gelles, R. J. (1980). Violence in the family: A review of research in the seventies. *Journal of Marriage and the Family, 42,* 873-885.

Gilligan, C. (1982). *In a Different Voice.* Cambridge, MA: Harvard University Press.

Glaser, R., & Thorpe, J. (1986). Unethical intimacy: A survey of sexual contact and advances between psychology educators and female graduate students. *American Psychologist, 41,* 43-51.

Gold, Y. (1987, August). *The sexualization of the workplace: Sexual harassment of pink, white, and blue collar workers.* Paper presented to the annual conference of the American Psychological Association, New York.

Goldner, V., Penn, P., Scheinberg, M., & Walker, G. (1990). Love and violence: Gender paradoxes in volatile attachments. *Family Process, 29,* 343-364.

Gruber, J., & Bjorn, L. (1982). Blue-collar blues: The sexual harassment of women autoworkers. *Work and Occupations, 9,* 271-298.

Gutek, B. (1985). *Sex and the workplace.* San Francisco: Jossey-Bass.

Gutek, B., & Morasch, B. (1982). Sex ratios, sex role spill-over, and sexual harassment of women at work. *Journal of Social Issues, 38* (4), 55-74.

Gutek, B., Nakamura, C., Gahart, M., Handschumacher, I., & Russell, D. (1980). Sexuality in the workplace. *Basic and Applied Social Psychology, 1,* 255-265.

Harassment charges reach record, US says. (1992, October 26). *The Boston Globe,* p. 5.

Harris v. Forklift Systems, Inc., 114 S. Ct. 367 (1993).

Henley, N. (1977). *Body politic: Power, sex and nonverbal communication.* Englewood Cliffs, NJ: Prentice-Hall.

Kanter, R.M. (1977). *Men and women of the corporation.* New York: Basic Books.

Katz, D., & Kahn, R. (1978). *The social psychology of organizations.* New York: John Wiley & Sons.

Kelly, J. G. (1979). *Adolescent boys in high school: A psychological study of coping and adaptation.* Hillsdale, NJ: Lawrence Erlbaum Associates.

Kelly, J. G., & Hess, R. (Eds.). (1986). *The ecology of prevention: Illustrating mental health consultation.* New York: The Haworth Press, Inc.

Keys, C., & Frank, S. (1987). Community psychology and the study of organizations: A reciprocal relationship. *American Journal of Community Psychology, 7*, 239-261.

Koenig, S., & Ryan, J. (1986). Sex differences in levels of tolerance and attribution of blame for sexual harassment on a university campus. *Sex Roles, 15,* 535-549.

Konrad, A. M., & Gutek, B. (1986). Impact of work experiences on attitudes toward sexual harassment. *Administrative Science Quarterly, 31,* 422-438.

La Fontaine, E., & Tredeau, L. (1986). The frequency, sources and correlates of sexual harassment among women in traditional male occupations. *Sex Roles, 15,* 423-432.

MacKinnon, C. A. (1979). *Sexual harassment of working women.* New Haven: Yale University Press.

Markunas, P., & Joyce-Brady, J. M. (1987). Underutilization of sexual harassment grievance procedures. *Journal of NAWDAC, 50* (3), 27-32.

Maypole, D., & Skaine, R. (1983). Sexual harassment in the workplace. *Social Work, 28,* 385-390.

McCain, N. (1983, November 2). Female faculty members and students at Harvard report sexual harassment. *The Chronicle of Higher Education,* pp. 1, 14.

Paludi, M. (in press). Creating taboos in the academy: Faculty responsibility in preventing sexual harassment. *Journal of NAWDAC.*

Paludi, M. (1988, April). *Working 9 to 5: Women, men, sex, and power.* Paper presented at the New York State Psychological Association, Catskills, NY.

Paludi, M., & Barickman, R. (1992). Sexual harassment of students: Victims of the college experience. To appear in E. Viano (Ed.), *Victimology: An international perspective.* NY: Springer.

Perry, S. (1983, March 26). Sexual harassment on campus: Deciding where to draw the line. *The Chronicle of Higher Education,* pp. 21-22.

Poole, M.S. (1985). Communication and organizational climates: Review, critique and a new perspective. In R.D. McPhee & P.K. Thompkins (Eds.), *Organizational communication: Traditional themes and new directions* (pp. 79-108). Beverly Hills, CA: Sage.

Pryor, J. (1987). Sexual harassment proclivities in men. *Sex Roles, 17,* 269-290.

Rappaport, J. (1977). *Community psychology: Values, research and action.* New York: Holt, Rinehart & Winston.

Rappaport, J. (1987). Terms of empowerment/exemplars of prevention: Toward a theory for community psychology. *American Journal of Community Psychology, 15*, 121-148.

Rappaport, J., Swift, C., & Hess, R. (Eds.). (1984). *Studies in empowerment: Steps toward understanding and action.* New York: The Haworth Press, Inc.

Rappaport, J., Davidson, W., Wilson, M., & Mitchell, A. (1975). Alternatives to blaming the victim or the environment. *American Psychologist, 30*, 525-528.

Reilly, T., Carpenter, S., Dull, V., & Bartlett, K. (1982). The factorial survey techniques: An approach to defining sexual harassment on campus. *Journal of Social Issues, 38* (4), 99-110.

Reilly, M.E., Lott, B., & Gallogly, S. M. (1986). Sexual harassment of university students. *Sex Roles, 15*, 333-358.

Remick, H., Salisbury, J., Stringer, D., & Ginorio, A. (1990). Investigating complaints of sexual harassment. In M. Paludi (Ed.), *Ivory power: Sexual and gender harassment in academia* (pp. 191-212). Albany: SUNY Press.

Riger, S. (1991). Gender dilemmas in sexual harassment policies and procedures. *American Psychologist, 46*, 497-505.

Riger, S., & Gordon, M. T. (1981). The fear of rape: A study in social control. *Journal of Social Issues, 37* (4), 71-92.

Robertson, C., Dyer, C., & Campbell, D. (1988). Campus harassment: Sexual harassment policies and procedures at institutions of higher learning. *Signs, 13*, 792-812.

Russell, D. (1984). *Sexual exploitation: Rape, child sexual abuse and workplace harassment.* Beverly Hills, CA: Sage.

Sandroff, R. (1988, December). Sexual harassment in the Fortune 500. *Working Woman*, pp. 69-73.

Schechter, S. (1982). *Women and male violence.* Boston: Southend Press.

Schneider, B. (1987). Graduate women, sexual harassment, and university policy. *Journal of Higher Education, 58* (1), 46-65.

Tangri, S., Burt, M., & Johnson, L. (1982). Sexual harassment at work: Three explanatory models. *Journal of Social Issues, 38* (4), 33-54.

Till, F. (1980). *Sexual harassment: A report on the sexual harassment of students.* Washington, DC: National Advisory Council on Women's Education Programs, US Department of Education.

Trickett, E. (1984). Toward a distinctive Community Psychology: An ecological metaphor for the conduct of community research and the nature of training. *American Journal of Community Psychology, 12*, 261-280.

Trickett, E., Kelly, J.G., & Vincent, T. (1985). The spirit of ecological inquiry in community research. In E. Susskind & D. Klein (Eds.), *Community research: Methods, paradigms, and applications* (pp. 5-38). New York: Praeger.

Walshok, M.L. (1978). Occupational values and family roles. *Urban and Social Change Review, 11*, 12-20.

Watzlawick, P., Weakland, J., & Fisch, R. (1974). *Change.* New York: W.W. Norton & Company.

White, M., & Epston, D. (1989). *Literate means to therapeutic ends.* Adelaide, Australia: Dulwich Center Publications.

White, M., & Epston, D. (1990). *Narrative means to therapeutic ends.* New York: W. W. Norton.

U.S. Merit Systems Protection Board (1981). *Sexual harassment in the federal work place: Is it a problem?* Washington DC: US Government Printing Office.

U.S. Merit Systems Protection Board (1988). *Sexual harassment of federal workers: An Update.* Washington DC: US Government Printing Office.

von Bertalanffy, L. (1968). *General systems theory.* New York: George Braziller Press.

Zalk, S. (1991). Men in the academy: A psychological profile of harassment. In M.A. Paludi (Ed.), *Ivory power: Sexual and gender harassment in the academy* (pp. 141-175). Albany: SUNY Press.

Index

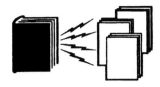

Haworth
DOCUMENT DELIVERY
SERVICE

This valuable service provides a single-article order form for any article from a Haworth journal.

- *Time Saving:* No running around from library to library to find a specific article.
- *Cost Effective:* All costs are kept down to a minimum.
- *Fast Delivery:* Choose from several options, including same-day FAX.
- *No Copyright Hassles:* You will be supplied by the original publisher.
- *Easy Payment:* Choose from several easy payment methods.

Open Accounts Welcome for . . .
- Library Interlibrary Loan Departments
- Library Network/Consortia Wishing to Provide Single-Article Services
- Indexing/Abstracting Services with Single Article Provision Services
- Document Provision Brokers and Freelance Information Service Providers

---

MAIL or *FAX* THIS ENTIRE ORDER FORM TO:

Haworth Document Delivery Service
The Haworth Press, Inc.
10 Alice Street
Binghamton, NY 13904-1580

or FAX: 1-800-895-0582
or CALL: 1-800-342-9678
9am-5pm EST

PLEASE SEND ME PHOTOCOPIES OF THE FOLLOWING SINGLE ARTICLES:

1) Journal Title: _____
    Vol/Issue/Year:_____Starting & Ending Pages:_____
    Article Title:_____

2) Journal Title: _____
    Vol/Issue/Year:_____Starting & Ending Pages:_____
    Article Title:_____

3) Journal Title: _____
    Vol/Issue/Year:_____Starting & Ending Pages:_____
    Article Title:_____

4) Journal Title: _____
    Vol/Issue/Year:_____Starting & Ending Pages:_____
    Article Title:_____

(See other side for Costs and Payment Information)

COSTS: Please figure your cost to order quality copies of an article.

1. Set-up charge per article: $8.00
   ($8.00 × number of separate articles) _____
2. Photocopying charge for each article:
   1-10 pages: $1.00 _____

   11-19 pages: $3.00 _____

   20-29 pages: $5.00 _____

   30+ pages: $2.00/10 pages _____
3. Flexicover (optional): $2.00/article _____
4. Postage & Handling: US: $1.00 for the first article/
   $.50 each additional article _____

   Federal Express: $25.00 _____

   Outside US: $2.00 for first article/
   $.50 each additional article _____
5. Same-day FAX service: $.35 per page _____

GRAND TOTAL: _____

METHOD OF PAYMENT: (please check one)

❏ Check enclosed ❏ Please ship and bill. PO # _____
(sorry we can ship and bill to bookstores only! All others must pre-pay)

❏ Charge to my credit card: ❏ Visa; ❏ MasterCard; ❏ Discover;
❏ American Express;

Account Number: _____ Expiration date: _____

Signature: ✗ _____

Name: _____ Institution: _____

Address: _____

_____

City: _____ State: _____ Zip: _____

Phone Number: _____ FAX Number: _____

MAIL or *FAX* THIS ENTIRE ORDER FORM TO:

Haworth Document Delivery Service
The Haworth Press, Inc.
10 Alice Street
Binghamton, NY 13904-1580

or FAX: 1-800-895-0582
or CALL: 1-800-342-9678
9am-5pm EST)